FORT ST. GEORGE
MADRAS

The Fort from the Island

FORT ST. GEORGE MADRAS

Fanny Emily Penny

Author of "Caste and Creed,"
"The Romance of a Nautch Girl," etc.

MJP PUBLISHERS
Chennai 600 005

First published: 1900

MJP's first reprint: 2008

 **MJP Publishers**

Dedicated
by Permission

To
His Excellency
Sir Arthur E. Havelock, G.C.M.G., G.C.B.
Governor of Madras
Who has watched with a kindly and
sympathetic interest the progress of this record.

PUBLISHER'S NOTE

India has a rich heritage of tradition and culture which dates back to the beginning of human existence. But unfortunately, most information of the past has not been properly documented. The few books published in the past are not within the reach of the needy, and in the present e-age with its modern communication techniques, many may not find time to preserve our heritage. But a few academicians and historians who may come forward in the future for research studies may lack the needed resources.

Keeping this in mind, MJP Publishers has endeavoured to revive the oldest rare books to serve the academic community and the society at large. In this effort, a series of rare books would be republished under the banner, "MJP's re-series". These rare books have been carefully selected based on the significance and authenticity of their contents as we perceive.

The books in the "re-series" have been recomposed in an elegant style and format to suit the interest of the present-day readers. Only slight modifications have been made for better presentation, and care has been taken to keep this to a minimum and to not affect the contents of the original edition.

The pen and ink sketches in this book were drawn by the Author, Fanny Emily Penny.

We hope that the "re-series" books would prove to be of immense help to researchers and general readers to have a better understanding of many important facts and happenings of the past, thus exposing the richness of our culture, tradition and knowledge.

MJP Publishers

PREFACE

I have consulted various books in compiling this little history, Talboys Wheeler's and Orme's in particular. But the most valuable sources from which I have drawn have been the records of Fort St. George which are kept in Madras. Through the courtesy of the Honorable Mr. G. Stokes, Chief Secretary, I have been able to consult the original papers from which Wheeler drew his information. I have also had access to the register books of St. Mary's through the kindness of the Reverend F. Penny, Garrison Chaplain of Fort St. George. My best thanks are due to these gentlemen, as well as to Mr. Sim of the Madras Civil Service to whom I am indebted for the interesting maps here reproduced; to Colonel Routh and Arthur E. Lawson, Esq., who have photographed the church and plate expressly for this book; and to Mr. J. Kelsall (Madras Civil Service retired) who has read the proofs and added some notes under his initials [J.K.]

Fanny Emily Penny

CONTENTS

ILLUSTRATIONS

GOVERNORS OF FORT ST. GEORGE

Names	Assumed charge	Remarks
Mr. Aaron Baker	1 Sept. 1652	First President and Governor.
Sir. Thomas Chamber or Chambers	1659	
Sir. Edward Winter, *Kt.*	1661	
Mr. George Foxcraft	June 1665	Imprisoned by Sir Edward Winter.
Sir. Edward Winter, *Rt.*	16 Sept. 1665	
Mr. George Foxcraft	22 Aug. 1668	
Sir. William Langhorne, *Bart*	1670	
Mr. Streynsham Master	27 Jan. 1678	
Mr. William Gyfford	3 July 1681	
Mr. Elihu Yale	8 Aug. 1684	Acting.
Mr. William Gyfford	26 Jan. 1685	
Mr. Elihu Yale	25 July 1687	
Mr. Nathaniel Higginson	23 Oct. 1692	
Mr. Thomas Pitt	7 July 1698	
Mr. Gulstone Addison	18 Sept. 1709	Died at Madras, 17 Oct. 1709.
Mr. Edmond Montague	17 Oct. 1709	Acting.
Mr. William Fraser	3 Nov. 1709	Acting.
Mr. Edward Harrison	11 July 1711	
Mr. Joseph Collet	8 Jan. 1717	
Mr. Francis Hastings	18 Jan. 1720	Acting.
Mr. Nathaniel Elwick	15 Oct. 1721	

(Contd.)

GOVERNORS OF FORT ST. GEORGE

Names	Assumed charge	Remarks
Mr. James Macrae	15 Jan. 1725	
Mr. George Morton Pitt	14 May 1730	
Mr. Richard Benyon	23 Jan. 1735	
Mr. Nicholas Morse	17 Jan. 1744	Fort. St. George captured, 10 Sept. 1746, and retained by the French till 1749.
Mr. John Hinde *at Fort St. David*		Deputy Governor of Fort St. David. Appointed President and Governor 24 Jan. 1747, but died before receipt of dispatch.
Mr. Charles Floyer *at Fort St. David*	16 Apl. 1747	Dismissed 6 July 1750.
Mr. Richard Prince	1749	Deputy Governor of Fort St. George.
Mr. Thomas Saunders	19 Sept. 1750	Seat of Government reestablished at Fort St. George, 5 April 1752.
Mr. George Pigot	14 Jan. 1755	Afterwards Lord Pigot.
Mr. Robert Palk	14 Nov. 1763	
Mr. Charles Bourchier	25 Jan. 1767	
Mr. Josias Du Pré	31 Jan. 1770	
Mr. Alexander Wynch	2 Feb. 1773	
Lord Pigot	11 Dec. 1775	Placed under arrest by majority of his Council, 24 Aug. 1776.
Mr. George Stratton	23 Aug. 1776	Suspd. from the Service.
Mr. John Whitehill	31 Aug. 1777	Acting.
Mr. Thomas Rumbold	1 Feb. 1778	
Mr. John Whitehill	6 April 1780	Acting. Suspended.
Mr. Charles Smith	8 Nov. 1780	Acting.
Lord. Marartney	22 June 1781	
Mr. Alexander Davidson	18 June 1785	Acting.

(Contd.)

GOVERNORS OF FORT ST. GEORGE

Names	Assumed charge	Remarks
Major General Sir Archibald Campbell, K.C.B.	6 April 1786	Also Commander-in-Chief.
Mr. John Holland	7 Feb. 1789	Acting.
Mr. Edward John Holland	13 Feb. 1789	Acting.
Major General William Medows	20 Feb. 1790	Also Commander-in-Chief.
Sir Charles Oakley, Bart	1 Aug. 1972	
Lord Hobart	7 Sep. 1794	
Lieutenant General Harris	21 Feb. 1798	Acting.
Lord Clive	21 Aug. 1798	
Lord William Cavendish Bentinck	30 Aug. 1803	
Mr. William Petrie	11 Sep. 1807	Acting.
Sir. George Hilaro Barlow, Bt., K.C.B.	24 Dec. 1807	
Lt. Genl. The, Hon. John Abercromby	21 May 1813	Commander-in-Chief and temporary Governor.
Mr. Hugh Elliot	16 Sep. 1814	
Maj. Genl. Sir Thomas Munro, Bt., K.C.B.	10 June 1820	Died at Pittakonda, 6 July 1827.
Mr. Henry Sulivan Graeme	10 July 1827	Acting.
Mr. Stephen Rumbold Lushington	18 Oct. 1827	
Lt. Genl. Sir Frederick Adam, K.C.B.	25 Oct. 1832	
Mr. George Edward Russell	4 Mar. 1837	Acting.
Lord Elphinstone, G.C.H	6 Mar. 1837	
The Marquis of Tweeddale, K.T.	24 Sep. 1842	Was also Commander-in-Chief.
Mr. Henry Dickinson	23 Feb. 1848	Acting.
Maj. Genl. Sir Henry Pottinger	7 Apl. 1848	

(Contd.)

GOVERNORS OF FORT ST. GEORGE

Names	Assumed charge	Remarks
Mr. Daniel Eliott	24 Apl. 1854	
Lord Harris	28 Apl. 1854	
Sir. Charles Eward Trevelyan, K.C.B.	21 Mar. 1859	
Mr. William Ambrose Morehead	8 June 1860	Acting.
Sir Henry George Ward, K.T.	5 July 1860	Died at Madras, 6 Aug. 1860.
Mr. William Ambrose Morehad	4 Aug. 1860	Acting.
Col. Sir William Thomas Denison, K.C.B.	18 Feb. 1861	
Mr. Edward Malthy	26 Nov. 1863	Acting.
Lord Napier of Merchistoun, K.T.	27 Mar. 1866	
Mr. Alexander John Arbuthnot, C.S.I.	19 Feb. 1872	Acting.
Lord Hobart	15 May 1872	Died at Madras, 27 April 1875.
Mr. William Rose Robinson, C.S.I.	29 Apl. 1875	Acting.
The Duke of Buckingham and Chandos, G.C.S.I.	23 Nov. 1875	
Mr. William Patrick Adam	20 Dec. 1880	Died at Ootacamund, 24 May 1881.
Mr. William Hudleston, C.S.I.	24 May 1881	Acting.
Mr. Mountstuart Elphinstone Grant Duff	5 Nov. 1881	
The Hon'ble Robert Bourke, G.C.I.E.	8 Dec. 1886	Created Baron Connemara.
Mr. John Henry Garstin, C.S.I.	1 Dec. 1890	Acting.
Lord Wenlock, G.C.I.E.	24 Jan. 1891	
Sir. Arthur Elibank Havelock, G.C.M.G., G.C.I.E.	18 Mar. 1896	

GOVERNORS OF BOMBAY UP TO 1810

Names	Assumed charge	Remarks
The Hon. Sir Gervase Lucas	5 Nov. 1666	Died 21st May 1667.
Captain Henry Gary	22 May 1667	Officiating [1669].
Sir George Oxenden	22 Sep. 1668	Died in Surat, 14th July.
Mr. Gerald Aungier	14 July 1669	Do. 30th June 1677.
Mr. Thomas Rolt	30 June 1677	
Sir John Child, Bart.	27 Oct. 1681	
Mr. Barth Harris	4 Feb. 1690	Do. 10th May 1694.
Mr. Daniel Annesley	10 May 1694	Officiating.
Sir John Gayer	17 May 1694	
Sir Nicholas Waite	Nov. 1704	
Mr. William Aislabie	Sept.1708	
Sir Stephen Strutt	1715	Officiating.
Mr. Charles Boone	1716	
Mr. William Phipps	1720	
Mr. Robert Cowan	1728	Dismissed from the Service.
Mr. John Horne	22 Sep. 1734	
Mr. Stephen Law	7 Apl. 1739	
Mr. William Wake	26 Nov. 1742	
Mr. John Geekie	15 Nov. 1742	Officiating.
Richard Bourchier	17 Nov. 1750	
Mr. Charles Crommellin	20 Feb.1760	
Mr. Thomas Hodges	27 Jan. 1767	Died 23rd Feb. 1771.

(Contd.)

GOVERNORS OF BOMBAY UP TO 1810

Names	Assumed charge	Remarks
Mr. William Hornby	26 Feb. 1771	
Mr. Rawson Hart Boddam	1 Jan. 1784	
Mr. Andrew Ramsay	9 Jan. 1788	Officiating.
Maj. Genl. Sir W. Medows, K.B.	6 Sep. 1788	
Maj. Genl. Sir Robert Abercomby, K.B.	21 Jan. 1790	
Mr. George Dick	1 Nov. 1793	Officiating.
Mr. John Griffiths	3 Sep. 1795	Officiating.
Mr. Jonathan Duncan	27 Dec. 1785	Died in Bombay, 11th August, 1811.

GOVERNORS OF BENGAL AND GOVERNORS-GENERAL OF INDIA UP TO 1810

Names	Assumed charge	Remarks
Mr. William Hedges	July 1682	
Mr. William Gyfford	Aug. 1684	
Sir. Charles Eyre	26 May 1700	
Mr. John Beard	7 Jan. 1701	
Mr. Anthony Weltdon	20 July 1710	
Mr. John Russell	4 Mar. 1711	
Mr. Robert Hedges	3 Dec. 1713	
Mr. Samuel Freake	12 Jan. 1718	
Mr. John Deane	17 Jan. 1723	
Mr. Henry Frankland	30 Jan. 1726	
Mr. John Stockhouse	25 Feb. 1732	
Mr. Thomas Braddyll	29 Jan. 1739	
Mr. John Forster	4 Feb. 1746	
Mr. William Barwell	18 Apl. 1748	
Mr. Adam Dawson	17 July 1749	
Mr. William Fytch	5 July 1752	
Mr. Robert Drake	8 Aug. 1752	
Colonel Robert Clive	27 June 1758	
Mr. J.Z. Holwell	27 Jan. 1760	
Mr. Henry Vansittart	27 July 1760	
Mr. John Spencer	30 Dec. 1764	
Lord Clive	30 May 1765	

(Contd.)

GOVERNORS OF BENGAL AND GOVERNORS-GENERAL OF INDIA UP TO 1810

Names	Assumed charge	Remarks
Mr. Harry Verelst	29 Jan. 1767	
Mr. John Cartier	26 Dec. 1769	
The Right Hon'ble Warren Hastings	20 Oct. 1774	Was Governor of Bengal from 13th April, 1772, and assumed charge as First Governor-General under Act passed in 1773, (13 Geo. III. Ch. 63).
Sir John Macpherson, *Bart.*	8 Feb. 1785	
Earl Cornwallis, K.G.	12 Sept. 1786	Also Commander-in-Chief.
Sir John Shore, *Bart.*	28 Oct. 1793	
Lieut. Genl. The Hon'ble Sir Alured Clarke, K.C.B.	17 Mar. 1798	Officiating.
Marquis of Wellesley	18 May 1798	
Marquis Cornwallis, K.G.	30 July 1805	Also Commander-in-Chief. Died at Ghazpur, 5th Oct. 1805.
Sir George Barlow, *Bart.*, K.G.B.	10 Oct. 1805	Confirmed, 11th July 1806.
The Earl of Minto	31 July 1807	

1

WHY FORT ST. GEORGE WAS FOUNDED

Fort St. George was founded in the year 1639–40. The reason for its foundation must be sought in the history of the preceding century. The European world was astir with the discovery of America and the new route by the Cape of Good Hope to the East Indies. Bartholomew Diaz rounded the "Cape of Storms" as he called it, in 1486. When the King of Portugal heard of his exploit he recognized its true import, and renamed it the "Cape of Good Hope." Led by Vasco da Gama, the Portuguese arrived on the West Coast of India at the end of the fifteenth century. The legend of their landing and the greeting they received is curious. Vasco da Gama carried a small body of condemned convicts who were destined to play the part taken by the rabbit and the guinea pig in vivisection; they were to form the subjects of experiment, and were to be sent ashore on arrival at any strange port where the sentiments of the native were not known. If the experiment proved fatal it would merely be the execution of their sentences. If they escaped assassination, so much the better for them. Fortune favoured the handful of men sent ashore at Calicut; and the worst that awaited them was the incorrigible gaze of curiosity from the mild Hindu, which gaze survives to this day in all its pristine vitality. Imagining that they were Moors, with whom, the natives had been familiar for centuries, the West Coast fishermen conducted them to the house of an Arab from Tunis. He recognized them as Europeans at once, and addressed them in Spanish with the thoroughly European greeting of, "Devil take you! What brought you here?"

Following on the steps of the Portuguese came the Dutch, a century later; and close on the heels of the Dutch, the English. The Englishman, however, made his way to the East as a private individual long before any company was formed.[1] The Portuguese trader was no stranger at Bristol, to which place he brought spices, silk and other Indian commodities for sale. Under the wing of the Portuguese merchant the Englishman left his native shores and took passage to the East to try his luck on his own account. Very modest indeed was his first appearance in India. He took no armed soldiers with him, and made no demand in his sovereign's name. No national jealousies were excited by his presence; and if he survived the dangers of the voyage, he returned to his native land rich in gems and highly prized spices, and full of tales of all the wonders he had seen. The sight of his wealth was convincing; the enthusiasm of his fellow-merchants was fired. Why should they not do as he had done?

In 1589, a body of merchants petitioned Queen Elizabeth for leave to trade in India, with a monopoly of Indian goods. The leave was granted, and three ships sailed in 1591 under the command of Captain George Raymond. Unfortunately, the little fleet met with bad weather and only one of the vessels ever reached India. It was probably not more than three hundred tons, if so much, and it was under the command of Captain James Lancaster. The venture was of a private nature, the money being subscribed by a small body of merchants, who divided the profits on the return of the ships and closed the accounts. This plan was adopted by the East India Company for the first few voyages, and the profit sometimes amounted to more than two hundred per cent on the outlay. But it was found better in the end of turn the funds into common stock, as it was difficult to separate the accounts of each voyage when the ships assisted each other abroad and worked, as it was convenient to do, into each other's hands.

In 1600 the first East India Company was formed, and it obtained a charter giving it the monopoly of the East Indian trade. The Company consisted of some two hundred and fifty members, knights, aldermen and merchants of London.[2] They sent out their first fleet under the same Captain James Lancaster, who had sailed in 1591. He was called the General of the expedition; and besides merchants, factors and agents, he had a surgeon and chaplain on his staff. He ruled in the name of the Company absolutely; and on him rested the responsibility of the expedition. His orders were to trade, and to found, if possible, a factory on some spot where the natives were friendly and trade was brisk. There seemed no great difficulty in getting cargoes, although it required some patience and perseverance. The jealousy of the Dutch and Portuguese, and the grasping character of the natives were the chief hindrances; but the merchants succeeded all the same in exchanging their

English broadcloth and bullion for calicoes on the West Coast, and in trading the cotton goods away at Bantam in Java for cloves, nutmegs and spices, which brought such rich returns in England.

The establishment of a factory was a far more difficult matter to accomplish. Captain Lancaster succeeded in planting one at Bantam in Java, where he left Mr. William Starkie in charge, in the year 1602–03. With this the Company had to be content for a few years; for though other attempts were made to establish centres, they did not prove permanent until 1612, when a footing was obtained North of Bombay, at Surat.

In 1611 the *Globe*, one of the Company's ships, rounded Cape Comorin and came up the Coromandel Coast. It was feeling its way with the hope of discovering some place where a permanent settlement might be made by rent or purchases, and where the holding rested on a firmer foundation than the caprice of the native ruler; or the tolerance of the Dutch and the Portuguese. It arrived before Masulipatam, a seaport between Madras and Calcutta, two cities that were not in existence then, only to find that the Dutch, as usual were before them. Captain Anthony Hippon, who was in command of the vessel, had two Dutch men on board, who were in the employ of the English Company. He sent one of these, Peter Williamson Floris, ashore with Mr. Robert Brown, an English factor, in the ship's skiff, having no notion what the surf on the Coromandel Coast could do. They were upset, and Brown, who was far from well, was nearly drowned. They were favourably received by the native port-officer, and they sent back at once to the ship for Mr. Lucas Antheunis, the other Dutchman, and Mr. Thomas Essington. By this time the President of the Dutch Company had heard of their arrival. He came forth in great wrath, flourishing his cowle or permission from the native ruler to trade and bade the strangers depart; an order they refused to obey. A quarrel ensued and the native port-officer or shahbunder, who evidently had good reason for welcoming the English, asked the gentlemen to refer the matter to the native lady who ruled Masulipatam in the name of her Sultana or Queen. When she arrived, she declared herself in favour of the Dutch, and would give no assistance and grant no cowle to the English.

But the Briton was not to be so easily beaten off the field. Essington and Floris determined to remain at Masulipatam whilst the ship went on a further voyage of discovery up the coast. When it returned, another effort was made to obtain permission to open a trade with the place; and this time the Company's servants were rewarded with some success, although they did not get all that they wanted.[3] They were permitted to trade on the payment of custom; and to leave some of their men to establish a factory. But they were not allowed to purchase land, and might at any moment be told to depart. Brown, Essington, Floris, Antheunis and Symon Evans were the five men chosen to work the first factory on the Coromandel Coast. Lucas Antheunis wrote from Masulipatam, "We are arrived here, upon the coast of Coromandel in Pettipoli[4] and in Masulipatam, in which two places we do hold our residence this 10th September 1611." The intention was to stay there three months to buy calicoes, and then to proceed to Bantam in Java, returning again to the new factory. Robert Brown was the chief; he had had experience in the Java trade, having been one of the Council of Merchants in the second expedition sent out under Sir Henry Middleton in 1604. Middleton left Brown at the factory at

Bantam with Gabriel Towerson, whom he was to succeed in case of Towerson's death.[5]

Brown was a valued servant, much respected and trusted by the Directors; but he did not live long to serve them. Whilst a Bantam he contracted dysentery, which he was never able to throw off. The water of Bantam was known to the Dutch to be deleterious in its effects, and this fact they carefully concealed from their rivals, the English. Middleton took a supply on board his ship with the most disastrous results to his crew on the journey home; and Brown received his death-warrant from the same source. He did not long survive his arrival at Masulipatam. He died and was buried September 8th, 1611, the first victim claimed on the Coromandel Coast from the ranks of the Company's servants. The second was Thomas Essington, who followed him shortly afterwards, May 17th, 1614. Their names head a long list, an innumerable army of able men, who have laid down their lives in the work of making an Empire, the like of which Asia has never seen before within her borders.[6]

The ships in which these pioneers of the English trade in the Eastern Seas set sail were no larger than the yachts of the present day, with which pleasure-seekers sail round our coasts in summer; and they were not nearly so well found. The ship-builders had no notion what a tropical climate could do in the way of decay. Cables rusted and cordage rotted with incredible rapidity; even the ships themselves were attacked by worms, which riddled their timbers in a manner unknown in England. The drinking water was kept in casks, which decayed before the journey was ended; and the food became weavilly and unfit for consumption. The merchants and factors who travelled as passengers had none of the luxuries which are to be found on a modern passenger-boat. A man was given a perfectly bare cabin in which he often placed,—unfortunate landsman that he was,—an ordinary English bedstead; it is to be hoped for his sake that he found some means of lashing and steadying it. He provided himself with looking glass, washbasin or anything else of that kind which he might think necessary for his toilette. If he required a bath he got a sailor to give him a douche of saltwater from a bucket. One advantage he possessed over the traveller of today; he had his cabin to himself, and he was allowed to fill it up very much as he pleased. He carried his clothes and personal effects in strong sea-chests, which he was glad to keep under his immediate eye, safe from the thieving fingers of the sailors. He also provided himself with a store of provisions and wine to supplement the very plain fare of salt junk, mouldy bread and boiled pease, which constituted the rations of the ship. He bought fresh fish, meat, vegetables and fruit at the different ports, the fruit being especially acceptable as it helped to mitigate the evils of scurvy, that curse of sea-voyaging.

The trip out took six or seven months, and was tedious and full of dangers without and within. Of the former, storms and pirates were the worst; whilst those within were disease and fire. In one of the earliest records of a voyage home, the captain relates how the cook, "o'er-guzzled with drink", dug a hole through the brick fire-place into the wooden side of the ship and set it on fire; "Thereby," the Captain plaintively observes, "giving us much trouble." The ships were absent from England two years, and it is a marvel how they survived their many perils.

Whenever a trading centre was opened by the Company, the community, however small, was organised and placed under definite rules previously laid down by the Court of Directors. Accordingly, the little Agency at Masulipatam was put under a Chief; and a Council was chosen from among the merchants. In spite of the permission accorded to them to trade, matters did not progress very favourably. They succeeded, however, in establishing two other stations on a smaller scale at Armaghaum and Pulicat, places lying between Masulipatam and Madras. As far as the market was concerned there was no lack of goods. The eagerly sought diamonds, the valuable silks, calicoes and saltpetre, were all there ready for exchange with the Englishman's broadcloth and bullion. But the jealousy of the Dutch increased yearly; and they undersold their rivals in the market, and did all they could to make mischief with the natives. The native ruler, presuming on the unprotected state of the English, blackmailed their goods under cover of exacting custom; and commercial enterprise was in imminent danger of being paralysed. It was distinctly recognised that if trade was to be developed with any success, a new and unoccupied field must again be sought, where a holding could be bought or rented from the native sovereign. The matter was reported home to the directors, who responded by commissioning Mr. Francis Day, one of the members of Council at Masulipatam in 1639, to seek for some spot where operations might be carried on under more favourable conditions.

The removal of a trading centre on a practically unknown coast was no easy matter. There were more requirements than one in choice of a new station. Good anchorage for ships was an essential; some natural protection from thieving hordes of horsemen was another; the proximity of good markets for exchanging commodities was a third; and an easy inland communication was a fourth important consideration.

When Day set out to search for the spot which should combine all these advantages, he turned his face to the South. Avoiding the Dutch settlement at Pulicat, where an attempt had already been made, unsuccessfully, to gain a footing, he directed his attention to St. Toma, as it was then called, the St. Thomé or Mylapore of the present day. It had been one of the largest of the Portuguese colonies on the Coromandel Coast; but its glory had departed with the decay of Portugal as a European power. A number of country-born Indo-Portuguese remained, whose blood was mingled with that of the people of the land, and who regarded India as their home. They met Day with a warm welcome, seeing in him a man who might infuse new life into the moribund trade of their town. The place was capable of renewed commercial activity. It possessed a strong fort which only needed repair; and the town was thronged with Portuguese and native merchants, whose experience in dealing with Europeans made them valuable as interpreters and middlemen between the English buyer and the Hindu producer. Day could probably have rented St. Thomé had be been so inclined; but he chose in preference a narrow strip of land directly north of St. Thomé, which seemed to him likely to prove an easier and more permanent holding. Here the Company could reign with greater safety and freedom, and maintain its independence with a smaller force in troublous times, than would suffice to hold St. Thomé. Here it could form its colony on its own lines, and it was unlikely from the appearance of the place that any other foreign power would ever covet its possession.

Aided by the friendly Portuguese, he effected the renting of a piece of land along the shore, a mile broad and six miles in length. It had nothing apparently to commend it. It was devoid of beauty of scenery; it had no harbour, although there was good anchorage in its roads. It was nothing but a dreary waste of sand, on which a monotonous sea broke in a double line of surf, giving it an inhospitable look, which it retains to the present day. A shallow lagoon-like river, running parallel with the sea for a short distance, formed the protection needed on the land side from predatory tribes of horsemen; but otherwise the river was useless. It afforded no shelter for ships; and its brackish waters were of no use for irrigation purposes. It often emitted an unpleasant and unhealthy effluvia from the rotting seaweed lying in its loathsome black ooze. The river, confined to narrower limits in the present day, with some of its mud banks reclaimed, is scoffingly dubbed "The Silvery Cooum." To atone for its defects, it has a trick of assuming in the tropical sunset a fascinating beauty and fairness. Its smooth waters reflect the gorgeous colours of the sky; the blue smoke of the wood fires in the native huts spreads in aetherial azure haze over the palms and banyan trees on its banks, and the eye of the artist is equally delighted as his nostril is offended when he gazes across its broad bosom. When the sky is purple with the gathering clouds of the monsoon, the Cooum ruffles its waters into a sheet of silvery grey ripples, and it gleams in its setting of dark green like a polished mirror of steel; even the black wet ooze glisters with delicate shades of pearl. But the Cooum is not remembered for its false and transient beauty; it is indelibly stamped on the memory of the Anglo-Indian by its odours.

Neither the smell of the river nor the acres of sandy waste discouraged the preserving servant of the East India Company, and Day concluded his negotiations satisfactorily on the 1st of March, 1639–40. And by his transaction his employers obtained their first territorial rights in India.

The Rajah of Chandragheri, who received the cash paid down as rent for the ground, must have laughed in his sleeve at the folly of the English in parting with gold for that dreary waste of sand and mud. He could not foresee that the apparently worthless spot might hold a Clive and a Munro, and that it might send forth mandates for the deposition of princes stronger than himself; that it might shelter and despatch a Job Charnock to found Calcutta in the name of his masters, a city destined to extend its rule from Cape Comorin to the Himalayas, and to stretch a powerful arm over the length and breadth of the country to protect the weak from the tyranny of the strong. Early visitors to Fort St. George thought scorn of the bargain; but afterwards, when the advantages of its strategical position were proved, Englishmen recognised the fact that Day had chosen well.

The price of the grant was a yearly rent of about six hundred pounds. The agreement was drawn up on a plate of gold, and it was dated March 1st, 1639 (old style). It was carefully preserved by the Company in Fort St. George until 1746. In that year the Fort was handed over to the French by treaty. During the occupation of the French between 1746 and 1749 the gold plate disappeared, and the Company lost, a valuable historical memorial of the founding of Fort St. George, and the acquisition of the first bit of Indian soil by the English.[7]

2

THE INFANCY OF FORT ST. GEORGE

FRANCIS DAY'S task was only half-finished when he obtained possession of the land. There was no building upon it but a half-dozen mud huts belonging to the muckwas or fishermen; he had to set about raising a warehouse for the Company's goods, and a house for the offices, wherein the Company's affairs might be transacted. Dwellings were also needed for the Company's servants, and it was necessary to attract the country-born Portuguese merchants who were the link between the exporter and the producer.

When the Dutch took Cochin on the West Coast a few years later, they committed the grave error of driving out all the Roman Catholics from the city. These men were the descendants of the Portuguese traders and native women, and they held the commerce of the inland country in their hands. When they were gone, the Dutch found themselves an isolated colony of exporters cut-off from their channels of supply.

Day made no such mistake. Sinking his religious scruples, if he had any, he invited the Portuguese traders from St. Thomé, and also any Englishmen not already in the Company's service who were trading there, to come into the Fort under certain conditions and settle. He gave them permission to build houses for themselves, and promised them the protection and countenance of the Company so long as they conformed to its rules. The advantages of such an offer were seen at once, and numbers of the traders availed themselves of it without delay. They were only too glad to leave a place which could no longer shelter them from the rapacity of the native ruler nor compensate them for a lost commerce.

Before long, substantial houses began to rise in the North West corner of the Fort, which looked towards a small native town; and at the same time the walls of the Fort itself were being erected on the north, south and east sides. The houses were built along the banks of the river, which then ran parallel with the sea coast; the walls of the houses, flanked as they were a part of the Fort wall. The North West corner of the original Fort was called Caldera or Caldere Point, Caldera being a Portuguese surname which occurs in the rent-rolls later on, as the name of one of the owners of a house in the Fort. It is also to be found in the Register books of St. Mary's church. Between Caldera Point and the point by the sea named Fisher's Point, a curtain or wall was erected, about one hundred yards long on the North, which was pierced by two narrow gateways. They led out to the native settlement called, at first, Gentu Town, and afterwards Blacktown, from the colour of its inhabitants, a name it retains to the present day. The colony inside the Fort was called White Town, but the White Town was dropped as soon as the English began to build houses for themselves outside the Fort.

The gates in the North wall were called the Choultry Gate and the Middle or North Gate.

One of the first to avail himself of Day's invitation was an Englishman named Clarke. He came from Masulipatam, where he held office under the Company. He built his house immediately after the concession of the land, and chose a site near Caldera Point. His name was given to one of the gates in the North wall, which gate is mentioned in a petition sent in to the Governor as "Tom Clarke's Gate". He had a son who was afterwards Portuguese interpreter to the Company, and who succeeded to the property. In 1675 the Company was obliged to deprive Clarke of his house.

The fortifications at Caldera Point and on the West along the river bank, consisting only of house and garden walls, were not strong enough to resist any attack made under the direction of a European power. In 1672 the French arrived at St. Thomé with a strong force, and threatened the English; and it became necessary to place Fort St. George in a suitable state of defence such as would resist their attacks. The houses at Caldera Point had to be pulled down, Tom Clarke's amongst the number. After it was done he sent in a quaintly worded petition to the President in Council, asking for an indemnity, in 1675. He admitted the necessity of the destruction of the houses which was "built thirty-four years since, when neither bulwarks nor scarce a house of noate appeared"; he claimed consideration on the score of his "ancestor having been ye first inhabitant through ye invitation of ye then Agent, who removed about that time from Armagon", (near Masulipatam).

In reply to his request he was assigned a sum of money, which was to be raised by a house tax levied on the inhabitants of Blacktown.

But they were not used to this mode of raising revenue, although they had had more than sufficient experience in various other ways of taxation, and they strenuously resisted its imposition. It is to be feared that Clarke never received his indemnity. He dies at Fort St. George, and was buried in the English cemetery lying between the Fort and Blacktown, a piece of ground which may veritably be called English soil from the number of our countrymen who lie there. His tombstone was removed with others from the cemetery to the compound of St. Mary's church in the Fort, after the attack by the French in 1758 under Lally. The old tombs in the cemetery gave cover to the enemy and enabled the French to bring their guns close up to the Fort walls; so the burial ground was levelled and cleared in its whole length, and some of the stones bearing inscriptions were preserved.

The inscription on the stone which commemorates Thomas Clarke says that he was the son of Thomas Clarke, an Englishman, who was formerly President of the English Company in the town of Masulipatam; and that he (Thomas Clarke, Junior) died October 6th, 1683. The stone lies on the north side of the church, and is cemented with others into a pavement, which is overshadowed by the oleanders growing so luxuriantly within the compound railings. The slab is broken in four pieces, the effect probably of a canon-ball to when the Fort guns were turned on the cemetery against the French. The inscription is in Latin, and it is surmounted by a coat of arms and a crest, manifestly hewn by a native sculptor. The tinctures are not given. The arms are: On a field—a fcssc—two plates. In chief two Maltese crosses. The crest is: On the helmet of a Knight a Maltese cross. At the end of the 17th century a Captain Thomas Clarke, Master of a ship, is mentioned in the records of the Company at

Fort St. George; and there were Clarkes at Masulipatam contemporary with Thomas Clarke, the Portuguese interpreter.

The first agent of Fort St. George was its founder. Like Charnock, the founder of Calcutta, he received no encouragement nor praise from the Directors for what he had effected. They were willing to pay custom and subsidise a native prince and to build a factory under the shelter of his wing. But they were not prepared to become territorial lords and to possess a fortified seaport of their own, where they might export and import their goods free of all charge. They did not know what political difficulties it might lead them into. A Fort seemed an expensive and dangerous luxury which was quite unnecessary. They were alarmed at the very word "Fort". It was diametrically opposed to the policy they had pursued for the first half century of their commercial existence, a scrupulously conciliatory policy of peace at any price. They therefore expressed their disapproval of his action, little knowing the true conditions of trade in the East.

One of the first lessons learnt by the merchant when he arrived in the country was the insecurity of property, and the necessity of building a stronghold for the safe warehousing of his goods. There was a time for buying, when the market, according to the season, was well stocked with merchandise; and there was a time for lading and despatching the ships, when the trade winds, or monsoons, as they are called on the coast of Hindustan, were favourable. These times did not accord, and the goods brought in by the merchants on contract had often to lie some months before they could be shipped. The merchants in Leadenhall Street never seemed able to grasp the state of affairs in those early days, nor to comprehend the state of affairs in those early days, nor to comprehend the many difficulties which beset their servants in the execution of their duties. Nothing shows this fact more plainly than the requests made by the Directors thirty years later, when they elaborated new rules for the government of the growing agency.

There was the dilatoriness and want of faith on the part of the native producer; the roguery of the middleman or broker, who swore that goods were not procurable when he wanted to raise the price; and the grasping dishonesty of the native ruler, who blackmailed and blockaded the Englishman whenever he wanted a little ready cash. Not only did the Court of Directors expect their servants to manage their commercial affairs with punctuality, as though they were trading in a well-ordered European market, and to safeguard their property, but they also asked them to control matters between foreign powers and the natives. They inquired what immunities from custom the Dutch had procured for themselves at the different native ports, and expressed a hope that the Governor and Council would prevent the grant of any "which might be to our prejudice". Considering that the Governor and Council could barely protect their own merchandise, and ensure fair treatment for themselves at the hands of the natives, it was hardly likely that they would run their heads into the lion's mouth by attempting to dictate terms on which the Dutch were to be allowed to trade. The Directors requested their servants to put a stop to blackmailing, and prevent native merchants from supplying inferior calicoes; also to see that the masters of English ships, whether in the Company's service or not, did not carry merchants of other nations to trade in the Southern Seas, where the Company claimed the monopoly of trade. Yet with all this they were constantly reiterating their peace-at-any-price policy. They did not appear to understand that an army-corps would have been needed to enforce the stipulations they wished to impose upon the Indian world. They also asked to be told the true price of commodities sold by the natives, a matter which to this day has not been ascertained satisfactorily; as the habit of the native dealer, from the merchant to the pedlar-hawker, is to ask one-third more than he hopes to get, and two-thirds more than he will take. A fixed price was ever the will-o'-the-wisp to the European in the Indian market.

When directions such as these reached the Governor he was apt to grow impatient, and his frame of mind evidenced itself in the replies he sent home. He then had to submit to reproof; and was told that the Directors highly disapproved of the tone of his letters; "and for the future we expect you will manage your pen with more respect," they said.

In spite of the disapproval of the Court, Day and his successors hastened on the completion of the Fort. He secured a small garrison of soldiers, whose duty, amongst other things, was to form an escort for the Company's property as it was carried in or out of the Fort. A small colony of merchants, factors and writers in the Company's service, was formed under the usual rules, and the Agency commenced its commercial life. It was governed from Bantam; its trade consisted chiefly in Indian calicoes and muslins which were needed for the Bantam market. It was a very small beginning, with not even the countenance of the Court to help it; and it speaks volumes for the pluck and judgement of its promoters that the little settlement ever maintained its existence at all. Certainly trade was very bad in England at that time. Society was disorganized by the Civil Wars, and merchants were generally idle and disheartened, expecting those who dealt in the necessaries of war, such as arms, ordnance and gunpowder. However, in 1652 the place was raised to the dignity of a Presidency, and Mr. Aaron Baker arrived from Bantam as its first President. The first general letter sent home to the Directors is dated November 5th, 1642, ten years before the place was raised to this rank.

As the records of Fort St. George do not date back earlier than 1670, there is not much material for the formation of a detailed history of its first years. A few facts may be gleaned here and there which suffice to give a general outline of its rise; and the monuments afford a few personal details of the men who passed a portion of their lives, and ended their days within the walls. The story of the growth of the place may easily be guessed. It was the record of a struggle between a handful of English merchants, who were bound down to a peace policy, and the native ruler, who already wanted to break faith over the bargain his predecessor had made.

The Agency was small and weak; but the men who ruled it were quick to perceive the advantages it offered, if they were given a freer hand and had the command of men and money; and this was the burden of the cry sent home. Baker could do no more than his predecessors, but he probably added his voice to the entreaty for ships, bullion and soldiers. One of the mementoes of Baker's Presidentship is to be found in St. Mary's compound. It is the saddest domestic tragedy that can happen in a man's live. He lost his wife, Mrs. Elizabeth Baker, at Bantam, just before he left the island. She is described as having travelled far over foreign seas, and having fallen a victim to the unhealthy climate of Java in 1652. This stone also bears a quaintly carved coast of arms without tinctures. It gives, on a field—a saltire engrailed; in chief a lion passant; impaling on a field—a fesse embattled—between three Catherine wheels. There is no record of Baker's death; it may therefore be supposed that he survived the climate and lived to enjoy his wealth at home.

Associated with Baker was a Mr. Henry Greenhill, who had been Agent before the place was raised to a Presidency. He signed a document with Baker in 1652. It was issued by the President for the purpose of settling some caste disputes which came before "President Aaron Baker, Agent Henry Greenhill and William Gurney." There is a curious epitaph on a mottled marble slab, which is let into the outer wall at the North-West corner of the church. The inscription is in Latin, and its tone conveys the complacent self-importance of the old East India merchants, an importance he had every right to assume by virtue of his pluck and endurance. It says: 'Wayfarer, whoever you are, standstill, standstill for a little while, nor shall I ask in vain if you are a good Christian. Not even tears will pay the price of your grief, when you know that the greatest ornament of his distinguished family, Henry Greenhill, who was the sole Agent of the Honourable Company of English Merchants trading in the East and second to none, lies here. For ten years, with the greatest attention and the strictest probity, he carried on his business. He died in the year of Christ 1658, aged forty-five."

He was one of the first settlers in the Fort, and built his own house, which he placed on the river bank. It was known as Agent Greenhill's house, and was occupied in 1672 by William Jearsey, a free trader. Jearsey asked to leave to raise it by a third storey, but his request was not granted. No houses were allowed to be above a certain height, lest they should obstruct the view of the surrounding country from the Fort House, as it was then called. Jearsey also built a pier into the river, which he was ordered to clear away. Greenhill, like Clarke, left descendants. A Thomas Greenhill owned a house in the Fort in 1687, and the name occurs in the register books in the following century.[8]

3

THE EARLY GROWTH OF FORT ST. GEORGE

In 1655 the Directors ordered the reduction of the Fort to an Agency again. The garrison was also reduced from twenty-six to ten men and the Company's servants to two factors. This was cutting Fort St. George down to the smallest dimensions possible short of annihilation. The promoters of its establishment must have regarded the action of the Directors with anxiety and dismay. Over two thousand pounds had been spent on the buildings and fortifications, not including the private money laid out by the inhabitants in dwelling houses. Within its walls the merchants had found at last the asylum they had so ardently desired ever since their arrival on the Coromandel Coast. Were their efforts to be of no avail? Was all their work to be undone?

Thomas Chambers, who held office as Agent after the reduction, must have had a good deal to say on the matter, and a good deal to do with the preservation of Fort St. George as a Presidency. He had gained a bitter experience at Masulipatam, where he had been serving from the year 1652 to 1659, at which date he was sent to Madras. The Factory at Masulipatam, unprotected by proper fortifications, had been through the usual vicissitudes of misfortune and humiliation, which attend an unarmed colony of foreigners in a treacherous land. He also knew that the animosity of the Dutch could effect, and he had felt the galling oppression of the native sovereign. A fort was to him the one desideratum of the merchant. He seemed determined to keep up the prestige of the one of which he now found himself the ruler; and ignoring the reduction, he wrote himself down as President of Fort St. George.

To him belongs the credit of organising the first Police arrangements for the protection of property in Madras. From the earliest times a kind of watchman duty had been performed by a native called the Pedda Naik. This man contracted to provide twenty men for a certain sum to watch over the property of the inhabitants. But both the Fort and Blacktown were growing in size, and the Pedda Naik's duties increased. He complained that the sum of money was insufficient to supply the requisite number of watchmen. His petition for a larger subsidy was entertained, and he was assigned certain paddy fields together with some small customs on common articles of consumption. For this he provided fifty watchmen, who were to be responsible for the orderliness of Blacktown, and for the good conduct of all the native inhabitants of the Fort, especially with regard to theft. These arrangements, made by Chambers, served very well for the next quarter of a century, when they had to be reorganised on account of the bribery and corruption that went on.

Besides organising the first Police corps, Chambers laid the foundation of the Governor's Body Guard. The Pedda Naik engaged to supply the Governor with a hundred and fifty to two hundred peons to attend him whenever he went through the native town, or abroad to take his pleasure, or on any state occasions. They were a very different set of men from the fine troop of mounted sowars who now accompany His Excellency the Governor whenever he appears in public, but they were the nucleus from which the present Bodyguard was evolved.

The written orders establishing the Police and Bodyguard are signed by "Thomas Chamber" in June 1659; and in them he calls himself "We, the President," as though he fully understood the dignity and power of the office, and were anticipating a speedy restoration of the Agency to a Presidency. The Directors manifestly approved of his general behaviour, for on his retirement the status of Fort St. George was restored, and Chambers, as he is more frequently called, received the honour of knighthood. His name appears subseqeuntly in the records in connection with commercial transactions. He was the last Agent, although the term is used in the Company's books for several succeeding years; and he was succeeded by Sir[9] Edward Winter, who was appointed President in the year 1661.

In 1660 the Restoration of the Monarchy brought peace at home and the revival of trade; and with the appointment of Sir Edward Winter, the Directors plucked up heart to put a little fresh life into their operations in the Bay. Fort St. George was once more made independent of Java, and held directly responsible to the Court for its actions. The lesser factories on the Coromandel Coast and Bay were again placed under its jurisdiction. Bantam was too far off to maintain discipline, and all the factories on the East Coast of India had got a little out of hand for want of a chief on the spot.

There were two matters which troubled the Court. One was the difficulty which so often occurred with the native ruler, who governed the country round Madras in the name of the King of Golconda. He was called the Nawab and was a most rapacious individual, always looking for presents, (or piscashes) for himself, which are nothing more than bribes. At the same time he demanded increased rent and customs for his sovereign. When his demands were refused, he seized upon the supplies of food and merchandise going into the Fort, half starving the Company's servants with a kind of blockade, and paralysing trade. The old account books of Fort St. George are studded with items of piscashes given to grasping natives, who were too strong to be resisted. The Directors grudged the expenditure over bribes even more than over fortifications. But it was impossible for the President to assure an independent front with no army at his back. There were actually at that time not enough men to man the guns on the walls; and, much against the grain, conciliatory measures had to be used, when the President would fain have tried the effect of powder and shot.

The private trade of the Company's servants was the other trouble, and it was a more difficult matter to deal with; for the Court of Directors and the Company's agents did not view it in the same light. The Company claimed by its charter the exclusive right to trade between India and Great Britain, except so far as it should grant concessions to those who would enter into a convenant to observe its rules. It paid its servants small salaries and expected them to profit by its concessions with regard to inland trade in India; but even there it laid down certain arbitrary restrictions which tied the hands of the merchant. Small salaries suited the Directors. They looked well in the accounts and reduced establishment charges to a minimum, which was hightly satisfactory to the shareholders. But the difficulty arose in regulating the private trade to the limits the Company deemed legal. The merchant, factor or writer readily subscribed to the rules of the covenant at home before starting, and entered into a bond to observe them. But when he arrived in the country and saw on all sides of him men of different nationalities engaged in a lucrative trade which was denied to him alone, he felt that his ignorance had been taken advantage of, and that he had been dealt unfairly, with by his superiors. Sometimes he left the Company's service, sacrificing his bond; but he more generally stayed, and traded just so far as his individual conscience would allow. The foreign merchants recognised no Company's rights. They laughed at rules made by a handful of unknown men on the other side of the globe; and it was impossible for the Directors to establish any right to any branch of trade in the East, such as they claimed in calicoes in the Southern Seas. Portuguese, Dutch, French, Spaniards, Danes, Moors and Gentus were all buying and selling in the great Indian market as they chose. And the market seemed to the new-comer broad enough, in truth, to hold half a dozen companies and yet leave room for the English free trader. He saw no reason why he should not do as others did, and take his share of the good things. It was an open and fair field; why should he be the only man excluded? Arguing on these lines, most men succumbed to the temptation. Some boldly carried on their transactions in their own names. Others went into partnership with the Portuguese, into whose families they sometimes married. Some traded under the wing of the native merchant or through him, merely placing their money in his hands; and one gentleman went so far as to conduct his commercial affairs in the name of the King of Bantam; a piece of British impudence typical of the nation.

When irregularities came to the ears of the Directors they meted out punishment in the form of recalling or dismissing the offenders. Naturally, in the scramble for the plums of the private trade, there were many heart-burnings, and men often fell out. A common method of retaliation was the despatch of private letters to those members of the Directorate who happended to be personal friends of the writers. The letters made insinuations, or openly accused the obnoxious person of illicit private trade. It was like a red rag to a bull with the Directors until they learnt to be wiser. They were only too ready to listen to any tale concerning the infringement of their rights; and many a man was recalled, or suspended from office, on the mere testimony of an enemy, without being given an opportunity of explaining matters. When he arrived home he had his tale to tell; and he did not spare the man through whose instrumentality he had lost his post. It was quite a case of the pot calling the kettle black. But neither the pot nor the kettle were so very black after all, and the Directors would often have done better to have attended to their own business, and taken no notice of the private affairs of their servants, so long as there were no graver evils in their ranks, such as embezzlement and falsification of accounts. It is due to the Directors to record the fact that they gave their servants a fair hearing on their return home, and made every endeavour to discover the truth of the accusations against them. If they found that they had treated a servant harshly, they reinstated him. But it was extremely difficult to arrive at the truth; for the men who bore witness took such different views of the question;

with regard to the inland trade in the East and the traffic in the Eastern and Southern Seas, what constituted legitimate trade could only be a matter of opinion, and it was impossible to draw a hard and fast line between it and contraband dealing.

Sir Edward Winter, who had been for some years past in the Company's service, was sent out with despotic powers to examine into the whole question. He was at liberty to dismiss and even imprison, and to confiscate the goods of any persons whom he detected in unlicenced trading, whether they were freemen or the servants of the Company. He set himself to his task with a zeal and energy which alarmed the little community of Fort St. George. They were soon made aware that their own private ventures would not bear the searching light of Sir Edward's investigations, armed as he was with new powers and a fresh code of rules drawn up for his guidance; and they did their best to hide their delinquencies and throw dust in his eyes. With such a man at the head of affairs life was not worth living, they thought; and they fell back on their old plan of trying to tar their Chief with the same brush as they were tarred with themselves. Voluminous letters were sent home containing hints that Sir Edward Winter was indulging in free trade himself, and feathering his nest to the detriment of the Company. There was no sympathy between the President and his subordinates at the commencement of his rule; and disgusted with society in general, and his thankless task in particular, he sent in his resignation.

The Directors accepted it, giving credit to the tales that had gone home as usual; and believing that their experiment had been a failure. The next President was chosen from their commercial ranks at home; he was a Mr. George Foxcroft and a business man to his backbone.

He was accustomed to the desk and the counting house; and he took life with all the Puritanical seriousness of the day. He sailed for India in 1665, carrying his commission with him.

Between the time of Sir Edward's despatch of his resignation and the arrival of his successor the atmosphere cleared, and the President, having realised what his position was worth with all its advantages, was no longer anxious to give up office; moreover, he had made good friends with his colleagues. However, he could not do otherwise than submit to the orders which he himself had originated. He accordingly received Foxcroft with the respect due to the coming man, and handled over charge in the usual courtly manner of the Cavalier that he was. Foxcroft's suspicions, if he had any, were lulled to rest; and he offered his predecessor a place on the Council as Second, until such time as it should be convenient for him to return home. Sir Edward hankered after his lost power; he could not wrest it by force from the hands of his supplanter, unless there were good reason for such an action. Could he find just cause for so doing? He awaited his opportunity and watched his enemy. The man was an uncompromising old Puritan; and it was not long before he expressed opinions about the King and his debauched court in words which were nothing less than treasonable in those days. Sir Edward was ready; he denounced the astounded President and his son, who had come out with him, as traitors. The Garrison and the majority of the merchants were on Winter's side, and an attempt was made to arrest the Foxcrofts. They resisted, aided by a few friends, and there was a fight between the two parties, in which one man was killed. The Foxcrofts were overpowered and imprisoned, and Sir Edward Winter once more resumed the reins of government.

He had now to justify his conduct to the Directors. He wrote home and made out of good case of disloyalty and treason against Foxcroft, whilst the friends of the latter had their tale to tell. Not content with writing to the Court of Directors, Winter also sent his story to the King and to the Archbishop of Canterbury. It took a long time in those days to settle matters when they were referred home. Perhaps Sir Edward thought of this when he closed the prison doors on Foxcroft and his son. Those unfortunate men were kept under restraint, though not confined to a felon's cell, for three years, in spite of the efforts made by their partisans to get them released. During that time Sir Edward ruled Fort St. George and its subordinates factories in the Bay, with a wisdom and judgement which filled the coffers of the Company.

Meanwhile the story that he sent home had had a very different effect on the recipients than he intended. It overshot the mark; and, to the suspicious minds of the Directors, it told a tale of deep-rooted, wide-spread disloyalty. The King and the Archbishop, as well as the Directors, were convinced that nothing less than wholesale sedition permeated the entire community of the Fort, from Sir Edward Winter himself down to the youngest writer on the establishment. This impression was strengthened by an insinuation on the part of Foxcroft's friends that Sir Edward intended to handover the Fort to the Dutch.

To the astonishment of Madras, at the end of three years a formidable armament arrived in the Roads, prepared to blockade the place and take it by storm. Explanatory messages were exchanged between the President and the Commissioners on board, and it seemed to be a great relief to the minds of the latter, when they found that no such measures were required. Indeed, the whole affair was only a storm in a teacup, the first of its kind, but by no means the last, in the Madras Council. The Commissioners took peaceable possession of the Fort; Foxcroft was released and reinstated as President; an investigation was held, and Sir Edward was exonerated from all blame. He was allowed to remain in Madras till he had settled his affairs; an order was issued to remain in Madras till he had with every respect, and he was subsequently given a passage home in one of the Company's ships. Freight was also allowed for his property, the order being accompanied by a prudent clause to the effect that no prohibited goods were to be sent amongst them.

Foxcroft was permitted to reign for a year, when he was superseded in his turn by Sir William Langhorne. Foxcroft's son, Nathaniel, who was imprisoned with his father, was to have had a passage home also, but he did not live to claim it. He lies buried outside the Fort; his tombstone has been placed by the side of that belonging to Aaron Baker's wife. The inscription is simple and touching. It echoes down to succeeding generations of strangers the bitter grief of the parent, who paid so large a price for the fortune he amassed on India's shores. It is as follows : "Here lyeth the body of Nathaniel Foxcroft, son of George Foxcroft, Agent and Governor in Fort St. George. He was borne into this World the 6th of September 1635, and translated into a better to the Resurrection of the Just, the 26th October 1670 after he had finished his pilgrimage on the earth, of 35 years, having always exhibited all the honour due from a dear and dutiful son to his parents, and by his universal obliging and ingenious conversation obtained a good report, and left a good name with all men."[10]

Mr. John Kelsall, I.C.S. (ret.) says that Winter was buried at St. Mary's, Battersea, the parish church. "The inscription on his monument states that he died in 1686, aged sixty-four, and that he was in India forty-two years. He was therefore born in 1622, and assuming that he went out when about twenty years of age, he can have returned home 'for good' only two or three years before his death." He may have come back to India after his deposition at Madras, but it was not to Fort St. George, as his name does not appear on the lists of the inhabitants, nor upon the nominal rolls of the Company's servants on the Coromandel Coast. Mr. Kelsall adds:

"There is an imposing monument to him on the wall of the south gallery. It is surmounted by a life-size bust of Sir Edward, in a full-bottomed wig, and he appears a truculent and stolid-looking man with a heavy moustache, but otherwise clean shaven. At the bottom are two carvings in high relief; the one representing him, unarmed and alone, wrestling with a tiger on the seashore; the other on foot with a drawn sword, pursuing four natives, one of whom is mounted. These incidents in his career are referred to in the inscription below. This ruins:

EDWARDI WYNTER.
Equitis qui ad huc impuber ex patria
Proficiens in Orientalibus Indys, mercaturam feliciter
Exercuit, magnas opes comparavit, majores conflaturus si
Non sprevisset, ibidem splendide vixit, et honorifice post
Annos 42 Angliam revisit
Uxorem duxit Emma filia Rich : Howe, armiger Norfolck
Decessit Mart secundo Anno aet : 64 Do 1685/6
Posuit marito optimo de se merito uxor moestissima.

"Below this again is an inscription stating that Catherine, relict of William Wynter, Sir Edward's grandson, who died in 1771, and her son William Woodstock Wynter, who died in 1747, are also buried here, and that the monument was re-erected and repaired by Edward Hampson Wynter, a great grandson of Sir Edward's. Also the following lines:

Born to be great in fortune as in mind
Too great to be within our isle confined
Young, helpless, friendless, seas unknown he tried,
But English courage all those wants supplied.
A pregnant wit, a painful diligence,
Care to provide and bounty to dispense,
Joined to a soul sincere, plain, open, just,
Procured him friends and friends procured him trust.
These were his fortune's rise, and thus began
This hardy youth, raised to that happy man,
A rare example and unknown to most
Where wealth is gained and conscience is not lost.
Nor less in martial honour was his name—
Witness his actions of immortal fame—
Alone, unarmed, a tyger he oppressed
And crushed to death the monster of a beast.
Twice twenty mounted Moors, he overthrew
Singly on foot, some wounded, some he slew,
Dispersed the rest : what more could Samson do?
True to his friends,
A terror to his foes,
Here now in peace his honoured bones repose.

"Sir Edward lived at York House, Battersea, which had once been a residence of the Archbishop of York, and has given its name to York Road, Battersea. There has always been some doubt what his actual rank was. In his evidence about the affray in Fort St. George he calls himself Knight and Baronet. His opponent Foxcroft writing in 1668, after his release, says: "It is now out of doubt that the title of Baronet was assumed." He appears in Courthhope's Knights as "Edward Winter of Zidney, Gloucestershire, 1661. Captain E.I. Service, Governor, Fort St. George. Died at Battersea." It will be noticed that there is on this monument no reference to a Baronetcy, nor to his having been Governor of Madras."

4

THE GARRISON OF FORT ST. GEORGE, AND THE SOLDIER OF TWO CENTURIES AGO

When Sir William Langhorne arrived in Madras in 1670 to succeed Foxcroft, he found a town within the walls of the Fort, a town which has sprung up in the space of thirty years. It was fortified and garrisoned, and every year saw it increase in trade and importance. But there was still much to be done in the way of regulating the little community that lived within its walls. The Fort House stood where the present Secretariat buildings now are, just in front of the sea gate. It contained offices, reception rooms, a dining hall, a room set apart as a chapel, and accommodation for a few merchants, factors and writers who were numbered on the staff. The original house had not been built with the solidity which marks the fine houses raised some fifteen years later under more experienced architects, and Sir William found it rapidly falling into ruin. The walls of the Fort also needed repair. Sun-baked mud, which is still commonly used for native houses, had been largely employed, with wood procured in the near neighbourhood. While ants and tropical rain play havoc with buildings made of such materials unless they are constantly renewed. In thirty years' time these agents of destruction had done their work, and it was necessary to set about rebuilding and repairing, if the President did not wish the fortifications and the Fort House to fall about his ears. It was not completed until some years later, but Sir William took upon himself to fortify Caldera Point, where, as has already been related, some of the original houses were sacrificed.

By the year 1673 the French had established themselves in strong force at St. Thomé and had formed a large camp in Triplicane, the present Mahomedan quarter of Madras, midway between the Fort and St. Thomé, where they laid out the handsome street still to be seen in Triplicane. The Dutch, uneasy and unfriendly with all other European powers, had advanced from Pulicat on the North, and were threatening to attack the Fort at Caldera Point. With dangers on both sides of him, the President felt that he had no time to lose, and he resolved in Council that it was "an absolute necessity to go on fortifying this place in the best manner we can." The walls were protected by seventy guns, described as ranging "from demi-cannon to saker," which could be utilized against an advancing force by land, or would cover the roads, where the ships lay at anchor.

A few words about the garrison and the kind of men who formed it will not be out of place. The little band, insignificant as it was, may be called the mustard-seed of the Madras Army. It was a very small beginning when ten men-at-arms were sent to protect the builders and merchants as they laid the foundations of Fort St. George. In all probability the men were drafted from Surat, where there was already an English settlement. They brought with them their quaint old armour and weapons of war, some of them being of the Tudor period. There were matchlocks, pikes, halberds, battleaxes and bucklers. In the Arsenal of the Fort may still be seen some curious breast-plates and helmets of metal, which were worn at one time by the garrison; the wonder is how Englishmen ever survived such an ordeal by fire, as a parade in full dress under the Indian sun must have been. At first half the men were armed with muskets and half with pikes eighteen feet long. Each man carried a sword as well. In 1665 the muskets were increased and the pikes reduced by a third. Instead of a bayonet the firearms were fitted with a dagger, the handle of which went into the muzzle. On parade the pikemen were placed near the colours in the centre of the corps, and the men on the outside, chosen for their strength carried hand grenades. This fashion of arming the troops lasted for twenty years, when bayonets were introduced. At the beginning of the eighteenth century pikes were abolished, but the sergeants still carried halberds, and these last were not done away with in India till the beginning of the 19th century.

The garrison was commanded in the early days by one of the Company's servants, who was called the Lieutenant or Captain of the Guard. He was usually a gentleman who never allowed his military duties to interfere in any way with his mercantile transactions. For some years Fort St. George was defended by a band of men whose number never exceeded twenty-six. They mounted guard at the gates and worked the guns under the direction of the Chief Gunner. And so long as the merchants had only the natives to fear it was sufficient.

In 1670 there were two companies of Europeans of eighty to a hundred in each, and these were further increased as necessity arose.

The attitude of the Directors towards its little army was curious. The merchants had a jealous fear of all military power. They openly expressed a wish not to have any commissioned officer higher in rank than a subaltern with the troops, whether they were the King's or their own. The superior officers who commanded the garrison were nominated from amongst their own servants; they were merchants by profession and had had no training in military matters. History shows, however, what such men could do, since Clive himself came out as a Writer, and was placed in the Accounts Office at a desk, with no thought at first of the brilliant military career that was before him. The effect of this arrangement was that the soldier was apt, in the absence of any senior officers, to get out of hand in times of peace. Sir William Langhorne found himself obliged to frame a number of orders for the regulation of the garrison. If we may judge by some of them, the discipline must have been very slack under the merchant Captain of the Guard. The soldiers were forbidden to dispute an order given by their superior officer; and when reproved and punished they were cautioned not to throw down their arms and refuse to perform their duties, as many had formerly done. For such an act of insubordination they were to be paraded before the troops and have their arms taken away from them by a cooly. In exchange they were to be given a spade or some agricultural implement, as a sign that they were to work for their daily bread by manual labour. On pain of fines and corporal punishment they were admonished not to drink more than half a pint of the country spirit, arrack; not to sleep on duty, not to climb over the walls of the Fort, and not to appear on parade or in church in anything but English apparel. This rule was extended to the offices as well. It seems to have been the general custom for the Englishman to discard the furbelowed dress of the Stuart period for a seminative costume, which, though comfortable, was scarcely dignified on parade. Duelling, lying, swearing and gaming were also prohibited.

The punishments for infringing the rules were various. In the case of the soldier they were flogging with a rattan, imprisonment in irons, sitting in the stocks, riding the wooden horse, tying by the neck and heels, and standing sentinel for some hours in armour, which last must have been another form of roasting alive. Tying by the neck and heels was an unpleasant process, not altogether without danger, as was proved in the case of a soldier named Thomas Savage, in 1677. His half-pint of arrack proving too much for him, "he did abuse with bad words, his officer". The Sergeant, John Waterhouse, ordered him to be tied to his bed; but his tongue still wagging, the order was altered to tying him by the neck and heels. The official memorandum thus concludes the story: "It seems that the Corporal not doing as he ought, the prisoner, Thomas Savage, complained— saying:

"Do not hang me." "The corporal, Edward Short, replied : "No, Thomas, I won't hang thee, but I will tie thee fast." "So after he had been bound the time of three of four inches of match were burnt out, which was, by the command of the Sergeant, lighted, he was unbound, and being loosed, was found dead and not seen to stir."

Riding the wooden horse was no joke either, though no danger to life was involved in the process. The horse was a kind of saddle-stand fitted with sloping ledges like the roof of a house. It was built on four legs and formed into a rough image of a horse. The unfortunate soldier who was condemned to act the part of jockey for the time being, had his arms tied behind him and his heels weighted. Three or four hours of this sort of thing in the sun was not a pleasant prospect for the disorderly drunkard on awaking. In 1676 a private was ordered to ride the wooden horse three several days, for three hours at a time, for being drunk; and another received "fifteen drubs at the brich of a gunn," for "contemning of the government."

The garrison gave the Directors some trouble over their love affairs. The Court was at first shocked at the alliances they made with the Roman Catholic and heathen women of the country, and at the careless way in which they allowed their children to be brought up, as Papists. The Gunpowder Plot was fresh in the merchants' mind, and it seemed flying in the face of Providence to permit this wholesale breeding of heretics. To remedy the evil, stringent rules were made relating to mixed marriages, compelling the parents to bring up their children in the orthodox Church. The Directors were not long in finding out that the British soldier was able to dispense with the marriage ceremony altogether, and they were obliged to modify their views. Instead of putting hindrances in the way of respectable alliances with the women of the country they began to encourage them, saying that such wives could be better maintained on the pay of the soldier than English women. The result of these unions and others of a similar nature has been the production of a race of English-speaking people, called at first Indo-Britons, and in the present day, Eurasians. The better class, who have had the advantages of education, are, to all intents and purposes, Europeans.

In times of peril, when the French and the Dutch threatened on one side, and the natives blackmailed and blockaded on the other, the British soldiers found life exciting enough. Their employers were by no means ungrateful; they knew how to reward their services with extra pay and clothing on occasions, and to send round the welcome bowl of punch with a liberal hand. The troops were feted and patted on the back and told they were fine fellows. They were paraded and exhibited to the native ruler in all their panoply of war, and they were sent to escort merchants and merchandise through hostile districts, which suited them exactly. But in times of peace it was quite a different thing. Whilst the merchant was busy with his peaceful buying and selling the men found life insupportably dull, confined as they were to the Fort. The forbidden pleasures of Blacktown with its "rack (arrack) house" and "punch-house" palled on them. Their thoughts wandered further a field and their inclinations with them. They slipped off to join the Moors or tried their hands at a little pirating; there was nothing dull or monotonous about either of these. In the court of the native ruler or on board the rollicking pirate vessel, they found themselves in an atmosphere of danger eminently suited to their adventurous spirits. There was a money in both, a free life and the sword of Damocles hanging above. The Company did its best to keep its men, and to get them back when they deserted, for it could ill afford to lose them, and the punishment inflicted for desertion was not severe. The soldiers were far too valuable to shoot unless they were utterly hopeless villains. Out of nine men of the garrison, who plotted to seize a sloop and set-up for themselves in the pirate line, the Council ordered four to be punished by riding the wooden horse. All being equally guilty, they decided who were to be the scapegoats by casting dice on the drumhead. The other five culprits returned to duty. The ringleader was expelled from the Fort, with a promise of being sent to England for trial if he ventured to show his face again within the walls.

It is curious that the native, highly as he valued the Europeans as an ally, could not appreciate him fully as an enemy in those early days. He could not understand his restraint; moderations and mercy were looked upon as signs of weakness. It was incomprehensible that the Briton could possess the power to take and keep, and yet refrain from following in the marauding steps of Sivaji and Aurungzeb. Fryer records in 1680 "The Language we have daily cast in our Teeth. Why vaunts your Nation? What has your sword done? Who ever felt your Power? What do you possess? We see the Dutch outdo you; the Portugals have behaved like men; everyone runs you down; you can scarce keep Bombain, which you got, (as we know) not by your valour, but by Compact; and you will pretend to be Men of War or Cope with our Princes? It's fitter for you to live on Merchandise and submit to us."

When Sir Edward Winter remonstrated with the Naik of Poonamalee on the blackmailing of the Company's goods coming into Madras, the reply was to the effect, that when the English horns and teeth grew, then he would free them from the duties. The English horns and teeth have indeed grown, and the native has learnt that the British soldier is not always panting to be on the war-path; that he can play the part of the protector, and is not an armed robber. He also understands that the presence of the Englishman of war has ensured to India such a peace as she has never known before.

Besides increasing the garrison, Langhorne added to the number of the peons from which his Bodyguard was drawn. In one document they are termed the Black Guards, not on account of their character, but of their colour. As many as seven hundred were at one time enlisted. There was also an attempt made to train some of the Indo-Portuguese for sentinel and other garrison duty. But the English had already discovered that little reliance could be placed on these men, and the real strength of the Fort lay in its European garrison. Faith in the native and Portuguese troops was further shaken when in 1686 they mutinied on being ordered to Bengal. They were under the belief that the Company intended to send them to Priaman on the West Coast of Sumatra, an unhealthy station dreaded by European and native alike. A gallows was erected in front of the Fort Gate, and the two ringleaders were threatened with death, which brought the men to their senses. Their arms were restored to them, and they were allowed to return to duty. But it was resolved to disband them as soon as the garrison should be sufficiently strong in European soldiers to permit of dispensing with their services. They were an unruly rabble without discipline, and officered by men whose hearts were in the counting-house, and who knew nothing of military work; men who were instructed by their employers "to keep the military subordinate to the civil authority." It was strange that which such good raw material at hand nothing better could be done. It was not from want of knowledge the French had shown during their occupation of St. Thomé how the natives might be trained. When Langhorne and his Council were increasing the body of peons, they directed that as many of the disbanded men from the French army should be secured as possible, on account of the military training they had received.

As a rule, however, the English were curiously indifferent to the kind of men they enlisted. Even the European soldiers, upon whom they relied so much, were drafted from the scum of their native land. The native troops for the first hundred years, whether peons, topasses or sepoys, were recruited from all sorts and conditions of men, including Hindus, Arabs, Caffres from Africa, Slaves from Madagascar, Indo-Portuguese and Mahomedans. They were armed with odds and ends of weapons, bows and arrows, spears and native daggers of sorts, and their dress was probably as varied as their arms. With merchants and factors for their officers, it was small wonder that they proved inefficient and unreliable. But there came a time when public opinion altered. Disciplined and led by men who knew their business, the native soldier retrieved his character. The first body of sepoys was raised in 1746, by the Governor and Council of Fort St. David, to defend Cuddalore against the French. In 1758 the pay of the sepoy was increased; European sergeants and commissioned officers were put in command, and Companies of a hundred men in each were formed. In the following year five battalions were organized, four of them being the 1st, 2nd, 3rd and 4th Regiments of the Madras Infantry of the present day. The Madras Sepoy received his baptism of fire from Hyder Ali; he more than fulfilled the expectations of those who believed in him then, and he has in no way disappointed those who have put faith in him since.

Although the European troops were largely composed of bad characters, there were those amongst them who were of a very different class. They were men who enlisted in England for one of two purposes: either to leave the ranks as soon as they arrived in India, and to obtain a writership through the influence of friends and relatives already established in the country; or to remain in military service and rise to a commission. Most of those who became Ensigns and Lieutenants began their career as Corporals and Sergeants. They were men of some education who were willing to climb the ladder of life from the lower rungs. They had to rough it at first, especially on the voyage out; but they had their reward, provided they proved themselves steady and reliable. In fact, they were just the kind of men to make good officers, being inured to hardship and possessing a personal knowledge of the raw material they had to deal with in the ranks.

This mode of getting out to India without the consent of the Company became so well known that the Directors were obliged in 1725 to take notice of it. They asked for the cooperation of their servants in putting a top to "the practice of getting persons sent out clandestinely as soldiers, midshipmen and the like, and their being entertained as Factors and Writers on arrival". In just such a manner John Goulding went out, and on paying the usual fee he obtained his discharge (1726). He then entered the Company's service and made himself useful to Benyon and George Morton Pitt, two successive Governors as Secretary. He was appointed Gunner, (Commandant of the Faith Artillery) and when he died a memorial stone was erected, recording his many virtues and accomplishments in a lengthy Latin inscription. John de Morgan, the ancestor of the mathematician, Augustus de Morgan, was another who obtained his Captain's commission about this period by passing through the ranks.

$$5$$

THE PECCADILLOES OF THE COMPANY'S SERVANTS

A check had been given to the development of trade by the reduction of the status of the Fort just before Winter's rule, and it took some time to recover from its effects. The reduction was made on the score of economy. The Company's dividends were low and the public faith in its stability was small. The system of salaries was one which lent itself to reduction, and was the frequent cause of misunderstandings between the Company and its servants. The salaries were paid at a certain fixed rate, and the sum was augmented by a gratuity. For instance, Sir William Langhorne received £200 salary as President and Governor, with another £100 as gratuity, making his income up to £300 a year. A Chaplain's salary was £50 with another like sum as gratuity, giving him £100 a year. By this means the Company always had it in its power to reduce the pay of its servants. They on their part ignored the gratuity system altogether, and regarded the sum total as the salary to which they were entitled. The result was that they frequently differed in opinion with their employers as to the amount which was due to them. The old records at Fort St. George often mention the overdrawal of salaries; and as each Chief of a Factory had to pay himself, it appears at first sight as though there was something dishonest about it. But a closer examination, shows that that this was not so, and that the stories of overdrawals as well as the stories of illicit private trade must be received with a grain of salt. Of course there were instances of dishonesty amongst the many individuals who came out in the Company's service, and some men were not as straightforward as they should have been. The records show undoubted defalcations occasionally, and the borrowing of money to make up the cash balance, when the inspecting Commissioner swooped down upon a factory; but this sort of thing was not the rule, and it is scarcely fair to class the man who disputed the question of salary, in the same category with the man who helped himself out of the Company's cash chest. It was a difficult matter from the very earliest days for a merchant to amass wealth without laying himself under the suspicion of dishonesty with the authorities at home. This was not peculiar to the English. Every Portuguese governor on the West Coast found himself similarly situated on his return to his native land; and sometimes he was thrown into prison and disgraced. So well known was the fact that one Portuguese nobleman insisted on having his private property valued and registered before taking up the appointment of Viceroy, so that he might be able to clear his name and reputation on his retirement. There was a wide difference between the sharp practice of the merchant over commercial affairs in the early days of the Company, and the shaking of the pagoda tree a century later by the Company's officials, when Cornwallis made war against rampant corruption within the Company's ranks. The careful, thrifty merchant was a child in iniquity compared with the extravagant princely official of later years.

An account of some of the internal difficulties of the Presidency at this period will give a very fair example of the ups and downs of fortune which were possible in a Company servant's life, even to the time of Clive and Warren Hastings.

One of the troubles originated at Masulipatam. The factory, after the foundation of Fort St. George, gradually deteriorated in prestige and importance. It was no longer the chief station in the Bay, and it was placed by the Directors under the Presidency of Madras. But apparently this authority was not recognized. The Chief at Masulipatam refused to show his accounts or to report the conduct of affairs at the factory to the President. He preferred to communicate directly with the Court of Directors and they weakly listened and permitted it. At the same time they complained to the Governor at Madras of the unsatisfactory state of things at Masulipatam, and remarked upon the attitude assumed by him and his Council at the Fort towards the subordinate factory, holding him responsible for the insubordination. They made no attempt to rectify matters and continued to issue their orders through the Fort Council. But when the servants of Masulipatam came to blows,—when Samuel Wales and Valentine Cullen threw a brickbat into Mathew Manwaring's window—whilst Walter Clavell and Mathias Vincent laughed at the authorities at Fort St. George, it was time to take stronger measures to stop such a shocking state of affairs. The story of the dispute was as trivial as the brickbat incident. The accusations and countercharges were—free-trading in the Company's monopolies, underrating the Company's calicoes, and overdrawing from the cash chest. Also of unbecoming personal conduct, including loose-living and levity. Finally, Vincent was charged with the heinous offence of witchcraft and dealing with the Devil; but this charge was not pursued until later, when those relating to the commercial affairs of the Company had been settled. As Langhorne seemed unable to reduce the unruly crew to order, the Directors thought it necessary to send out a commissioner to investigate the matter. A Major or Mr. William Puckle arrived in 1676 with full powers to examine and question as he thought fit. His reception by the Governor and Council was not very cordial; they resented the presence of a man holding such powers, who was inexperienced in Indian mercantile affairs and already prejudiced against them. Their attitude may be distinctly seen in some of their answers to his queries, and their irritation was extended to the Court. When Major Puckle directed that extravagance was to be avoided, and the maintenance charges of each factory was to be reduced to the smallest amount possible, Langhorne and his Council replied, that they "would be very glad that anything in this Fort and Factory could be better regulated than it is." In answer to a recommendation that all complaints from subordinate factories and servants should be sent through the Governor and Council of Fort St. George, they said that they had long desired it, and that there was no way to remedy it, but by discountenancing the transgressors at home; implying that the fault lay with the Directors when they gave ear to irregular complaints, and not with themselves. When the disorders at Masulipatam were pointed out, the Governor and Council suggested that the evil might be avoided by a better choice of those whom the Directors placed in authority.

After his enquiries at Fort St. George, Puckle went on to Masulipatam to settle the brickbat and other affairs. The two principal antagonists were Richard Mohun and Mathew Manwaring who were in the Company's service. Mohun had been the first to be aggressive. He, as Chief of Masulipatam, had thought fit to stop Manwaring's salary, or in other words to fine him for alleged private trade. Manwaring retaliated by accusing Mohun of using the Company's money and name for his own private benefit. On receipt of this information, the Directors, without waiting to prove the truth of it, sent orders for Mohun's immediate dismissal. The Governor of Fort St. George did not care to take upon himself the onus of executing this order. He contented himself with merely suspending him, and appointed Manwaring as Chief in his place. But the Directors refused to recognize the appointment, and nominated their commissioner, Major Puckle, as Chief of Masulipatam on £100 a year. On his arrival he took up the post and set about his enquiries, with the result, that Mohun not only managed to clear himself in Puckle's opinion, but to bring the Governor under suspicion. Mohun followed up his victory with a piece of assurance which is amusing. He proposed that the Governor and Council should pay the Company £100,000 compensation, the sum which he estimated his employers had lost through being deprived of his valuable services during his suspension. As his dismissal had come from the Directors themselves, and as the Governor and Council had tempered the wind to the shorn lamp by modifying the decree to suspension, the sublime impudence of the man may be gauged. Mohun was not allowed to remain at Masulipatam, but was sent to Madras, where he was placed on the Council of Fort St. George. The turn of Fortune's wheel left Manwaring under a fresh cloud, and he was anxious to go to Madras to see about a passage home, as he wanted to tell his story at the fountain head.

At this juncture Major Puckle fell a victim to the climate and died; Manwaring took up the reins in the absence of any other competent person, and once more ruled as Chief pending orders from Madras. It was not likely, with Mohun on the Council, that he would be left to reign in peace. Manwaring was told to handover charge to Vincent and come to Madras. When he arrived there, he made two requests: one that his wife at Masulipatam might have the protection of the Chief; and this was accorded, "she being reckoned a lady soe obliging and discreet." The other was that he might be restored to the Chiefship. This was refused, and he then asked for a passage home, which was granted. He prepared for his journey, promising to make it very hot for the Governor and Council when he reached England. But he never got there. On March the 14th, 1682, he was buried in the cemetery whither Wales, a free merchant and one of the gentlemen of the brickbat incident, was also carried in October 1687. So often the tale ended thus. The struggling Englishman who had built his fortune and added his mite to the planting of the British power in India, found a grave in the foreign soil, and never saw his native land again.

Walter Clavell's bones were laid in Bengal after having served the Company many years.

Mohun enjoyed the confidence of his employers for some time; he wisely made it his business to pull with his colleagues; and when, soon after Puckle's death, he was asked if he wished to pursue the charges he and the Major had brought against Sir William, he was glad to withdraw from such an unpleasant position. He had got what he wanted in his restitution to office, and he was ready to let the matter rest. But Langhorne was not satisfied that it should drop in this fashion. He called upon his Council to place on record their confidence in his honesty, during the time he had served them. This they did, declaring unanimously, Mohun amongst them, their belief in his integrity. Mohun kept his appointment in the Company's service until 1680 when he once more fell into disgrace, and this time he did not escape his fate. He was dismissed, the Directors being firmly convinced that he was "notoriously and vilely culpable," and no longer to be trusted. His name does not disappear entirely off the books with his dismissal. In 1684 we find him renting the disused factory at Acheen, and his late employers were of an amicable kind, indicating that their adverse opinion of him had been modified.

Vincent was the most fortunate of them all, but at the same time he may be considered the most culpable in offence against the rules of the Company. After governing at Masulipatam he was transferred to the Bay, and became Chief of Hugli, succeeding Clavell. Pitt, a free trader, was infringing the Company's charter at this period in the Bay. He (Pitt) married Miss Jane Innes, a niece of Vincent's wife. Vincent became very friendly with his nephew, "Pirate Pitt," as the Directors called him, and probably found him a useful and accommodating relative. We are indebted to Hedges, who wrote a diary of the times, for many little personal details of his contemporaries. He was not an impartial historian by any means, nor was he particular as to the sources from which he gathered his information. He was ready to listen to the tales of the natives as well as those of the aggrieved Europeans. Moreover, he had a grievance and a mission himself. Like Puckle he was sent out to deal especially with an abuse. The private trade had developed, and men no longer contented themselves with what could be done in the country; they aimed at the more lucrative business of the home trade, and for this purpose the free merchants possessed vessels, which were unlicensed by the Company. The owners and commanders of these ships were called interlopers. William Hedges was commissioned by the Directors to put down all interloping, and went out to India for that purpose.

The tale he tells of Vincent's iniquity is as follows. Hedges left England in a ship called the *Defence*, commanded by Captain William Heath. He was armed with evidence against Vincent and others, and intended on arrival to mete out justice right and left impartially. Pitt, the interloper, sailed for India just a month later in Captain Dorrel's ship, the *Crown*, an interloper. The Directors, knowing Pitt's character and what his mission to the East was, did their best to stop him; but he eluded them and got safely away to sea. They trusted that he would fall into the hands of their Commissioner on his arrival in India, for Hedges was well aware of the reputation Pitt bore. Captain Dorrel proved either a better navigator than Captain Heath, or he possessed a better ship. The *Crown* overhauled the *Defence* and was the first to arrive in the Bay. Pitt had taken the precaution to hire and bring out twenty soldiers under the command of a corporal. He landed his Bodyguard and established himself at Chinsurah, having duly warned his Uncle Vincent of the rod in pickle which Hedges was preparing for him. Vincent was not inclined to leave the matter to chance; he followed the example of his nephew, and gathered a strong Bodyguard of Portuguese and Rajputs round him, and took up his position in the old Dutch quarters, from which it would have been no easy matter to dislodge him. Both men gave out that they were acting on behalf of a new Company whose orders Pitt had conveyed from home. Thus prepared they awaited the coming of Hedges. That gentleman was astounded on landing to find that he had been outsailed by Pirate Pitt; and his feelings of vexation and chagrin may be imagined when he was received by Vincent with all the display of gubernatorial power. Hedges' orders were to arrest Vincent immediately on landing and send him on board the *Defence*, to be kept a close prisoner under Captain Heath until he could be sent to England. Needless to say such a course was impossible. Whether aided by the "Diabolicall arts" he is said to have practised with the Brahmins and others in the Bay for bewitching men, or by his own shrewd mother wit, Vincent escaped scot-free. After a short time he realized his wealth and returned to England, sailing in the *Crown*. There seems little doubt that he made the most of his opportunities, and that his conscience did not trouble him on the score of his covenant with his employers. But there is no accounting for Dame Fortune's favours. Whilst she frowned on Manwaring and looked coldly on Mohun she chose to smile on Vincent. She crowned his wealth with a title, and he became Sir Mathias Vincent in less than two years after his return to England.

Closely connected with the Company's servants at Madras was a native merchant whose name figures frequently in the public records. It was the practice of the Company to procure the products of the country through brokers or merchants as they were called. They were the middlemen and took the European merchandise on credit, undertaking to supply certain goods in exchange, according to patterns which they exhibited. Sometimes they received sums of money on account, given on the advance system which is so generally in use in India. The transaction was a pledge of good faith and bound the broker of the terms of his verbal contract. The Company's servants observed great care in the choice of their native brokers, dismissing those who were unsatisfactory, and refusing to have anything to do with them. On the other hand, they treated their approved brokers with liberality and consideration, receiving them courteously and presenting them on occasions with gifts. The chief of the brokers was Cassa Verona or Viranna. He is first mentioned as acting in partnership with Timanna in 1665–70 in Winter's time. The sums of money which passed through the hands of the firm were very large, and great confidence was placed in the two men. But now and then there were disputes over the charges they made, and at one time Timanna was imprisoned by the Company. But after his death matters went more smoothly; Verona carried on the business alone, increasing his wealth and his power till it approached a princely magnificence. The Directors at home were not so well satisfied with Verona as their servants were in India. They suspected strongly that Verona bought his popularity and his privileges by assisting the merchants and factors in their own private trade. They tried to discountenance the monopoly, and gave ear to the usual tales accusing Langhorne and Winter of making use of Verona's services, and of receiving large douceurs from him. There was no proof of the truth of the stories. Verona, moreover, made himself useful in diplomatic dealings with the native rulers, and was more than once entrusted with a delicate mission of propitiation, when the Company had everything to gain by an amicable settlement, and when the alternative of compelling the people by force was not possible. Verona lived in great state, and when his wife and child died he was allowed the much coveted honour of a salute from the Fort guns, which proclaimed to the Hindu world his princely importance. His star was at its zenith in the time of Langhorne and Streynsham Master. At that period he was able to rent whole towns, St. Thomé being one of them. He was the object of jealousy to other native merchants, and a Hindu named Lingappa tried hard to ruin him and his employers, but did not succeed. Verona managed to maintain the favour of the Company and to make himself indispensable until his death. When that event happened the Directors had just sent out a gold medal and chain, which was to have been presented to Verona as a reward for all the services, political and commercial, which he had rendered. Under the circumstances, however, the economically minded factors and merchants had the gift melted down and coined into pagodas for the Company's use. After Verona's death the Council appointed another chief merchant from amongst the brokers, stipulating that he should not live in such magnificence and state as his predecessor; and no native merchant ever obtained such power again, or enjoyed such a monopoly of trade, as Verona.

Langhorne is said by some historians to have been weak in his government. Fort St. George was weak; the garrison was weak and the British power, as compared with the French and Dutch who had approached so closely to the Fort, was very weak. But Langhorne seems to have been diplomatic, and to have steered his frail bark successfully over a stormy and difficult sea. He returned home in 1677 with the usual trail of the serpent behind him in the shape of vague charges of free trading, and pilling the pagodas unfairly. He left his mantle of rule and calumny to the shoulders of Mr. Streynsham Master, who had been on his Council for some time previously.

6

STREYNSHAM MASTER, PILOTS AND DIAMONDS

Streynsham Master was the eighth son of Richard Master, Esq. of East Langdon Court, Kent. He was a man of very different character from his predecessors, having been better educated. He possessed the gift of expressing himself in a scholarly fashion, and he wrote a bold flowing hand. He entered the Company's service in 1659, some years before he came to Madras; he distinguished himself at Surat in 1670, by a determined and courageous defence of the factory against the forces of Sivaji, with a party of seamen from Swally, for which act he received a gold medal from the Company. He was appointed to Fort St. George with the understanding that he was to succeed Langhorne. A strong man was needed at the head of affairs to establish discipline amongst the Company's servants. So long as the place was small and unimportant it did not matter if the discipline was not particularly strict; but when the Fort increased in power and had subordinate factories placed under its government, it was necessary to establish a dignified order of things at headquarters. Langhorne had done his best to lay a foundation for Master to build upon; but the former shrank from bringing himself into open conflict with either his fellow-countrymen within the walls, or the natives outside. Master had no such scruples; he brought the same spirit to Madras as he had displayed at Surat, and governed like his name, with a masterful hand.

There had been trouble in the Council at the Fort as well as at Masulipatam during Langhorne's time, and an extraordinary scene of nose-pulling had occurred in the Council Chamber in 1676. A merchant who dealt in precious stones, named Nathaniel Keeble, made some defamatory remarks upon the wife of Mr. Edward Herrys. The latter had been under a cloud a few years previously, but was now restored to favour, and was enjoying an important position on the Council. Herrys took up the cudgels on behalf of his traduced spouse, and used his fists upon Keeble's face with such good effect as to make his nose bleed. The merchant vowed vengeance if he were hanged for it, and his antagonist had him bound down to keep the peace. Keeble was confined to his room till he found the necessary security; and not liking this curtailment of his liberty, he broke bounds, and tried to escape by jumping off the Fort wall. He sprained his ankle and was recaptured. The Governor ordered him to be imprisoned until he could be shipped off home. He could not afford, however, to leave India just then, his fortune not having been realized to his satisfaction, so he ate humble pie and was forgiven.

Another curious scene in the Council Chamber happened two years previously, when Mr. John Crandon was dismissed from the service. He emphatically denied having erred, but the Governor

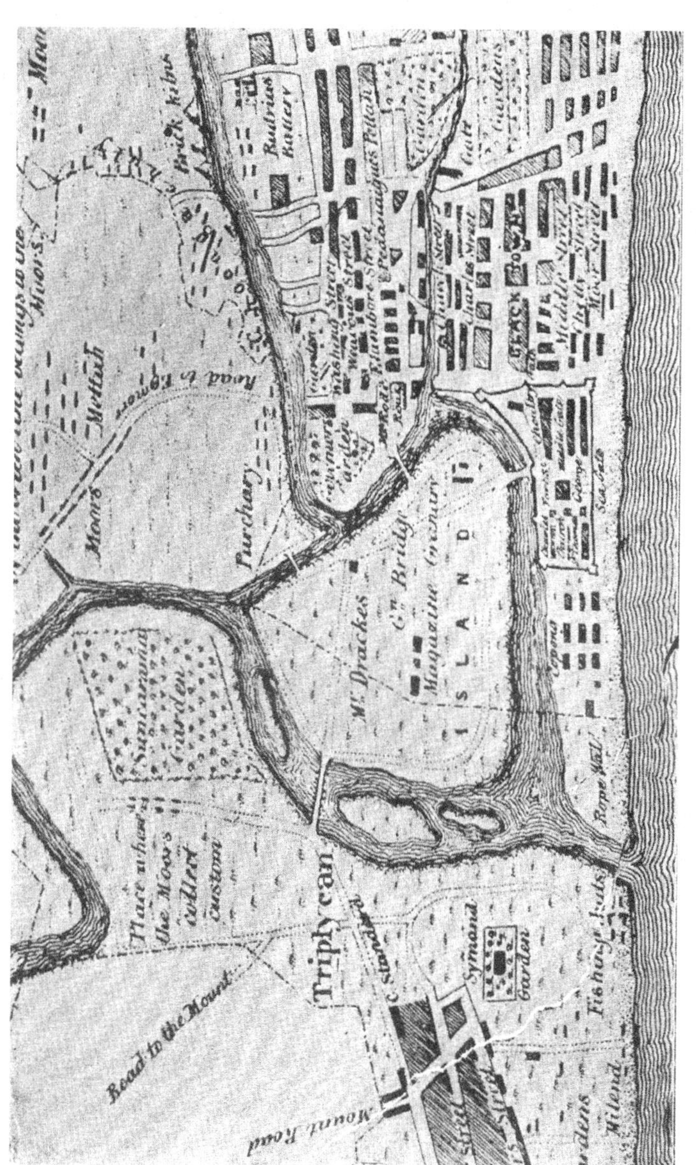

The old Fort in 1733

possessed written evidence against him in his own handwriting. When confronted with this Crandon made an end of his denial, confessed that the charges were true, and accepted the sentence which had been passed upon him. There was no shame or disgrace about dismissal in those days. The covenant began and ended at the will of employer or employed, without regard to age or length of service. William Jearsey had undergone the sentence of dismissal in 1669, and he remained in the Fort, trading as a free merchant, paying customs and dues to the Company, and enjoying the friendship and society of his old comrades, without any disgrace being attached to his name.

Sir William Langhorne left India with Mr. Herrys at the beginning of 1676; at the same time the Sergeant and Corporal who caused the death of Savage through tying him by the neck and heels, went to take their trial in England.

Masters first act was to remodel the rules which governed his Council, and introduce a more orderly system of keeping the books, which he had seen in use at Surat. His next was to look to his fortifications. His old enemy, Sivaji, had penetrated South to within a day's march of Madras, and there were all sorts of disturbing rumours of his hostile intentions against Fort St. George. But Sivaji had had his experience of the English once before, and he did not care to risk his prestige by being again frustrated in his designs; so he merely requisitioned the English Colony for medicines, which he called cordial-stones and counter-poisons. These were despatched by his messengers, and master and his colleagues were relieved after a few months suspense, by hearing of his departure.

The Fort was strengthened and partly rebuilt under the direction of a clever engineer named Edward Fowle. He was also

Commandant of the Artillery, an appointment which went under the title in those days of Chief Gunner. The Company had its own brickfields and kilns where it employed native labour, and made all the bricks needed for building purposes. The mortar used was particularly strong and binding. It was made according to the native plan, with jaggery or palm sugar mixed with it. All the old masonry exhibits in the present day a hardness and cohesion which suggests the Norman builder of Great Britain, and it is difficult to break it up. The walls were strengthened and partially rebuilt. The Middle or North Gate and the Choultry Gate in the North wall were enlarged. The dimensions of the Fort were still on the original lines, about half the size that they are today and arm of the river which exists now only as a small covered drain, remained flanking and protecting the West curtain or wall. The wall on the sea face had been undermined and damaged by the sea. It was repaired together with the sea-gate battery. There was a fourth entrance, called the Fort Gate, which was in the West wall and faced the Fort House on the land side opposite to the sea. Some of the stones used for the gateways came from the Island of Johanna in the Mozambique Channel. The island was in the direct route then taken by the ships from England, and it was usual to water there on the way out, and stay a few days to procure fresh meat and vegetables. In an account of it given in 1783 it is described as fertile, and containing beautiful scenery of hills and valleys, well-wooded and abounding in fruit and grain. The people, who were of Arab extraction, were friendly, and quite alive to the advantages of trading away their produce for English gold. Warren Hastings was said to have visited the King of Johanna on one of this voyages, and to have been received with great friendliness. The island is mentioned by the earliest navigators, and its name occurs in the records of

Entrance hall of one of the old houses, Fort St. George

Fort St. George in a letter dated Dec. 12th 1677, from the Directors to the Governor and Council of Fort St. George. The letter intimated that arms and armour were sent for the garrison, and that stones for the fortifications were to be taken on board at Johanna. The timber used was procured from Balasore at the mouth of the Hugly.

The renovation of the Fort was not a matter of a few weeks or even months; it seems to have been a work which was constantly necessary and always going on. The houses at the South East corner, towards the St. Thomé Gate, were erected in Fowle's time and probably under his direction. They are built upon a magnificent foundation of laterite, a ferruginous clay, which in its pristine conditions quarried as soft as ordinary clay. The blocks are cut-out with an iron implement, and on exposure to the air they harden into a building material which equals granite in endurance, and forms a lasting unalterable foundation on the sandy soil of Fort St. George. The laterite was well known to the natives who used it for their own better class of buildings; they procured it from the Red Hills, a few miles from the Fort; and it had the additional advantage of being cheap. Probably the English were able before long to get stone nearer than Johanna, but they preferred laterite and bricks for ordinary work; and the buildings of the Fort are made chiefly of those materials. A dry ditch was cut on the South side in very early days, and later on, it was extended on the East.

The old Fort House, or castle, as it was sometimes called, was absolutely unsafe in Langhorne's time, and he had it repaired. Fryer, who visited the place in 1674, described it as having four turrets, each armed with ten guns. It was eventually pulled down and replaced by another building, which was ruined by the shot and shell of the French in 1758, and which had to be pulled down. Some few years later the present house was built. The wing containing the Council Chamber on the South was added afterwards, together with the wing on the North.

The banqueting hall juts out like the stem of the capital letter T, and runs towards the sea gate. It is used as a record room in the present day, and has been flanked by side rooms required for the same purpose. The hall contains some very fine black polished porphyry pillars, which were taken from Government House at Pondicherry, when that town was rendered, up to the English in 1751. At its restoration to the French the pillars were not sent back, and they are the most interesting feature of the old banqueting hall.

A fine house, erected probably in Master's time, which is now used as the Accountant General's office, served as a residence for the Governors when circumstances obliged them to live in the Fort. It faces the West end of the church; and at the South extremity of the same line of buildings stands a corner house, also used now as Government offices, where Colonel Wellesley stayed when he came to Madras. The Duke's old house has a handsome teak staircase, and a large reception room highly ornamented with mouldings of fruit and flowers of the Jacobite period, giving evidence of the native artist working under the guidance of the European. The houses are two-storied, with here and there a third storey added later; the walls are enormously thick, and the lower rooms appear to have been intended for warehousing goods rather than living rooms. But there came a time when the crowded condition of the Fort made it necessary to use every available corner. Many a young Writer and Ensign has grilled and panted in those lower rooms now pronounced unfit for

St. George's Gate and the Barracks

House in which the Duke of Wellington lived, and
St. Thomé Gate

habitation, wondering what fate it was that had brought them to India's coral strand.

Edward Fowle well deserves the praise bestowed upon him by the Company; for some of his work still testifies to his ability as an architect. Having planned the Fort, he was asked by the Governor and Council to go to Bencoolen on the West coast of Sumatra, to superintend the erection of a fort there. Unfortunately, he fell a victim to the malarious climate and died soon after his arrival. He left a widow in Madras. His daughter Elizabeth he had given away in marriage in the beautiful church of St. Mary's, which he doubtless designed and helped to build. She became the wife of Benjamin Northey, one of the Company's servants in 1685, and was widowed in the following year. She soon consoled herself and took for her second husband John Pitt. She died in 1688, after giving birth to a son who did not survive her. Another of Fowle's daughters, (Mary,) married John Beard, who was Chief in the Bay. It was a common thing in those days for widows to marry again. European women were few and the men greatly outnumbered them. There was a large mortality amongst the men, who had not learnt how to protect themselves from the tropical climate; it was not unusual for a woman to have as many as three husbands in a comparatively small space of time. Mrs. Fowle, the widow, married Robery Ivory, who succeeded Fowle as Chief Gunner of the Fort.

Master did his best to settle the disputes at the factories in the Bay. He visited each in turn and introduced the same method of keeping the books as he had established at Madras. He enquired closely into matters, and allowed his strong hand to be felt amongst the lax factors and merchants. It was not a pleasant task, and it helped to make him enemies, who did not fail by-and-bye to throw mud at him.

He travelled in state with a suitable retinue, and Mohun went with him as Second in Council. The different officers of his Bodyguard are enumerated in the diary of his journeys which he kept. One was a "roundel fellow", another a "kittesal fellow" and a third an "arrowe fellow." The roundel and the kittesal were umbrellas; the first was an emblem of power; it was ornamental and was borne in front of the person. It was of immense importance in the eyes of the natives, and apparently was also of some consequence in those of the Europeans, as an order was issued about this time that no person below the rank of a Factor or Ensign, was to use a roundel; the order was extended to their wives as well. The kittesal or quitasol was for use as a shelter from the sun, and was probably made of palmleaf; there was no honour attached to it.

Master went first to Masulipatam, and thence by sea to Balasore at the mouth of the Hugly. There he had to tranship into a budgerow or river boat, as the river was difficult to navigate owing to want of pilots. It will not be going beyond the province of this gossip to say a few words about the origin of the present Calcutta Pilot Service, which was organised before the city was founded; especially as the first members of the body were Madras men and had their families living at Madras.

It was known that Portuguese ships of 600 tons burden went up the river; but the Directors, could not persuade their captains to take vessels further than Balasore, where they transhipped their cargoes to the great detriment of the goods. For some time past the Directors had been sending out orders concerning the establishment of a system of pilotage, and offering premiums on freightage to the commanders and mates of all vessels that should reach a certain point on the river. But beyond putting down a few buoys with flags at the entrance, nothing had been done, and no commander would venture up. It was not work that the ordinary sea-going captain could do; it needed men who were always on the spot studying the changes in the riverbed and noting every movement of the fickle current. The pilot service is said to have been established as early as 1668, when a small vessel was built to take soundings from which charts were to be made; but it was not until some twenty years later that there were men enough with sufficient knowledge to serve as pilots. George Heron or Herron was the first man to make a chart of the river and to draw up any regular instructions, and these the Directors caused to be printed. The first British ship to go up the Hugly was the Falcon in 1679, which was commanded at the time by Captain Stafford.

There lies buried in the old cemetery on the glacis a Captain Titus Oates, the son of Samuel and Mary Oates of Great Yarmouth. He is described as a "pilote of the Bengall River." He died in 1723 aged forty-four. His descendants remained in Madras, following the sea and becoming commanders of country vessels.[11]

The premiums given to pilots were usually large, and those offered by native ship-owners were a great temptation to the men to leave the Company's service. In 1679 a man named Downing entered the service of the King of Golconda, on a salary of six hundred pagodas a month, in charge of a vessel bound for Persia. Downing was a deserter from the Company's ranks, and the Governor complained to the native official who ruled in the name of the King, that it was contrary to the laws of the King of England that his subjects should thus serve other nations. He advised him to get rid of Downing, adding that all such men were runaways and would do no good to their employers. The King's Viceroy replied that it was inconvenient to have the man removed, and he asked that he might be left where he was for the present. As Master had no means of securing Downing by force he was obliged to consent, and the matter was dropped, the defaulter taking good care to keep out of the reach of the Company.

During this trip Master was brought into contact with Job Charnock, and his name appears frequently in the records of Fort St. George; but his story must be told in another chapter; it is only necessary to say here that Master misunderstood the man entirely, as indeed did most of his contemporaries. Master made him Chief of Cassimbazar on the Hugly, and directed him to join immediately so that they might meet. Charnock was otherwise engaged in the affairs of his employers, and he refused to leave Patna until his business there was completed. This caused a coolness between the two men; and perhaps helped to spread and perpetuate tales, which awakened the suspicions of the Directors and aroused thoughts in their minds unworthy of them. It seems to have been a great opportunity thrown away, as both men were undoubtedly earnest and single-hearted workers in the Company's service; and at a time too, when there was laxity and disorder. Charnock, if Master had only known it, would have made a valuable coadjutor in the work the latter had taken in hand in settling matters on a better footing in the Bay. Though very difficult in education and polish, they possessed certain characteristics in common. Both were determined and firm in their line of action; both had the Company's interest at heart, and both were gifted with a clear perception of what the policy of the Company ought to be towards the natives. But this very strength of character helped to cause the misunderstanding through which they drifted apart. Master cancelled the appointment he had made and put another man in Charnock's place. Charnock said very little at the time, but his unfriendly attitude towards Master showed later on that he resented the treatment and felt the indignity of it.

Whilst Master was up in the Bay, Masulipatam was overwhelmed by a disastrous tidal wave which swept inland over the country. The sea flowed twelve feet deep in the Dutch factory and did great damage. The English factory escaped with only three feet of water. A great part of the town was washed away, and thousands of the natives were drowned. The after effects brought evil consequences in disease and malaria from decaying vegetable and animal matter, and it was some time before the place recovered from the catastrophe. A similar thing happened at Masulipatam in 1864, when a tidal wave swept the coast, and some sixty thousand people were drowned.

Master took the opportunity whilst at Masulipatam of visiting the diamond mines so celebrated in the 17th century. The trade in diamonds was one of the Company's most lucrative monopolies, and the free merchant, who dealt in precious stones, was obliged to pay duty on them and ship them by the Company's vessels. The market where they were to be purchased was the town of Golconda, but the mines were some distance away, some in Kurnool and some in the present district of Hyderabad. In Master's time the Moghul claimed all stones above a certain weight, found by the people who purchased the right of mining. A staff of watchers was placed over the mines to see that no diamonds were carried away above the prescribed weight, the punishment of defaulters being death. Diamond mining was a speculative pursuit and consequently fascinating to the native, who no doubt frequently succeeded in evading or bribing the Moghul's officers. The stones, whether fairly or unfairly acquired, found a ready market with the merchants of Fort St. George, who were always glad to do a deal on their own account if they had the opportunity. The gems were easily carried by passengers returning to England, or by interloping captains; and as a means of transmitting money they offered superior advantages to any other commodity. The Company was always on the alert to discover diamond smuggling, and in 1682 David Basew, described as "a very antient man," who wished to return to his native country, was ordered to be strictly examined as to whether he was taking home any stones. Master thus described his visit to Gullapullee, where Mr. Cholmley had bought diamonds for the Company the year before.

"We went to the mines upon a hill to see them dig and look for the diamonds, which is done after this manner. The ground is loose, of a red, fat (sic) sand and gravel; great and small, black, red and white stones. One or two of the miners loosen the earth with an iron crow (bar), and others with iron spades heave it up to a heap, whence others with baskets wind (winnow) the small dust from it with the wind. Thence it is carried to a trough made up of stones and earth, filled with water, which is brought thither above a mile upon men's heads, where all the gross earth is washed away from the gravel. For the earth melts like sugar, and run out of a hole with the water, so that the gravel all remains. That they carry thence and spread upon a smooth plain place prepared for the purpose, where the same men (that dig, dust and wash the earth) sit all the heat of the day in a rank (row), one by another, with their faces towards the sun, looking for the diamonds; and the man who employs them sits over against them, to see that what they find they deliver to him. And in this manner they find the diamonds in the same fashion and shape as they are sold rough; and to an observer the cost and labour of finding them countervails the value and worth of the diamonds. Those that employ the miners do not buy the ground, as some have reported, but they, or anyone that has a desire to employ his money that way, first acquaints the governor of the mines with it; then he grants him licence to spring a mine where the employer thinks best, paying three pagodas per mensem if he employs no more than ten, twenty or forty men; if more, then four, and of some, five pagodas per mensem. The miners, or those labourers that work in the mines, are paid one and a quarter pagodas per mensem in money and corn; and this is all the charge the adventurer in the mines is at; except it be that they overbid one another sometimes for a good piece of ground which one hath lit upon, and another hearing of it, bids the governor money for it, and he that gives most has it. But besides the rent of three to five pagodas per mensem to the governor for the King, there is a custom or excise set upon all corn at about fifty per cent above the market (price); upon salt, betel (nut), and tobacco at above double and treble the market rate; and all the miners and those that deal there, except a privileged Englishman or such like, are compelled to live upon the miners in those towns where that excise is raised. The whole rent of these mines is reckoned to the King worth sixty thousand pagodas per annum, and as much more to the governor to bribe the courtiers to hold the place."

That is to say, the governor or manager had to allow the courtiers round the Moghul a share in the plunder, otherwise they would procure his dismissal. The mines seen by Master were merely pits; none were more than three feet below the surface, and most were only two. The diamond mines have proved of absorbing interest to all generations, and they have been examined more than once by Europeans with a view to reworking them. The diamond alluvial deposits are pretty well exhausted, the ground being honeycombed with shallow pits. To this day occasional search is made in the old localities by the natives, who firmly believe that the precious stones grow. The diamond matrix or bed is of considerable extent and by no means exhausted. Comparatively it has been very little worked, although there are signs of gunpowder having been used for blasting, and pits to the depth of fifteen feet have been excavated. But the process was difficult and expensive; it required stone-breaking machinery, which was beyond the reach of the native speculator; and consequently the larger portion of the diamond beds of India remain still untouched. There is every reason to believe that the out-turn might be as good as it was in Tavernier's time, when sixty thousand miners were employed. There are two drawbacks, however, which have caused the European to hesitate. One is the expensive machinery required and the scarcity of fuel. The second is the unreliability of the native workman. The stones are so easily secreted and sold; and the Hindu is so superhumanly expert at thieving. European labour would be necessary to a large extent, and in such a climate it would be difficult to obtain and very costly.

There are many tales told by the natives of wonderful finds; one is of a fine stone which gleamed for years in the mud wall of a villager's house before its true nature was recognised. There are also stories of stones hidden in the village temples of the district; but there is not much truth in any of them. If there ever were valuable stones in the temple, which is quite possible, the probability is that they have long since disappeared and glass or crystal has been substituted. The Hindu shows no ignorance in the matter of gems; he knows as well as the European what their value is, and his cupidity is great. Even in the large temples of the South where the jewels are catalogued and placed under the guardianship of chosen trustees, the stones, occasionally disappear, and carefully imitated gems in glass are discovered in their places. The native jewellers of the Golconda district possessed the art of cutting and polishing the stones, although they never equalled the English workman in that respect. They understood the use of diamond dust and emery powder, which last was also quarried in the neighbourhood. Garnets were found in Kurnool and Hyderabad and were cut into beads; also amethyst, rock crystal and rose quartz, all of which were readily bought by native and European merchants for the Hindu women or for the fashionable London dames.

The Nathaniel Cholmley mentioned in Master's account was the Company's agent at Golconda at the time. He did not escape the usual accusations which every man seemed to think it necessary to hurl at his neighbour. He was accused of buying as much for his own profit as his employers', with the result that the Directors sent out orders that he was to be shipped off to England in the shortest possible time, an order which he seems to have resisted. Pringle conjectures him to have been the same Nathaniel Cholmley who married Mary, only daughter and heiress of Sir Hugh Cholmley, Baronet of Whitby.

7

ST. MARY'S CHURCH
AND THE VESTRY

On Master's return from the Bay he set about consolidating and building up the status of Fort St. George. He may be called its second founder. He had already made reforms in the method of transacting business and in keeping of the books. He remodelled Langhorne's rules for the governance of the community, and appointed a Provost Marshal to see that they were enforced. The personal behaviour of some of the Company's servants was not all that it should have been. There was no actual crime except such as arose from drink. Drink was the chief weakness of the times and was at the root of all disorderliness. The Company provided wine and beer, as well as food, domestics and lodging for its servants. Madeira was one of the favourite beverages, and Shiraz wine from Persia, a strong liquor made by the Armenians and sometimes called Armenian wine. It was coarse and fruity compared with the soft delicate wines of

Europe. As the Englishman lived a community life his conduct was brought into public notice and his excesses were observed. Master's rules for the guidance of the private individual read quaintly, and many of them would not be tolerated in the present day. All the inhabitants of the Fort were obliged to be in their houses by a certain hour at night, when fires and all unnecessary lights were extinguished. Prayers were read morning and evening in a room set apart for a Chapel in the Fort House until the church was built; and if any young writer or officer ventured to cut chapel he was fined. Alas! history says that he had to be fined also for coming to church in a state of elevation, and offering to fight a friend on the way. Fines were also imposed for swearing, lying, quarrelling and Sabbath breaking. No social gatherings were permitted on Sunday; the guests ran the same risk as their host in assembling round his hospitable board. If fining was not sufficient to bring the contumacious to their senses, they were shipped off home by the first vessel leaving port. The Company certainly did its best to foster good manners amongst its servants; but it now and then verged on the ridiculous, when it took serious notice of such misdemeaours as that of Thomas Burrett. This gentleman in 1682, to use the words of the Governor and Council, "most impiously drank the health of the Devil." For this crime "so notorious and of so black a dye," he was condemned to "run the gantlope," and to be imprisoned till he could be sent to England. The record adds that it was hoped that this would deter others from "committing crimes so hellishly wicked."

Whenever the Governor went out either for business or pleasure he always moved with regal state. He was attended by a strong Bodyguard of armed peons, and he usually rode on horseback, preceded by the state umbrella-bearer and trumpeters, who announced his coming with flourishes of music. If the sun was too hot he used a palanquin, which was borne by horses or men. A visitor to the Fort, a little later than Master's time thus describes the Governor's progress to church on Sunday.

"Twixt eight and nine the bell tells us the hour of devotion draws near. A whole company of above two hundred soldiers is drawn out from the inner Fort to the church door for a guard to the passing President. Ladies throng to their pews, and gentlemen take a serious walk in the yard if it be not too hot. On the Governor's approach the organs strike up and continue a welcome till he is seated; when the minister discharges the duty of his function, according to the forms appointed by our prudent ancestors of the Church of England."

Master's reign was a short one, yet in that time he left two lasting memorials of his energy. One was the Fort church, dedicated to God in honour of St. Mary; the other was the Court of Judicature[12] out of which was by-and-bye evolved the High Court. Hitherto justice had been administered by two of the merchants, who had no more doubt concerning their judicial ability than they had of their military capacity. They sat in the Choultry or native court which was situated near one of the gates of the North wall, and unhesitatingly gave their judgement without the aid of lawyer, barrister or jury. And until Master's time this course had contented the people, European and native alike. But complaints began to reach the Governor's ears of the imperfect administration of the Choultry Justices, and a change was necessary. The Justices had never been allowed the power of life and death, consequently all murder cases had to be tried in England unless a warrant signed by the King was sent out. The accused person thus often suffered a long term of imprisonment before opportunity could be found of shipping him home, as was the case with the Corporal and Sergeant who had caused the death of Savage. The Company had lately obtained a new charter from Charles II; and by this charter Master discovered that he, with his Council, was empowered to try all cases, civil and criminal, which were beyond the capabilities of the Choultry. Accordingly the new court held its first sitting at nine in the morning of March 27, 1678, in the room used as a chapel, and heard a civil suit, Tivill versus Jearsey. In 1683 it was ordered by the authorities in England, that the Court should consist of one person learned in civil law, two merchants and such other officers as the said Court should think necessary, the appointment being made by the Governor in Council. The Directors promised to send out a Judge Advocate as soon as possible, and in due course Sir John Biggs arrived. He was received with honour and was given a seat in Council. He died in 1689, and was buried in the old cemetery, just after having laid his wife Jane to rest in the same spot.

Within a few days of the first sitting of the Court of Judicature the foundations of St. Mary's church were dug. It was the first church of the Anglican Communion raised in India, and it was built by the liberal subscriptions of the merchants of Fort St. George. From the earliest times when the merchant adventurers sent forth their ships they remembered the religious needs of their people; and they attached paid chaplains to the staff of each little fleet. When factories and forts were established the chaplains were appointed to them, and were no longer required to move about with the merchantmen. Fort St. George was too small a place to be given a chaplain at first, and the few English inhabitants made use of the services of two French Capuchin friars, who performed their rites for them in English.

The gulf between the national churches of France and of England was not so wide as it became subsequently, when Napoleon placed his Church in the hands of the Pontiff of Rome; and the little Anglican community at the Fort had no difficulty in accepting the ministrations of the good friars. They were infinitely preferable to the Portuguese, who had introduced all the horrors of the Inquisition into India. One of the French priests was afterwards made to feel its strength, and suffered five years' imprisonment at Goa, for having served the English as he did.

As early as 1655, mention is made of a Protestant chaplain at Madras and from that time the place was never long without one. The Revd. Patrick Warner had a good deal to do with the urging on of the building of St. Mary's but he did not see the work completed, having returned to Europe before the church was consecrated. His successor, the Revd. Richard Portman, had the privilege of performing the dedicatory service at its opening two years later, in 1680.

The first sod was turned on Lady-Day 1678 (hence the name St. Mary). The edifice, which rests on a firm laterite foundation, testifies to this day to the excellence of the masons' work in brick and polished chunam (a fine sea-shell plaster, having the appearance of white marble). The roof is bombproof, and the walls, six feet thick, are massive enough to have sustained a siege in those days. It has been slightly altered at the east end by the introduction of a chancel, a vestry and an organ chamber, but otherwise the building remains very much as it was originally designed.

The spire was added in 1692, and quarters were built at the West end adjoining the Tower for the Chaplain.[13] The house has disappeared together with other houses near the church, so as to open out the edifice and let in more light and air. The present tower of St. Mary's is not the original one. In 1759 it was so much damaged by the shot and shell of the French during the siege by Lally, that it was found to be beyond repair, and the Vestry decided that it would have to be entirely rebuilt. There was some delay owing to want of funds, and it was eventually done at the expense of the Company, under the direction of Colonel Gent, H.E.I.C.S., who, as a reward for his trouble, was presented by the Vestry with the scaffolding. The new tower is finer and considerably taller than that which was first built.

The church has been put to various uses during the last two centuries. In 1758, during the siege, it was used as a barrack for the soldiers. In 1782 Lord Macartney, the Governor, asked that it might be handed over to him as a storehouse for military stores. The war with Tippoo was going on, and the Fort, which had only been partially restored, was full of soldiers and war material. It was considered absolutely necessary in the interests of self-preservation to turn it into a storeroom; it was accordingly handed over for a period of nine months, and the services were held in the banqueting hall close by. The furniture was safely stored; the only thing that suffered was the organ presented by Mr. John Smith, which no one seemed competent to rebuild. In 1800 Brigadier General de Meuron asked for the loan of the church, when it was not required for the English services, to give his Swiss Regiment a service in French. Gericke, the Lutheran missionary, was able to act as their minister, and performed the service for them once a week. The same concession had been made to a Hanoverian Regiment a few years previously, when a service had been held regularly by the Lutheran missionary in German.

At no time has the edifice shown to better advantage than in the present day. It holds its own against all the modern churches of the Presidency, not excepting the Cathedral, which, however, is considerably larger than St. Mary's. Lockyer, who visited the Fort in 1703, thus describes the Fort church:

"The church is a large pile of arched building adorned with curious carved work, a stately Altar, organs a white copper candlestick, very large windows, etc. which render it inferior to the churches in London in nothing but bells, there being one only, to mind sinners of devotion, though I have heard a contribution for a set was formerly remitted the Company."

The altar was beautified with a fine copy of a well-known picture of the Last Supper. It is now skied above the chancelarch. The Vestry books do not begin till the year 1746, so that there are no records to give the history of the painting or the name of the donor. It is mentioned as the altar piece in 1782 when the church was handed over to Lord Macartney, and it was put back into position after the restoration of the building. In 1795 the Vestry ordered it to be removed and hung in the vestry, so that the East window might be opened.

The church possesses some handsome silver plate. This was more fortunate than the gold tablet in the time of the occupation of the Fort by the French, as it escaped confiscation. There is a fine massive alms-dish which was given by Elihu Yale in 1688 on the death of his only son David. There is also an old cup which is too large for present use, the names of the donor is unknown. A beautiful silver font-basin and flagon were presented in memory of Lady Mary Goldsborough in 1689, and they have her arms engraved upon them.

Church Plate and Master's Bible

The basin, which is like a deep soup-plate, fits into the stone font and is still in use.

Master was present at the consecration of St. Mary's and the Bible that he used to that occasion is in the strong box of the church. It forms one of the most interesting possessions of the Chaplaincy, and was presented by one of the Master's descendants, on retirement from the Madras Council, towards the end of the 19th century.

The church is full of mementoes of men who have helped to make history, and is the last resting-place of several Governors and Commanders-in-chief to the Madras Army, Francis Hastings, Sir Thomas Munro, Sir Henry George Ward, Sir Alexander Campbell, Sir Samuel Hood, Lord Hobart, Lord Pigot and others. Some of the monuments are fine bits of sculpture by Flaxman, the younger Bacon, Richardson and Turnouth. Flaxman's figures of the high-caste natives are excellent. The colours of the old Madras Fusiliers[14] hang on the chancel-wall just above the pulpit. They were carried into Cawnpore immediately after the massacres; then through the six engagements during the first and second advance on Lucknow by Havelock, and into Lucknow itself at the first relief. They have been the silent witnesses of some terrible scenes. Within the last twenty years most of the pensioners of the Fusiliers have died. They were tough hard Englishmen, acclimatised, but British to the backbone. It was always interesting to hear these old fellows talk of their campaigns; they could never speak of the mutiny without excitement, and a spark or two of the fire which led them on through every obstacle to the relief of their countrywomen and children, or to avenge their death. Yet, with all their bitterness, it was touching—the testimony they bore to the fidelity of their camp-followers, the bhisti

The staircase to Governor's seat in Gallery, and
the Tombstone pavement

and the cook-boy, who went with them and ministered to their wants on the march and in the trenches.

The carved work mentioned by Lockyer is on the gallery. It is beautifully designed and executed by heathen hands under Christian superintendence. The figures of the elephant and parrot, familiar in Hindu temples, appear on the balustrade, intertwined with rich arabesque foliage, surmounted by cherubium, and the faces of middle-aged men with full-bottomed wigs, suggestive of the Governor and his Council of that date. Formerly the Governor sat in the gallery, in state, with his colleagues round him; but of late years the historical old Fort church has been forsaken for the more modern Cathedral; the gallery has been set further back, and it is now relegated to the military prisoners, who attended service under a guard. The approach is by two handsome staircases outside the North and South walls.

When Lord Hobart died in 1874, the vaults under the chancel steps where the great men have mostly been laid, were opened to find room for him. One vault was empty except for a single nameless coffin. There was no inscription above to record the burial of anyone. It was known that Lord Pigot, one of the Governors of the eighteenth century had been interred in the church, but no one knew where; it was surmised that this coffin must contain his remains. The Duke of Buckingham, Lord Hobart's successor, ordered a granite slab to be placed above the vault with the words, "In Memoriam," engraved upon it.

Lady Hobart beautified the East end of St. Mary's, in memory of her husband, with carved choir stalls, stained glass, encaustic tiles, etc.

and the public erected a marble bust of Lord Hobart, which is placed just within the chancel arch.

From the time of the consecration of St. Mary's church a Vestry was formed to govern its affairs. The history of this Body is unique as being the story of irresponsible effort nobly sustained for the general good of the settlement. The Governor usually presided at the Vestry meetings, supported by the Members of Council and the chief people in the Company's service.

Unfortunately the earliest records are lost. There is a note at the beginning of the existing books to this effect: "The minutes of the Vestry prior to this date appear to have been lost at the capture of Madras by the French under La Bourdonais (sic) in 1746." The first meeting of which there is any record was held in 1749, immediately after the restoration of the Fort of the English, and a new minute-book was then commenced. Deputy Governor Richard Prince was present, with the Members of Council and principal residents. From that time to the dissolution of the Vestry, names well known to history constantly recur in the minute-books; Palk, Morse, Pigot, Lord Macartney, Colonel Clive, General Stringer Lawrence, Warren Hastings[15] and others attended and took their part in the administration of Church affairs.

The most important duty of the Vestry was the administration of the St. Mary's Charity Fund. This Fund was commenced with the foundation of the church. In 1685 mention is made of the investment of six hundred pagodas in the Company's stock on behalf of "the Church Orphans." Money was at first accumulated by subscription and donation. Then people gave their houses to the Vestry by deed of gift, in trust for the support of their wives and children whilst they were away in the far East—a journey from which they frequently never returned. Or they bequeathed their houses by will for the benefit of their widows and children; the property becoming the Vestry's when they no longer required support. Sums of money were deposited and devised in the same manner, and the trust was faithfully and conscientiously kept. The Vestry nursed and increased the Fund, making every effort to extend the charity for the support of disabled soldiers, for widows, and for the benefit of a school for Eurasian children.

The method adopted by the Vestry was to purchase house property in the Fort, where it was increasing yearly in value; and also to invest money in "respondentia" bonds (which was placing money in the hands of ship owners and masters for the purpose of licenced private trading). In 1758, at the siege, some of the houses were severely damaged and a new policy was inaugurated. The Fathers of the settlement sold the houses and lent the money to the merchants on security of their houses in the Fort. No house security outside the Fort was taken till after 1792 when Tippoo Sultan had his wings cut. Later still they lent money to the Nabob of the Carnatic through the Government, the security being a portion of his landed property. For this loan they obtained twelve per cent. Later again they put all their property into the hands of Government and bought the Government ten-per-cent bonds, which now yield three and a half per cent.

Once a year the Vestry met regularly to elect two church wardens and two sidesmen, that is to say, to see that two such officers were duly provided. The officers were progressive; a man began as junior sidesman and became senior in his second year, junior churchwarden in his third and senior churchwarden in his fourth. As senior warden he had charge of the bonds, papers and accounts, and at the end of his year of office he resigned. The proceedings were orderly and serious; the accounts accurately kept. All were impressed with the importance of their proceedings and with a desire to make the charity go as far as possible.

They modelled their constitution on that a Vestry Body in England, and fully believed that they had the same legal powers to hold property, make rates and do anything anyone asked them in the way of administrating trusts and funds. Acting under this belief, their deeds were admirable and their conduct altogether dignified; they innocently created for themselves an official position and rigorously lived up to its requirements; and herein as a Body they were unique in British India.

The Vestry proceedings show the old merchants of the eighteenth century in their very best light, kindly, charitable, acknowledging the claims of the European and Eurasian poor, and manifestly putting themselves out and giving up their valuable time to try and better the condition of their indigent neighbours.

The school grew from a small beginning of twenty-five boys to more than double that number, and the greatest interest was taken by the Vestry in the well being of the children. The Charity boys were brought before the Vestry annually, to show their copybooks and their sums, and to repeat their catechism. It was an important function and a momentous day to the young people. The ushers, as they were then called, were complimented and rewarded; a resolution was passed recording the satisfaction felt by the Vestry at the progress made by the boys, and congratulations were offered to the Chaplain in charge. At the age of sixteen the boys were apprenticed out to a trade. Some were sent to sea, some bound to surgeons, some were made writers or clerks; others were apprenticed to watch-makers, ship-builders and carriage-builders. Nor were the boys lost sight of when they left the school. Enquiry was made as to their conduct, and the names of several who did credit to the school are left on record.

In 1805 the St. Mary's Vestry proceedings came to an end, and the Body was dissolved in the hundred and twenty-fifth year of its age. During that period the fund had grown, by careful nursing, from the six hundred pagodas of the "Church Orphans" money to sixty thousand pagodas, just two lakhs of rupees.

The immediate rock upon which the vessel split was the Marmelong Bridge between St. Thomas Mount and Madras. Peter Uscan, an Armenian merchant, died and left fifteen hundred pagodas in 1754 to the Vestry; the interest of this sum at five per cent was to be used in keeping the bridge in repair. Any interest made on the capital over and above five per cent was considered to be perquisite of the Charity Fund, and was given to the poor. In 1804 the bridge wanted widening and strengthening. It had been originally built for the accommodation of foot-passengers and small country carts. But during the war with Tippoo it had frequently been used by the Company for the passage of troops and heavy artillery in preference to the more laborious road through the river bed and ford. The Vestry was asked to do the alteration, but refused on the ground that their trust said nothing about rebuilding, but only repairing. The refusal was given by the majority; it was not unanimous. An account of monies spent was then asked for, and it showed that the interest at five per cent had not been expended entirely upon repairing the bridge, for it had not always been needed. The Vestry were asked to pay up the arrears; this they refused to do as the money had long ago been given away in charity. There were great divisions in the Vestry, where a personal element had sprung up, and the matter was referred to the High Court. The Court ruled that there was no authority in the Vestry as a Body, because there was no parish, and that the Vestry had no legal right to administer such a trust as that imposed by Peter Uscan. It was useless to dispute the judgement of the Court, and the Vestry paid nine thousand pagodas, being the sum adjudged due, including interest and compound interest, into the hands of trustees legally appointed on behalf of the Marmelong Bridge Trust. They were also recommended to place their own funds in the hands of proper trustees whose legal rights as such would be recognised in a court of law.

There was probably no intention on the part of the dissenting members of the Vestry to bring about this total extinction of the Body when they raised their voices; but there were several causes at work to produce such a result in the course of time, even if there had been no Marmelong Bridge to split upon.

The system which had answered the purpose of a small community was scarcely sufficient to administer such a large and important charity as the St. Mary's Fund had became. The relief of the poor, the upkeep of the church, and the maintenance of the Charity School grew beyond its means as time went on. The Vestry appealed for help to enable the fund to keep pace with the demands upon it; they proposed to do a great deal more than met with the approval of the residents of Madras, upon whom would fall the responsibility of carrying on whatever was initiated. The Vestry proposed to build a workhouse on the model of a similar institution in England, that at Royston in Cambridgeshire being named as a pattern; and the proposition was made without looking into the future to see if a plan of such immensity could be carried on by a handful of private individuals. The scheme was Utopian and too large for the charitable enterprise of private persons who were colonists in a foreign country. Then the more prudent began to question the wisdom and judgement of the men who administrated the Fund.

Secondly, there was the personal element already mentioned, which had crept in through having dealings with members of the Vestry. In order to invest a portion of the money on better terms, the Vestry foreclosed on a young merchant for eight thousand pagodas. It put him into difficulties at the moment, and he had the sympathy of the community. Offence had also been given to another merchant by the Vestry. One of the Charity boys had been apprenticed to a Mr. E. Roebuck.[16] "In 1804 the boy complained of ill-treatment, and the Vestry—apparently without making sufficient enquiry—passed a rather severe minute on Mr. Roebuck's conduct. These two men were greatly instrumental in raising the questions which proved so fatal to the Vestry.

A third cause was to be found in the fact that there had lately been established at Madras a Supreme Court of Judicature (1800) and there had been a consequent immigration of lawyers. These wanted to know the nature of the trust by which so large a sum was administered by the Vestry. They were influential in getting the case taken into Court, and in the appointment of official trustees for that

St. Mary's Charity Fund. All this combined to kill the old management, and after the settlement of the Marmelong Bridge question in 1805 there were no more Vestries held to take in money at five per cent and lend it out at eight, ten and twelve per cent. From that time the trustees of the Fund received a regular sum from the Government Treasury for the specified objects of the church, the school and the poor, and there has been no increase of the capital since then. It seemed a pity to have to take the management out of such hands and virtually kill a self-constituted body of unpaid workers who had successively, for a hundred and twenty-five years, so admirably performed their duty towards their neighbours; but it had to be done.

After the administration was taken from the Vestry there was a loss of interest in Vestry concerns, if conclusion may be drawn from the absence of records. Between 1805 and 1830 there is no record of a Vestry meeting, no appointment of churchwardens and sidesmen, no letters, no accounts. The old parochialism was killed. And when the records were commenced again in 1830 the Chaplain was expected to do everything, and was held responsible for everything.

8

THE EXCHANGE MASTER'S CHARACTER AND FAMILY

Trade during Master's rule became brisk and the Company was able to make larger investments than it had ever done before. All commercial business was transacted at the sea gate. Every morning the native merchants assembled outside on the sea face. It was a convenient place of meeting and within easy reach of the Englishmen's residences; it was protected by the walls on one side and the sea on the other. To this spot the native dealers, who were never allowed inside the gates, brought specimens of their merchandise. The English merchants, many of them dressed in turban and native costume, chaffered and bargained on behalf of the Company and themselves. Diamonds smuggled from Golconda, pearls from Tuticorin, rubies from Burmah, sandalwood from Mysore, grain , spices, saltpetre, indigo, calicoes, etc. for exportation; salt, betel nut, ghee, straw, etc. for inland traffic, all found their way to this strange improvised market, and changed hands at the sea gate. Amongst other commodities the Directors asked for different kinds of waterfowl, which were required for the King, and which were to be placed in St. James' Park. There was something very fascinating about this Oriental market, and few escaped the fever of speculation. Even the English ladies tried their hands at a quiet deal now and then, and traded on their own account. Very few of the Europeans could speak the language, although the Directors encouraged the study of it by offering rewards for proficiency; it was this which obliged the English to employ brokers like Verona. If the old sea gate could speak, what tales it could tell of the shaking of the pagoda tree!

A few years later the Company built a fine town-hall within the walls of the Fort, about a hundred yards to the North of the sea gate, and business was transferred there. It is said that dungeons were constructed beneath it, but they were probably merely the lower rooms, which were used for storing merchandise, and which gave the hall the nickname of "the Company's Shop." It was usually known, however, as the Exchange, and it has been put to many and various uses since it was forsaken by the merchants. Before there was any club or general meeting place for the English gentlemen living in the Fort they used it as a tavern. A tavern was another name for an hotel. It was the fashionable resort, the punch-house being relegated to the soldier and his companions. General Welsh in his Reminiscences says, that on landing as a cadet at the end of the 18th century, he passed his first night in India on the hall table of the Exchange. General Conway, Adjutant General of the Madras Army, whose marble effigy is one of the ornaments of St. Mary's church, had a curious accident in the house. He was a raw youth just beginning his military career. One day he was standing at a window in the Exchange, looking towards the sea gate, when one of his young companions came up to him in a very excited manner, exclaiming, "Conway, the house is on fire! Save yourself." Without a second thought Conway sprang out of the window, which was some distance from the ground, and broke his leg, only to find afterwards that he had been hoaxed by his friend. The tavern was closed on the foundation of a club; and the Exchange became the home of a much milder form of dissipation in the shape of a library started by private enterprise. Instead of the noisy Ensign and the practical-joking Sub Lieutenant, its halls welcomed the gentler sex, who gathered to gossip and look for the latest literature out from home. The Madras Gazette, one of the first of the local newspapers, was printed at the Exchange early in this century. Later on the building was used as a Government office, and the Revenue Board held its sittings there. The old Madras light, or Pharos, as it was sometimes called, was placed at an early date on the top of the Exchange. A skeleton cage was erected on the roof and the lantern was secured inside. It was guarded with weather-boards on the land side and only showed its light seawards. The oil that supplied the lamp gave a dull yellow flame which appeared of a reddish tinge out at sea, not unlike the end of a lighted cheroot. But poor as it was, it was better than nothing, and a great boon to navigators who were making the port. The Fort light was replaced early in the 19th century by a light house erected on the North glacis. When the Law Courts were built in 1895, the light was removed to a handsome tower rising from the building, and its revolving flash may be seen many miles out at sea. There is a large room on the upper floor of the Exchange, which served at one time as a Council-chamber, probably when the present Secretariat was built. The ceiling is of a peculiar pattern in chequered moulding, which is unique, plain and yet handsome. The house still stands intact, and it now serves as the Mess house of the European Regiment of Infantry which garrisons Fort St. George.

Towards the end of Master's time Madras was blockaded, and the supplies of food and fuel were stopped by the native authorities. Lingappa, the Naik of Poonamalee, had endeavoured to blackmail the Company, but Master had vigorously resisted all such attempts. The Naik then had recourse to force, and tried to blockade the fort by stopping the food and forage supplies, which the natives were accustomed to bring in daily. Master sent Lieutenant Richardson, the Captain of the guard, with a party of soldiers on foraging expeditions, and compelled the people to supply what was needed. The latter were not long in discovering that the English Governor was more to be feared than the native ruler. The Naik's orders were gradually disregarded and the blockade ended. It was the only policy to pursue, and it was one which had to be adopted later on. But it was not understood by the Directors at the time; they disapproved of Master's action, and recalled him at a moment when he had just succeeded in gathering the reins of Government firmly in his hands, and had produced order and strength out of disorder and weakness.

Master, like his predecessors, Winter, Langhorne and others, did not escape calumny. Notwithstanding the fact that he had consolidated the power of the Company, raised its status, increased its trade and shown a firm front to the tyrannical native ruler, he was accused of neglecting the interests of his employers and enriching himself at their expense. As Wheeler says: "They attributed all the troubles that befell the Presidency to his pride and presumption; and because it was morally impossible for him to send off the ships with the usual despatch, whilst Madras was almost in a state of blockade, they had the meanness to ascribe the delay to his being so much engaged in private trade. In vain, Master proudly referred to the increase in the population and revenues of the town during his administration; the Directors declared that the amount was more than counterbalanced by the increased expenditure during the troubles. In a word, just at the moment when Master seemed to be on the eve of defeating Lingappa, and of finally placing the foreign relations of the settlement on a satisfactory footing, he was recalled by the Court of Directors."

The charge of enriching himself by private trade was particularly unjust as he had been openly encouraged by the Directors to make certain speculations on his own behalf. In a letter dated December 24th, 1675, written from London to the Council at Fort St. George, the two following paragraphs occur.

"We have permitted Mr. Master to send to and bring from the Bay yearly 15 tons of goods on his own account, freight free, in our shipping. All others are to pay 30s per ton freight from the Fort or Masulipatam to the Bay, and £3 per ton on the return trip.

"And we have permitted Mr. Master to send home yearly 2 tons of goods on our Tonnage, of goods not prohibited, and to be consigned to us, and this principally in the hope that he may find out some sorts proper for this Market which are as yet unknown to us."

It is not at all likely that a shrewd and experienced merchant such as Master was, would speculate wildly and unwisely. It is far more probable that his ventures were successful, and whilst he profited, the Company gained knowledge and an increased trade without having taken any risk.

On his retirement he was worried by a tedious enquiry, and when his accounts were examined a mistake was found to which the most was made. Some elephants belonging to the Company had been sold and the money was not accounted for in the books. Master did not deny having received it, and he pleaded forgetfulness as an excuse for the omission. It was quite sufficient to give his enemies an opportunity of saying many hard and bitter things against him.

His health was impaired by a long residence in India, and his memory was not good at any time. He made no attempt to excuse himself in this case, although he might have done so by throwing the blame on to his clerks whose duty it was to draw his attention to the mistake. Many of the charges were founded entirely on the word of native merchants whose ire had been raised by the rejection of their contracts.

Master's pride prevented him from replying to them. At no time in his career did he condescend to conciliate his enemies, and his conduct was misunderstood by the Directors, who gave ear to every complaint. In the light of modern times, Master appears to have been a man in advance of his day. The charges seem frivolous, spiteful and without support. It was a period of plain speaking. The Directors themselves were guilty at times of the most intemperate language towards their servants, and they seem to have been in no way astonished at receiving the same kind of thing in return. The value of the Director's praise or abuse was well understood, and it is unlikely that Master took their words to heart or vexed himself on account of their hasty judgements. There were many men on the Directorate as well as in the service of the Company who had no sympathy with one of Master's birth and education. His pride of family was probably an offence to many of his associates, who would not have been sorry to have seen a man of his class fall under temptation.

His character was cleared after his return to England in 1682. His differences with the Company were satisfactorily settled by certain payments which he made into the Treasury, and he received knighthood. It seems possible that the Directors altered the opinion they had formed and recognised the debt of gratitude which they owed him. They elected him a member of the Court, and in 1697–98 he was Chairman, a position he could never have occupied had they considered him guilty of fraud and embezzlement. He died April 28th, 1724, at the age of eighty-five and was buried at Macclesfield.[17]

From a pamphlet privately printed by a member of the family we have an interesting account of the Masters, and a peep at the personal character of the man himself from his own letters. In one written from Madras to his sister Mary at East Langdon, he says:

"As business comes on so I find the state of our family to creep out of my mind, which I am willing to retain so long as possibly I can. Wherefore my petition to you is that you would please to honour me so far, as by the next return of these ships, to send me a true account of our family of the Masters; from what house they came and where was their own seat. So likewise of the Streynshams and also of the Oxendens; an account of all our Uncles and Aunts and ourselves taken exactly; of what day and year we were born; that

I may know all our ages, together with the distinct mark in heraldry for the distinctions of brothers; and if there be any ancient histories of such things that you think fit to send, they will be very welcome to me, for I am a great lover of such stories."

In answer to the above letter, Master received replies from his brother and his sister. The brother expressed his belief not founded, however, on historical proofs, that the family originally came from the low Countries and settled at Sandwich, where they traded and acquired land. The first known ancestor was John, a wealthy merchant of Sandwich, who became Mayor of that place several times between the years 1528 and 1558. He bought lands and the manor of East Langdon from King Henry VIII., which previously belonged to the Abbey of West Langdon. This estate was left by John, on his death in 1558, to his son James, the great-grandfather of Streynsham. James left it to his son, Sir Edward Master, Knight, who married Awdrey, the heiress of Robert Streynsham of Ospring; and on his death it came to Richard, Streynsham Master's father. Miss Streynsham, the heiress was a distant connection of the Master's family; she brought the Streynsham coat of arms and personal with her.

Miss Mary Master's letter went into more personal detail. She mentioned John of Sandwich and described James his son as being "in his youth wild; spent and lost almost all by cards and dice; but hearing people oft say, 'Yunder goes Master had land', it so struck him that he resolved as he had so he would have." And thus he purchased back his lands and rebuilt the fortune he was in a fair way to dissipate. John Master "lived nobly, kept three-score men in blue coats which was the livery all gentlemen formerly gave." She quaintly concluded by saying, "My mother is not willing our ages should travel so far," but all the same she managed to send her brother the information he needed, mentioning amongst them Robert, "an Indian merchant, and hope one day President." (Robert died unmarried at Karwar).

Her description of the various brothers and sisters was as follows. One was "a fair, fat, middle-sized woman", another "a tall, brown woman"; and a third "an ingenious, witty, flaxen-haired, beautiful, middle-sized, hasty woman." One of the brothers was "a ready (ruddy?) well-complexioned boy, now at the free School at Canterbury, ready to go to an employment"; and another was "a little risselled boy and consumptive; now at Canterbury School, and if he live he has chosen to be a Doctor of Divinity, and pleads much for it.

Streynsham Master's mother was an Oxenden; his maternal Uncle, Sir George Oxenden, Knight, who was President of the Factory of Surat in 1656, and Governor of Bombay in 1668, was instrumental in getting him the appointment in the Company's service.

The Masters were a prolific family; Streynsham's great-grandfather James had ten children, his grandfather Sir Edward had fifteen, and Richard his father had twenty, Streynsham being the thirteenth child and the eighth son.

At the present time there is a descendant of his living in Madras, the wife of the Revd. Henry Goldsmith of the Church Missionary Society. Her father, Charles Gilbert Master, Esq., was a Member of Council in Madras in the year 1887, when he presented the Bible belonging to his ancestor Streynsham to the Chaplain of the Fort.

9

TAXES, SLAVERY AND INTERLOPERS

Master was succeeded by William Gyfford, who was the exact opposite to him in character. Whereas the former was "a statesman among traders," the latter was eminently a merchant among traders. Gyfford instead of having profited by a long experience in the country seems to have acquired some of the weakness, the shiftiness and the want of straightforwardness of the natives amongst whom he had lived and worked. In 1657 he was a factor, and he rose to a seat in Council in 1662. In 1671 he was made Chief of the factory of Tonquin. During those years he had seen Fort St. George rise from weakness and insignificance into something like a power in the land. But he had early learnt the lesson inculcated by the Directors before Sir Josiah Child's influence was felt in the Court. He was a peace-at-any-price man, quite ready to conciliate the native traders and bow low to the native rulers so long as it brought in the desired wealth. Fortunately he held the reins of Government for only three years, but during that time he managed to upset a good deal of the work of his predecessor. The Directors' opinion of him went through several modifications. They began by calling him their "worthy Agent." A few years later he was "that heavy President," and "our too easy Governor"; and they accused him of having "not only lost his first love for our service, but his understanding with it."

It is quite possible that his health had something to do with his weakness. He was always ailing whilst at the Fort and frequently pleaded ill-health as an excuse for not calling his Council together to transact business. He got his nickname of "our too easy Governor," on account of his leniency with regard to municipal taxes.

It will be remembered that there was an attempt to tax the inhabitants of Madras as early as 1675, in Langhorne's time, when the old houses, built by the first batch of colonists were demolished. A very small sum was assessed to each house, but the people absolutely refused to pay it; they declared that they would rather leave their houses than submit to the yoke. It was the thin end of the wedge; though accustomed to a variety of taxes of different kinds, they had never suffered the imposition of a house-tax. There was no means of forcing them, and so it was never collected.

Streynsham Master made another attempt at taxation to pay for the cleansing of Blacktown, which from all accounts was in the usual condition of a pristine Eastern city. The streets were made the receptacle for rubbish and filth of all sorts, and the natives could not understand that this arrangement was capable of improvement. Master did not revive the obnoxious house-tax, but imposed a duty on arrack and paddy, (rice before it is husked,) and increased the customs on tobacco and other goods. The people remonstrated, but paid the tax. At the same time they sent in a petition to the Governor and Council praying that they might be allowed to keep the streets clean themselves, remarking that in their opinion scavengers were not necessary.

When Gyfford succeeded Master, the protest against taxation was renewed; he was weak enough to listen, and to remit the municipal dues. But soon after doing so, he received an urgent order from the Court of Directors to insist upon the taxation of all the houses in Madras, to supply funds for the cleansing of the town, and for the upkeep of the fortifications, together with the garrison charges. The Directors pointed out forcibly that the safety of the inhabitants of Blacktown depended on the strength of the Fort, and that the security of the people's lives and property was in the Fort guns. The expenses over repairing the fortifications had been heavy, the sea having encroached to the very walls, and undermined the foundations of a part of them. Looking at it in the present day, when the sea is a quarter of a mile distant, it is difficult to believe that it could ever have touched the walls of Fort St. George. Yet up to the middle of the 19th century the waves beat within twenty or thirty yards of the sea gate; and wreckage after a storm was thrown up to the very path beneath the walls.

Gyfford's inability to cope with the difficulties which he himself had in a great measure caused, obliged the Directors to make other plans, for they were determined to enforce their wishes. Sir Josiah Child,[18] the President or Chairman of the Court, began at this period to make his power felt; and his strong hand was seen in all the organisations of the period. He conceived the idea that a Mayoralty and Municipality for Madras would meet the case, and that the people would submit to taxation more readily if it came from themselves instead of the Company. He formed a scheme and drew up a plan for its constitution, throwing out seductive hints as to the gorgeous robes of office that might be adopted; and described the titles and signs of authority that might be assumed. He hoped that the pageantry and semblance of power would cajole the wily Hindu and careful Gentu into parting with their fanams for the public good. But Gyfford was not the man to carry out any scheme of the kind, however well organised. He did nothing; and it was not in his time that the Madras Municipality saw birth.

Blacktown had increased considerably in the last twenty-five years, and many fine houses had been erected in its streets. Some of these were inhabited by Europeans. The Fort, crowded as it was, would not hold all the servants of the Company especially those who had married, and an arrangement was made by which they housed themselves outside, receiving what is now called Presidency allowance to cover house rent. These allowances were made as early as Langhorne's time, and they have continued down to the present day. Gyfford succeeded, after much pressure from the Directors and a great deal of opposition from the people in gathering a certain amount of revenue for municipal purposes; but he was boycotted and otherwise worried by the rebellious tradesmen, and was often obliged to be content with promises that were never fulfilled.

A pleasanter event that marked his rule was the establishment in 1683 of the Bank of Madras. The rules were formulated by the Directors, who sent an order for "raising a Bank to the value of one hundred thousand pounds sterling at six per cent." Deposits were invited for not less than six months' duration. The Bank has flourished ever since with varying fortune, chiefly good; and it is one of the oldest institutions of Madras dating only three years later than the foundation of the Court of Judicature and St. Mary's church.

A curious item in the records of Gyfford's time throws a light upon the Company's method of making money wherever money was to be made. It is not unknown in the present day, when boots and shoes, vests and shirts and other articles of wear are shipped home for sale in the cheaper shops of our English towns. The Directors discovered that labour was cheap in India. They had already established their own weaving, buying up yarn and employing weavers, dyers, fullers, etc. to manufacture the particular articles for which there was the greatest demand in England. These worked on the advance system, without any bond or written contract, probably because it was the custom of the country. In England the largest demand was for calico, which was so called from having been first bought in the Calicut bazaars. It was rapidly superseding the more expensive flaxen-stuffs, being cheaper and more healthy to wear. An order was received from the Directors to make and send home a large number of calico garments for underwear. Some were to be of strong blue material, suitable for the workpeople; some were to be finer, for the middle classes, and some of the finest make possible to tempt the rich. The merchants were warned to be careful of their choice of stuff, and to put in nothing but the best workmanship; they were also to have some of the garments embroidered. These seem to have been intended for the ladies. One wonders what the merchants with their old-fashioned Cromwellian notions thought of the sudden demand for such fallals; and how they liked having to play the part of M. Worth in superintending the fashioning of the mysterious underwear. A handsome profit on the transaction, however, probably went a long way to salve the puritanical conscience.

Slavery "of a mild type" was allowed throughout the land, but it in no way resembled the system which disgraced our American colonies. The slaves in the houses of natives occupied important positions in the domestic circle, and they identified themselves with the members of the family. The English, whatever their principles may have been, were obliged to adopt the custom of the country if they wished to obtain domestic servants, and each household had its little band of slaves numbering from one to two dozen men, women and children, the last being learners. They were fed and clothed by their masters, and they received a small sum monthly for pocket money which was frittered away in betel nut and sweets. But slavery was not without its abuse; and frequent orders were issued for the protection of the class. About this time a great number were exported yearly from Madras, and the traffic in human flesh became so extensive that it led to the abduction of children. The culprits were natives themselves who deported their fellow-countrymen by country vessels. The exportation of slaves was prohibited; and punishments by fines or loss of ears were inflicted on all those convicted of stealing children. The possession of slaves was allowed in the country, not only amongst private people, but also in the Company's service; the Company purchased them for the purpose of manning the masulah boats required for the shipping. A little later the order was relaxed on account of there being "a sore famine in the land, reducing the people to great straits." Slaves were then to be had for very small sums, and children were given away by parents who did not wish to see them die of starvation before their eyes. When the famine was over and the supply was lessened, abuses again crept in which necessitated legislation. A capitation fee was demanded for each slave leaving the port, and those who went abroad were obliged to register their names in person. This was to prevent a slave from being deported against his will.

The slaves in private houses were quite as well as off as the hired servants of the present day. Besides food, clothing and pocket money, a schoolmaster was provided for them, and they were taught reading and writing in their own tongue and the principles of Christianity. The Company went so far as to find them in prayerbooks and give them a service on Sunday. There are various entries in the register books of St. Mary's recording their baptism, their masters and mistresses usually standing sponsors for them. They had their faults; and when beyond the management of their owners, their crimes were dealt with by the law. It was very severe, death being the punishment of theft. In the case of a certain slave under sentence of death for stealing, the sentence was commuted to branding with a hot iron, treatment which would not be tolerated in the present day. The register book also mentions the baptism of illegitimate children of slaves, which points to another abuse of domestic slavery.

In Gyfford's time frequent mention is made of the interlopers who were then at the height of their notoriety. The character of the interloper is best defined by the word "smuggler"; but whereas the smuggler tried to evade the law of the land and cheat the revenue, the interloper endeavoured only to encroach on the rights of a company of merchants and infringe their charter. By this time the Honourable East India Company had shown the mercantile world of England how money was to be made in the East; its successes had aroused the envy and jealousy of less-fortunate men, and these were inclined to dispute the rights of the monopoly and claim a place in the Indian market for themselves. Ships were fitted out for trading illegally in the East; and in the year 1682 as many as seven sailed from England with the avowed purpose of infringing the Company's charter and of opening new ports if necessary to carry on their trade. In India another form of interloping had sprung up which was still more difficult to deal with, as it was grafted on to legitimate trade and was almost impossible to detect.

It will be remembered that the Company's servants were allowed certain privileges in the Eastern ports. Their salaries were so small and inadequate, that unless some such privileges had been granted, the Company could not have tempted men to come out to India. As the country was too much unsettled by internal wars to allow of goods being carried inland without an expensive armed escort, the traffic was almost entirely confined to the sea. The first thing a merchant needed was a ship to carry his merchandise from port-to-port. He might, if he liked, ship his goods on one of the Company's vessels, provided there was accommodation. But a more general method was the employment of private ships which paid duty at each port. Excellent vessels were built in the country at comparatively small cost, of materials which lasted far better than those supplied by English ship-builders. The fittings, ropes, sails and iron work were brought from England and a European crew was employed under an English or Eurasian captain. The ship was owned frequently by the merchant, or he took a share in her with the commander. She carried a supercargo who was half trader, half diplomatist, a man who was always on the watch to open out new markets and speculate in fresh commodities. There were many risks to run from storms and pirates on the ocean, and hostile natives on shore; but an ordinarily successful voyage round the coast was a lucrative affair, often yielding cent per cent, or even more. The duties in all the Company's ports were heavy, and there was as great temptation to evade them as the opportunity of doing so offered. It is probable that every private ship did some smuggling which was connived at by the merchant, who was quite ready to share in the profits, though not to take an active part in it.

Captain Alexander Hamilton,[19] who command a private trader at the latter end of the seventeenth and the beginning of the eighteenth centuries, has left an account of his adventures which exhibits the attitude of the owner of the private trading ships. His sympathies were manifestly with the interloper and not with the Company. On a certain trip to the Company's port at Bankok in Siam, he complains bitterly that he was obliged to pay five hundred pounds sterling as duty on a three-hundred ton vessel before he was allowed to sail. He wrote a letter of complaint to the Governor of Fort St. George under whose direction the Agent in Siam acted. But he could obtain no redress; and he was reminded that if he rebelled against the just dues of the Company, he would be declared an interloper and a pirate. He never forgave the Madras Council this threat, and his pen was sharpened with acrimony as he wrote what might otherwise have been a graphic and faithful description of the Fort and its inhabitants.

Some interlopers made no secret of their ill-doings. They appeared in the roads of a port and departed without paying a single rupee in duty. Yet the authorities were morally certain that they did not arrive in ballast nor depart without profit to their owners. No one knew better than the Governor what the ships came for; but he could seldom get any proof of cargo being shipped or landed.

Or, if he had the proof, he failed to catch the culprits. They had pulled up their anchor and were slipping down the coast before the proofs came to hand. Yet the Governor possessed considerable powers and might fire upon a ship if it refused to give an account of itself; or seize its cargo if there was evidence to show that it was smuggled.

The king of interlopers two hundred years ago was William Alley, usually spoken of as "Interloping Alley." He did more than smuggle from port-to-port in Indian waters; he carried diamonds and pearls to Europe in direct violation of the Company's charter. John Bridger, a merchant in the Company's service, readily admitted when accused, that he had sent diamonds to England, but vowed that he was not involved with Alley. Sir Josiah Child, however, stated that he had evidence of Bridger's correspondence with Alley, and of the forwarding to England of a quantity of diamonds by the *Sampson*, which was an unregistered ship. Bridger was dismissed, but he continued to live in the Fort, trading on his own account, the loss of a salary of forty pounds per annum being a little consequence.[20]

The Directors became at length almost rabid on the subject of interlopers, declaring them pirates and treating them as such if they could find the smallest pretence for doing so. They prosecuted as many as twenty-three interlopers in the year 1683 in England. In India the Governor bribed and threatened; and confiscated goods whenever he was able, which was not very often. Declarations were set up against them, and a proclamation was read out in St. Mary's church after service, warning the congregation not to have dealings with them. But it was all of no use; the interlopers flourished, and counted among their ranks Thomas Pitt, who subsequently became Governor of Fort St. George. Before he attained to this honour he was part owner with another man of two private vessels which were subsequently bought up by the Company.

The appearance of an interloper in the roads of Madras occasioned as much excitement in the Council as that of a smuggler on the coast of England in the old days. The Governor had no coastguards to help in detecting the irregularities of suspected ships. He had to do his best with his peons and his military men, none of whom were above suspicion themselves. He was, moreover, morally certain that half his merchants and factors were more interested in the movements of the vessel than the affairs of the Company warranted. He not only therefore watched the ship, but kept a sharp eye on his subordinates. There were others who needed watching besides the Europeans. These were the Portuguese and native merchants. Lingappa did not scruple to threaten that he would employ the interloper when he could not come to terms with the Company; and some of the European free merchants of Madras who married into Portuguese families made use of their wives' relatives to trade irregularly from St. Thomé.

In 1682 an interloper appeared at Tuticorin. The Governor was informed of it and he sent two Englishmen from Fort St. George to deal with it. James Bett and Charles Fleetwood,[21] the two gentlemen chosen for the business, proceeded overland. Their orders were to bribe and threaten; and they carried five hundred pagodas with them. Their chief object was to get the crew of the interloper to desert the ship by money presents and promises of preferment at Fort St. George. Tuticorin was several days' journey from Madras by land through a country ruled by more than one native chief; nevertheless they undertook it cheerfully. When they reached "Tittycorin", as they called it, they found the ship had sailed. The story savours of the wild-goose chase, but though they did not catch their wild goose, they probably utilised their official trip by looking for new markets. Pearls were then to be had at Tuticorin, and the merchants were eager to secure them, Bett and Fleetwood were old inhabitants; and though Bett was Captain of the Guard, he was as keen a trader as the rest, in no way likely to miss an opportunity of turning a penny. He died at Fort St. George in 1692. The entry in the register book says "He died by the bite of a mad dog about two months before, and continued in his senses to the last minute."

A ship suspected of being an interloper appeared in the St. Thomé roads a few years later. The doctor and purser were Englishmen and strangers. They came ashore and reported the vessel to be the *Resolution*, Captain Etherington, commander, and that she had put in for wood and water. The suspicions of the Governor and Council were aroused. They met and issued orders for the watching of the ship; also for the shadowing of certain people on shore. Some dubashes, (native clerks,) belonging to Fort St. George, having been to St. Thomé, were arrested and confined temporarily as a warning to others. Senhor Lucas Luiz of St. Thomé, who entertained the strangers, received a letter from the Governor cautioning him not to assist any of the merchants in trading with the interloper, under pain of being prosecuted and severely punished. The inhabitants of the Fort were forbidden to receive the strangers, or to go outside the walls without permission. Certain Portuguese and Armenian merchants were also bound over in writing not to have dealings with the vessel. There was a good deal of saltpetre lying at St. Thomé at the time, and it was reported to the

Governor that this would be exchanged by the interloper for sugar. In spite of all precautions and warnings it came to the ears of the authorities that three gentlemen belonging to the Fort had been seen at St. Thomé in Company with some of the ship's officers. They were promptly sent for and asked to give an account of their journey. They obeyed the summons at once with the alacrity of injured innocence and replied readily to every question put. Yes, they had gone to St. Thomé; they were only taking the air in their palanquins. As they passed Senhor Luiz's house, he asked them to stop and drink a glass of wine, which they did. But on entering his house they found two strangers there, who in course of conversation admitted that they belonged to the suspected ship. Mr. Meverell, Mr. Lovell and Captain Parham, the three gentlemen in question, instantly put down their glasses and departed, shaking the dust of Senhor Luiz's house off their feet; they were shocked at the thought of having been unwillingly in such evil company. The Council had to be content with the explanation given. Whether the saltpetre was "trucked", as they called it, for sugar, or was only a blind to divert suspicion from the smuggling of the more profitable pearl and diamond, it is impossible to say. There was no evidence forthcoming, and in a day or two the ship disappeared as mysteriously as she had come, and was seen no more.

In 1684 an exciting chase took place off Madras, when Captain John Smith of the interloping ship *Constantinople*, was pursued by Sir John Wetwang, commanding the *Royal Fames*. Smith, who was one of the Alley's associates, escaped through the fleetness of the vessel, and Wetwang had to return empty-handed to Madras. The latter died that very year, and lies buried in the old cemetery. Two others of the same name followed him to the grave there, Samuel Wetwang, his son, who was a factor in the Company's service, buried in 1685, and Captain John Wetwang, also described as Commander of the *Royal Fames,* who died in 1687.

There are constant references in the records to incidents connected with interloping; but they are too numerous to relate. One more story may be told, however, to illustrate how easily the free trader could do a little interloping and how great was the temptation to the merchant-servant of the Company to wink at it.

It was the custom to entrust a sum of money to the legitimate private trader at a fixed rate of interest; the rate was high in consideration of the risk incurred; but it was a legal transaction in the eyes of the Company so long as the customs were paid by the trader. In the event of a successful voyage, even at the high rate of interest, the owner of the vessel found it very remunerative. The bonds were called "respondentia"; and to make them recoverable in a court of law they had to be duly registered for a small fee.

A Captain named Perrin took five hundred pounds from Mr. Ralph Sheldon, Governor in the Bay, to trade in Persia. Perrin had a successful voyage, disposed of his goods advantageously, and brought back a cargo of Persian wine, which was then a fashionable drink with the Europeans. Having plenty of time and fine weather he called in at Goa on his way back, a Portuguese port on the West Coast. There he found a Surat-built ship for sale, cheap. He bought her, manned her and effected a snug little bit of illicit trading in pepper with the vessel. When he reached his destination he was rash enough to take Sheldon into his confidence, offering him half profits on the sale of the cargo. By this means he no doubt hoped to secure the cooperation of the Governor in the disposal of his goods. But

Sheldon was not to be tempted; he refused to have anything to do with the transaction, and asked for his money back, together with the stipulated interest. Perrin alarmed, paid it at once and demanded the bond in return, as was customary, to be destroyed. But Sheldon refused to part with it, saying that he retained it as a hold upon a man who was interloping. This was indeed springing a mine upon Perrin; and it placed him in a very awkward position; in short he found himself branded as an interloper. No one dared to have any dealings with him, and he was unable to dispose of his cargoes. In his dilemma a friendly brother-commander came to his assistance. The wine which was good and worth a considerable sum, was secretly transferred to the friend's ship, where it was sold without difficulty and realised a handsome price. Perrin was glad to get out of the trouble without further loss, and was doubtless more careful in future where he placed his confidence.

Note: Captain John Powney, Commander of our ship *Brittannia*, delivered in a protest against Captain Alexander Hamilton, Commander of the ship *Morning Star*, together with an attested copy of a letter from the said Captain Hamilton to the President, dated at Siam barr, wherein he insinuates a design to take satisfaction of Captain Powney for some injuries he says he has received at Siam, through Captain Powney's means.

(Copy of part of a letter from Captain A. Hamilton.)

"To the Hon. Joseph Collett.

"Dated at Siam bar, December 27th, 1718.

"Falling into an unprecedented Dilemma, or rather a Gulf of Perplexitys by the means and contrivance of Captain John Powney and his Associates herein no less matter than the breach of the Treaty of Commerce with Siam settled by Charles the second of happy memory and the ruin of my voyage, I think myself obliged to acquaint your Honour of it, and with the new stipulations he has settled here for his fellow subjects.

"Imprimus. That all shipping belonging to the subjects of Great Britain, except those employed by your Honour or himself, shall pay measurage for their ships or vessels, according to Siam conscience, for there's no settled rule; and all Goods or Merchandise imported here by the said subjects of Great Britain, excepting from your Honour or himself, shall pay 8 per cent Customs in specie if they are landed, whether they can be sold or no, but if not landed to pay nothing; but the last part of this paragraph was conceded to by the King of Siam the 4th of the last month. Otherwise we must have paid for our whole Cargo according to the first projection by Powney, etc.

"Item. Whoever buys our Goods shall be obliged to pay the money into the King's Treasury that he may deliver us Goods out of his Royal Warehouse (when he has any), at his own established prices, which at present are higher than Suratt.

"And that all English Shipping that comes here, except those of your Honour's or his, shall be obliged to stay one year for the disposing and receiving of their Cargoes, (for silver and gold are prohibited exportation on pain of confiscation of Ship and Cargo, besides slavery to the Ship's Company,) that the Ships so remaining may be a pledge for the good behaviour of all their fellow-subjects, if any should dare to take satisfaction of the Siamers, for being robbed and oppressed by them, and that there may always be victims of Bloud and Treasure ready to be sacrificed by the Siamers, if any such accident should happen.

"All which conditions Captain Powney's Associates, Cia Seneratt and Paipatt, would have put upon me with the greatest rigour, if I had not used both presents and threats to prevent them. Captain Dalgleish and I designed to have addressed the King with Petitions and Presents to have these unjust impositions and Calamitys removed; but Mr. Collinson, who Captain Powney left here to be Seneratt's Intelligence, discovered our design to him, and next day came an order from the King that no Europeans, Moors or Gentues, except his own subjects, should approach the Palace on pain of Death. One day I discoursed Seneratt about the Injustice and the Oppression we lay under; but he deny'd he had any hand in it: I told him I had asked the same question of Paipatt and that we would give a sum to have it removed, for if it continued the consequence would endanger a rupture with the Company. He bid me to go to Seneratt, who could best give an account of its rise; I told Seneratt of it before Collinson, and a few days after Collinson was summoned to a Court, who gave a declaration, which brought my life, Ship and Cargo in question. About a week after I was summoned to another Court where an impeachment was drawn up against me, that I had told Seneratt before Collinson (and some others who were ready for Witnesses, though never any one but Collinson was near) that Seneratt and Paipatt had inculcated ill notions into the King's head for laying customs and other Impositions on all the British subjects, excepting those aforesaid; I deny'd the whole accusation. My Judge frankly told me that I must take care what I said for if I was cast, I must lose my head, which condition I was forced to accept on for want of other remedy. On which Mr. Collinson was sent for to confront me, who declared to the Judge before Captain Dalgleish and Mr. Saunders that what Seneratt had asserted was true; but I proved by Seneratt himself that Collinson did not understand Moors, which was the Language our discourse was in; I was acquitted by the Judge and the Evidence ridiculed by the whole Court. The Evidences folly and ignorance, (though no doubt mixed with malice or his Master's Orders,) I pity and deem him far below my resentment, otherwise I should have sent him home without his ears. Amongst other discourses at our table, (which was a common one,) some words might have passed that for all the Siamers precaution in making us leave our great guns at Bencock, anybody that had a mind to disturb the repose of this great King might bring Guns under their ballast, and plague him more than a Spaniard did forty years ago, forcing his way down the River in spight of all the Force of Siam, though the King then headed them; Next day Seneratt was Master of the Secret, and designed to have persuaded the King to make me unlade my Ship in order to search her; And though I have ne'er a spare great Gun, (which I am sorry for,) yet for fear of farther trouble, was forced to strike up a pretended friendship with Seneratt to divert the charge and trouble.

"After a month's stay at Siam, and finding no appearance of Trade, except on the base slavish condition aforesaid, and all the doors of Justice fast bolted against it, I solicited for me Tara or Dispatches in order to try my fortune somewhere else, but could not obtain one in less than two months and a half, though solicited every day.

"Before my departure from the City, I thought the Dutch Chief might have some more interest than myself with this pollitik Court, and made an overture of letting him have about thirty thousand rupees worth of Suratt Good at Suratt prices, he paying the 8 per cent Custom; but after ten days' try all found that nothing but my money paid into the King's Cash could do, so am forced to leave this Glorious Port (as the King styles it) without selling half as much as I have paid away in port charges, wherein is one thousand rupees measurage for my ship as per stipulation aforesaid.

"For which damage and losses, which have or may come on this part of my voyage. If I meet with Captain Powney, I shall use my powerfullest Eloquence to persuade him to reimburse my Masters.

"And am in great hopes that this foolish Brother of the Sun (the King of Siam) who by ill advice has broken our Commerce and opprest us, shall find the 'Morning Star' has beams eno' to attract all the glories that Japan sends him this year, and convey them to Bombay; for Madras maxims are very good in such cases as ours. And because we are unjustly debarr'd trading here and plagued with insupportable affronts and abuses, 'tis but reasonable to undeceive the Siamers, and teach them so much of the constitutions of our laws, that their King, nor any subject of Britain, can alter the established Commerce of Siam without the consent and the approbation of the Legislature, or those that they have made it over to.

"And am in great hopes that this simple King, (whose avarice and lazyness is like to make a revolution in his country,) will be the first that will taste of his folly, and that the complaints of his slaves or subjects will awake him to bring the authors of this new Project of Tyranny to condign punishment, some of whose heads are already in no small jeopardy about my leaving the country without paying the Customs, or at least very inconsiderable for a few shawls and dates.

"I have two good chances to encourage me, one about the latter end of next month, and if that miscarries, I shall call at this barr about the beginning of May for a few teculls, and I hope Captain

Powney when he comes here will fall into the snare that he has laid for others.

"There's one thing more that I can't forbear taking notice of to your Honour. A letter of yours came to Seneratt and one to the King which were accounted spurious till one came from Powney, and then it was made legitimate about a month after; however, Dalgleish had no benefit by your Honour's certificate because he once asked Seneratt for some money he had owed him above a year.

"The reason why Seneratt gave me (when we were good friends) for laying on those impositions, is, because Madras makes the King pay 8 per cent, therefore we ought to pay as much and Madras be clear.

"I had almost forgot to acquaint your Honour that when Captain Dalgleish, Messrs. Emmerson and Saunders and I went to visit the Vizier about business, he treated our Honour to some unhandsome epithets for writing to Seneratt as Vizier about business of consequence and not to him, and he told us that if anything spoiled our business at Siam it would be your Honour's friendship with such villains.

"I am, etc.

"Alexander Hamilton."

10

PIRATES AND PRINCES; AND THE RETIREMENT OF GYFFORD

Interlopers were so closely connected with pirates that an account of one is not complete without some mention of the other. The very word pirate is attractive. It suggests romantic adventure and daring crime in the storybooks of our youth. The real thing is an abhorrent creature with a great deal more of the crime and much less of the romance than is represented in fiction. The race is not extinct; pirates are still to be heard of on the high seas of the Far East; but piracy in the Red Sea, the Indian Ocean and the Bay of Bengal is a thing of the past. The interloper was not a pirate, though he degenerated into one occasionally; there was a very wide difference between the two, but the Company, for its own purposes, did not always choose to see it. The interloper was unscrupulous and not strictly honest in the eyes of the law; but he was not a common thief; and he never resorted to violence. The pirate was nothing more nor less than a murderous thief or a thieving murderer, according to circumstances. He made no pretence to respectability and did not trouble himself to trade with or without permission. His sole business was robbery, barefaced robbery with violence; and he attracted to himself a choice assortment of scoundrels drawn from all countries.

From the earliest times pirates infested the western coast of India. Marco Polo speaks of their fleets, and describes how they extended their ships in a line to watch for their prey. Each ship was placed five miles away from its neighbour, by which means twenty vessels could scour the seas for a hundred miles. On sighting the prize a signal was given, and the whole fleet was in readiness to cooperate for its seizure. At no time were the English ships safe from piracy. The danger began as soon as they left the shores of Europe and neared the coast of Algeria. Madagascar was another stronghold, and the danger continued until the friendly Indian ports were reached. For this reason the ships travelled in company as a rule; the Globe, being an unusually fast sailer, ventured to make the voyage alone and was an exception to the rule. Down to the middle of the eighteenth century, when the power of the pirates was broken, the rich Indian merchantmen belonging to the Company were obliged to sail under the protection of armed cruisers provided expressly for the purpose.

The earliest European pirates in Eastern waters were Portuguese. They scoured the seas during the sixteenth century from the reign of Henry VIII to the time of Charles I. They were the bane of all traders, European and native, and preyed alike on Portuguese, Spanish, Dutch, Arabian and Moorish vessels, always seeking for bullion and precious stones. The only trade they ever engaged in was the slave trade, kidnapping their human freight and finding a market for the same up the Hugly. Their depredations extended from Madagascar on one side to the Straits of Malacca on the other. Their chief stronghold was on the coast of Arracan to the North East of the Bay of Bengal, from which point they also sailed up the Hugly.

The native rulers complained bitterly to the English of the outrages committed by pirates, holding them partly responsible because the piracies were committed by Europeans. But the English were powerless to suppress them, especially as the pirates had a strong ally in the Kind of Arracan, whose fleet they manned and made into a formidable naval power in the Indian seas. The fleet numbered two hundred large galleys, and there was no other like it at that period in the East. It was Sheista Khan who succeeded in breaking their power; but he had to use guile instead of force. As Viceroy of Bengal he picked a quarrel with the King of Arracan, and obtained an excuse for destroying his fleet. He bribed the numerous gang of Portuguese, who were the backbone of the King's naval power, and persuaded them to turn their arms against their late master. Being nothing but mercenaries or the worst sort, they readily consented to destroy the fleet of Arracan and enter the service of Sheista Khan on more advantageous terms. But no sooner had they effected this than the Viceroy showed himself in his true colours. He dismissed them summarily and ordered them to be gone. They were overwhelmed with dismay; but fearing death were obliged to submit. Without money, arms, or ships they were harmless, and there was nothing before them but starvation; their power was broken and the band was dispersed. The galley or galliasse used by the Arracan pirates was a large long boat of great swiftness, propelled by oars and sails.

There were two men to each oar, and the largest galleys were said to have fifty oars a side. It was easy to overtake and capture an ordinary sailing vessel if the wind was light; the pirates attacked in such numbers that they did not hesitate to seize any large-armed merchantman that was rash enough to allow them to approach under cover of pretended friendliness.

Dutch and English pirates succeeded the Portuguese, and frequent mention is made of them in the records of Fort St. George. The Company was given a Commission to deal as it pleased with piracy, felony, and robbery on the high seas; and it did not spare those who fell into its hands. Robbery was punishable by death; and pirates usually suffered the extreme penalty of the law and were hanged or shot. In 1689 nine Englishmen were sent from Pulicat and tried for piracy. Two of them were condemned to death and six were sentenced to be branded on the forehand with the letter P. The guard was assembled to witness the executions and the branding of two of the unfortunate men. Two men were branded on board the *Williamson*, and the other two on the *Resolution*. This was done as a warning and deterrent to others. There is no entry in the register books of St. Mary's of the burial of the two men who were executed on that occasion; but in the previous year, early in 1688, there is a record of no less than four burials of "pyrates". The first, Charles Lane, is simply designated "pyrate"; the second, James Smith, is described as having been hanged; the third, Ralph Shackley, was shot; and the fourth Alexander Hunter, was hanged on board the *Royal Fames*. In December 1687 the burial of Jeremy Nichole took place, "Seamen and pyrate", who was probably shot or hanged. In 1719 the records speak of another tragedy of the same kind. Bullmore, who helped in pirating the brigantine *George*, was caught and brought to trial, and he

Register book of St. Mary's, showing Elihu Yale's marriage

too suffered the extreme penalty of the law. When an execution took place the gallows were erected just outside the Fort Gate in the West wall under the bastion, and the men of the garrison were paraded to witness it.

William Kidd was the prince of pirates, the Council called him the "Grand Pirate". He was sent out in command of the *Adventure* to suppress the pirates of Madagascar; but instead of doing so he threw in his lot with them and turned pirate himself. He is mentioned by Captain Watts of Fort St. George, Commander of the *Sedgwick*. In 1697 Kidd chased Watts for three days and three nights off Anjengo on the West Coast of Travancore, and Watts seems to have escaped only by the skin of his teeth, as he was more or less becalmed. Watts eluded the Scylla of Kidd only to fall into the Charybdis of a well-known Dutch pirate, called Chivers or Sivers, who pursued him in an Algerine galley for nine hours. By the aid of oars Chivers overtook the *Sedgwick* and boarded it. When he and his men discovered that there was nothing but a cargo of pepper on board they were much disgusted. They consoled themselves, however, by taking all the stores they could find, cordage, anchors, tar, etc. Captain Watts put a good face on the matter and lost none of his men in useless opposition to superior numbers. Instead of fighting he treated his uninvited guests right royally and gave them as much punch as they could drink. This put them into such a good humour that they abandoned their intention of taking the ship as a cruiser, and let Watts and his cargo of pepper go. The *Sedgwick* was afterwards employed to carry men and ammunition to Tranquebar, at the request of the Governor there, who asked for soldiers and arms to protect the Company's ships from pirates.

The adventures of Captain George Weoley, another Madras man, were no so happy, when a few years later his ship was captured by pirates. The *Pembroke* did not surrender without a tough struggle. The pirates were Englishmen, and possessed two good ships which they had taken. The larger vessel was the *Prosperous*, originally commanded by Captain Hillyard, who had been killed. Its pirate-captain as a man named Howard. The vessel carried forty guns and nearly two hundred men. The smaller ship was the *Speedy Return*, under the command of a man named Bowen, and it carried twelve guns and seventy men. The pirates ransacked the *Pembroke* for money and arms, and then talked of burning her. But they thought better of it afterwards and let her go; she arrived safely in the Madras roads, and the tale of her misfortunes was duly laid before the Governor and Council.[22] "Captain Weoley (Weoley is a Dutch name, the eo being pronounced like oo) was not with his ship; he was detained by the pirates as a prisoner on board the *Prosperous*, and was made to serve as a pilot down the Straits of Malacca. He escaped, however, a few months later and returned to Fort St. George.

William Kidd's fate was curiously bound up with a Madras ship. Early in the year 1698 he took a merchant vessel off Cochin, called the *Quedah*. She belonged to Armenian merchants, and was commanded by an Englishman named Wright. Her cargo was worth £30,000 and Kidd was offered £20,000 as a ransom for the ship, but he refused it. Leaving the *Adventure*, he sailed in the *Quedah* to the West Indies, where he left her in charge of the Captain of another vessel whilst he proceeded to Boston via New York on business of his own. The news of his latest piracy had reached Boston, and on arrival he was questioned closely by the Governor as to the whereabouts of the *Quedah*. He refused to answer and was thrown into prison. He could not be tried for piracy in America, and was therefore sent to England where he was "wanted" for other matters. He was found guilty of piracy and murder on the high seas and suffered the full penalty of the law in 1701.

There was a strong band of native pirates on the West Coast of India that attacked ships coming up to Madras from the Cape. It was headed by a Mahratta chief named Angria, who, at the beginning of the 18th century, held an almost impregnable position in the fortress of Gheria, a small Gibraltar on the Mahratta Coast. For years Angria, and his sons after him, were the terror of the Indian Ocean, and no merchant ships could leave Surat or Bombay without a strong armed escort. It was long after Gyfford's time that the power of these pirates was broken. Angria himself was never caught, he died at this castle of Gheria and his sons continued his nefarious calling under his name. Many expeditions were made against them, but in vain. In 1717 Charles Boone, Governor of Bombay, whose early days of service were spent in Fort St. George and whose marriage to Jane, daughter of Daniel Chardin, is recorded in the register books of St. Mary's, sent a force against Angria after the capture of the *Success*, a valuable merchantman belonging to the Company. In 1718 a second expedition was despatched which met with no better success than the first. Gheria proved far too strong a fortress for the forces sent against it. It was protected by heavy artillery which was under European direction, and it possessed a formidable fleet of ships of all kinds, which were fully armed with guns. The crews were composed of Dutch, Portuguese, English, Arabs, Negroes and others who fought desperately and spared neither themselves nor their enemies. It was not until 1747 that the pirates received a check. In that year Commodore James of the Company's Marine Service, commanded the *Guardian*, 28 guns. He was convoying a fleet of seventy valuable coasters when he sighted Angria. He signalled to the coasters to run into Telicherry on the West Coast, which was near at hand, and then boldly attacked the pirates, who, although not defeated, were beaten off and obliged to retire to Gheria. In 1756, James, who had kept them in check from the time of his first encounter, determined to beard the lion in his den and take Gheria. He left Bombay with a large well-armed fleet. Clive, who had lately arrived in Bombay, accompanied him with eight hundred soldiers and three hundred native troops. There was a big sea-fight off the fortress, in which the pirates were defeated. Behind the rock lay an excellent harbour with docks which were completely hidden from the sea. James penetrated into the harbour and set fire to the shipping. At the same time Clive landed with his troops, scaled the heights and took the fort. At its capture it contained two hundred cannon, six brass mortars, a quantity of ammunition, £125,000 in treasure, and eleven prisoners, eight of whom were Englishmen and three Dutch. The power of the pirates was broken and it never revived; and from that time they gradually disappeared from the coasts of India, under the vigilance of the Indian Marine.

To return to Gyfford; he was not only impeded in his government by his weak policy and want of decision, but he was also hampered by having an empty treasury. A great deal of cash had been wasted in bribery over the interlopers; and a further drain had been made on the Company's purse by the conclusion of some expensive investments. The native dealers had discovered that they only had to threaten the Governor with selling their goods to the interlopers to obtain their price; and there is little doubt that some hard bargains were thus driven with the English. Added to this the Directors had a difficulty in England of raising funds. Their credit was at a low ebb and their dividends at zero. This was the more vexatious as just then, under Sir Josiah Child, the Court was endeavouring to open out new ports and establish new factories. The Bay was no longer under the Governorship of Fort St. George; but there were several factories on the Coromandel Coast which still looked to Madras for money and for supervision. Ralph Ord, who came out as a schoolmaster to the Fort, had been taken into the service of the Company, and a very able servant he proved. He and William Cawley were sent across the Bay to Sumatra to negotiate with the native powers there. They persuaded three influential Rajahs of Sumatra to make the voyage to Madras where they could treat in person with the Governor. Their arrival in the roads caused great excitement, and preparations were made for a suitable reception. The ship anchored opposite the sea gate, and the landing and reception of the Rajahs is thus described in the minutes.

The Sumatra Princes being seated in the Masulah (boat), the ship saluted them with nine guns. Some of the Council with Mr. Ord and Mr. Cawly, with our chief merchants went to the seaside, and courteously received them to the Fort, the whole way being lined with a guard of soldiers, accompanied by most of our chief black merchants; as also the town music and dancers—the usual state of the country. Entering the hall, they were received with courteous salutes and embraces from the Chief (Governor) and thence brought to their seats; where, after the usual compliments and welcomes, Mr. Ord delivered the Queen of Acheen's letter to the Chief, which was received by him with the accustomed salaams, and a glass of wine passed round to her health, with seventeen pieces of ordnance (fired) to it and their welcomes. After the ceremony of betel and rosewater, they took their leaves, and were attended to their lodgings by Chinna Vencatadry and the chief people of the town; where all necessary servants were appointed in readiness for them, with which they seemed well pleased and satisfied.

There was a long palaver with the Princes extending over several days; but terms were at length settled and ratified by the exchanging of diamond and gold rings as evidence of good faith. The English were to be allowed to build forts and factories at Priaman and Bencoolen, and trade free of duty in the rich produce of the islands.

They set about executing their design at one and despatched men and ships from Fort St. George. But there was one factor in the business which they had not reckoned on, and that was the climate. Sickness attacked merchant, soldier and cooly alike, and men died in alarming numbers. The colonies at both places were decimated and paralysed. Priaman fell into the hands of the Dutch, and Bencoolen, having killed Fowle amongst others, remained unfortified and insignificant.

At the end of Gyfford's[23] governorship there seemed every prospect of Fort St. George being attacked by the Moghul's army, and the Council had to look to its defences at home. Workpeople were engaged to finish what had been begun under Fowle's direction in the way of fortification. The place was provisioned with salt pork, beef, fish, etc. and grain was stored in the godowns. Guns and small arms were examined and ammunition laid in. A freshwater tank was made and filled with sweet water, the wells of the Fort being brackish. Nothing that might be necessary was forgotten. Even the medical men were charged to have their "salves for wounds" ready and to be sparing of the small surgery box "that we may not want upon great occasion."

In the midst of all these preparations Gyfford was called upon by the Directors to retire in favour of Yale. He had been Governor from 1681 to 1687 with the exception of a few months interval in 1684–5, when he went to the Bay; he acted as Governor in place of Hedges; and Yale being second in Council at Madras, took up the reins temporarily during his absence.

Note: The arms assigned to the Company in 1601 are very beautiful. The shield is divided into two compartments, the upper bearing, between two conventional namely a four-divided square, having, in its first and fourth quarters, a golden fleur-de-lis on a blue ground, and in the second and third a golden lion, "passant guardant," on a ground of red; and the lower, three quaint-fashioned ships, with streaming ensigns of St. George, in full sail on the tranquil azure of the new-found Southern Seas. The supporters are blue sea-lions, flushed with gold, one on either side; and the crest a sphere celestial between standards of St. George and overhung by the motto "Deus indicat." Below all is a second motto: "Deo ducente nil nocet." In 1698 the new English Company received new arms, having for motto: "Auspicio Regis et Senatus Angliae," for crest a little lion, "regardant". holding a crown, toward the right, in the paws of its outstretched forearms ("the Cat and Cheese" of the old Indian Navy), and for supporters two big lions, "regardant," each holding in its left paw a St. George's pennon, and resting its right paw on a large white shield divided boldly by St. George's Scarlet Cross, and displaying in its right upper quarter the reduced shield of the royal arms of England (English roses quartered with French lilies) surmounted by the Imperial Crown of the realm.

11

ELIHU YALE, THE MAYOR'S COURT AND OTHER MATTERS

Elihu Yale's name is best known in the present day in connection with Yale College in America. In gratitude for munificent donations towards its endowment, the authorities called the institution after him. Curious to relate, he was born in America whilst his father, Thomas Yale, was on a visit there. Elihu came out to India as a young man, drawing a salary of five pounds a year as Writer in 1672. When he stepped into power he was a seasoned old Anglo-Indian, having been already fifteen years in the country. He had served under Master, and had seen the change of policy advocated by the Directors and carried out by that Governor. Like him in some respects, Yale possessed a strong character, but it was the character of the bold enterprising merchant without the political qualities which contributed so much to Master's success. Though he was no politician, there was nothing weak or undecided about Yale; his attitude towards the shifty native was firm and confident. He was quite ready to carry out Sir Josiah Child's policy of showing an independent front to the native ruler and of resisting the demands made so often for money. Under his hands the mercantile interests of the Company prospered, and its dignity was preserved. Yale's long residence in the country had enabled him to establish friendly and even intimate relations with his colleagues. When he became Governor he did not allow his new honours to interfere in any way with his friendships. The register books of St. Mary's name him frequently as sponsor the children of his neighbours, and "Father" to the brides. His own marriage was solemnised in the Fort Church; it was the first to take place within the new building. He married the widow of Joseph Hynmers or Hinners, a servant of the Company, formerly of the Bombay staff, who had died in Madras, and several children were born to Yale and baptised at St. Mary's. The great trouble of his life came to him at Fort St. George when he lost his only son David, a promising little lad and the apple of his eye. The child was laid to rest in the old cemetery, where his monument may still be seen in its original position over the grave or vault.

Gyfford, who pleaded ill-health to the Directors, had taken up his residence in the new Garden House on the banks of the Cooum. The house is described by Wheeler as being near the spot now occupied by Munro's statue. He lived at the expense of the Company, and naturally the Directors complained of having to keep up two houses. As has been already explained, it had been the custom of the Company's servants to live a community life. Merchants, writers, and factors dined together in the middle of the day at the Fort House, the Governor taking his seat at the table, and presiding. Yale resumed the old custom; he lived in the Fort where he had his own private house, mixed freely with his neighbours and entertained right royally. Like many of the other merchants, he owned a garden house, but he used it only as an occasional retreat for pleasure. His private house in the Fort was situated on the North side which suffered so severely in the siege of 1758–9, when all the houses on that side were destroyed.

The Moghul did not appear before Madras; but the country was in such an unsettled condition, that Yale not only placed the Fort in readiness to sustain a siege, but also made a wall round Blacktown, portions of which may still be seen. The work was not sanctioned by the Directors, and Yale ultimately had some trouble over it, as they came down upon him for its cost. Had the enemy appeared and the fortifications of Blacktown proved of use, the money would have been paid readily enough and Yale's forethought commended. But as Madras was not attacked, the Directors grudged, as usual, all monies laid out in fortifications and defences.

Soon after Yale's accession the Union Jack was hoisted "upon the standard on the English bastion" in place of the Company's flag, a flag which showed two roundlets on a red field. It was made the occasion of a great gathering of English and natives. On the 12th of June, 1688, the Company's servants, and the chief inhabitants of Blacktown, English, Portuguese and natives, met in the Fort. Thirty-one guns were fired in honour of the King; twenty-one for the Company and nineteen for Sir Josiah Child, the Chairman of the Court in England. The poor were fed, several prisoners were released and the soldiers were "as merry as punch could make them". Yale presided at "a handsome collation" on the Fort House terrace, when healths were drunk and toasts given in Madeira and Shiraz wine.

The chief event during Yale's governorship was the foundation of the Madras Corporation with a Mayor and Aldermen. Child had pushed it on with persistence, believing that it was the only solution to the difficult question of the town conservancy. He even went so far as to send out the maces and swords without waiting to hear whether the Corporation had been successfully formed, and gave orders for the making of gorgeous robes of office. He also promised to allow the Corporation to retain half the fines levied by them in their Court, the other half going into the Company's coffers. The Directors in doing this were closely following the Dutch, whom they took for a model more than once in administering Indian affairs. But whilst liberty and self-government were given to the town of Madras, a jealousy of power was shown in the warning issued to the Governor. He was told to be careful in his choice of Aldermen and Burgesses amongst the influential natives, and not to admit those who might form a combination; "but so mix the heads of all castes in that Court that you may always hold the balance." There was a large assembly of the people, and the various members of the Corporation were nominated. The proceedings wound up with a dinner "at three in the evening" in the room used for the Town-hall. The first Mayor of Madras was Nathaniel Higginson, who stood high in the Company's service and succeeded Yale as Governor. Sir John Biggs was appointed Recorder of the Corporation. The Governor administered the oaths to the Mayor and Recorder, and they in turn administered the oaths to the Aldermen and Burgesses. The robes of office were donned and the new Body marched in state to the Town-hall.

The Mayor's Court began its work immediately and to this day it continues, although it now goes by the name of the Presidency Magistrate's Court. The Mayor has also merged into the President of the Municipality and the Aldermen and Burgesses into Municipal Councillors.

Although such an imposing show had been made and the Corporation formed with flourish of trumpet and beat of drum, the taxation did not come any the easier. The people resisted as strenuously as ever the imposition of anything approaching a house tax; they would not even submit to a small ground rent. The new Mayor, of whom so much was expected in the way of town improvements, was unable to do anything. The new Town-hall, schools and sewers which had been proposed as the first works of the new Body could not be thought of; and he had to ask to be allowed to take certain customs on articles of consumption brought into the town, that he might provide the necessary funds for cleansing the streets.

When the establishment of the Corporation was being formulated in England there was a curious discussion as to the source from which the charter should proceed, whether the King James II., should grant it under his seal, or whether it should come from the Court direct under the Company's great seal. The Directors were jealous of their powers in India and claimed absolute rule over all their affairs. When the Chairman of the Court was asked his opinion, he replied diplomatically that what the King thought best the Court would also think; but if the King wished for his private opinion it was this: that no person should hold office in India except by a commission direct from the Company. Any other would be prejudicial to the Directors' authority and likely to cause trouble; and he cited an instance which had occurred in another part of India where men appointed by the King had looked to his Majesty as head instead of to the Directors. The King saw the wisdom of the argument and at once gave way in favour of the Court.

The Mayor's Court was empowered to pass sentences which would not be permitted in the present day; but in the absence of proper prison accommodation it was necessary to inflict summary punishment as often as possible. Fines were imposed where there were the means of paying them. But more often than not there were no means, and then branding, flogging, the stocks and loss of ears were substituted, the execution of the sentence taking place, as in the case of the privates, in public, as a warning to others. The power of capital punishment was not given to the Mayor's Court of judicature except for piracy, with regard to Englishmen; but it was different with natives. In 1718 three of the latter were hanged on the Island for murder and robbery. In the case of two English soldiers found guilty of murder, the sentence of death could not be passed, and the men were severely whipped instead, the punishment being repeated weekly.

The form of administering oaths to Hindus was curious. Natives were not sworn on the Bible like Christians; they took their oaths on flowers and sacred water brought from the large temple in Blacktown. In the Supreme Court the method was a little different; sacred tulsi grass being used instead of flowers; and the blades of grass with the water were swallowed by the witness after the oath was administered. This custom continued as late as 1873 when it was abolished.

With the establishment of the Mayor's Court Madras was satisfied that its provision for the administration of the Law was complete, and for many years it asked nothing better. But in the beginning of the 19th century the Supreme Court came into existence and the first Chief Justice was appointed (1800). The sittings of the Supreme Court were held in the building which is now used as an arsenal. At that time it presented a fine colonnaded front on the South side, facing the St. Thomé curtain. The colonnade has since been filled in and shows nothing but a blank wall, which is not conducive to the beauty of the Fort. Sir Thomas Strange was the first Chief Justice. He was a man of great ability and had already acted in the same capacity at Halifax in America. He was the son of Sir Robert Strange, the artist and engraver, who married Miss Isabella Lumisden. A romantic tale is told of that lady by the Honourable Mrs. Forbes, in her book, "Curiosities of a Scots Charta Chest, 1600–1800". Sir Robert threw in his lot with the Stuart cause in '45, and after the battle of Culloden, at which he was present, he was obliged, like many other men, to fly for his life. His steps instinctively led him to the house of his lady-love in Edinburgh, "When, hotly pressed, Strange dashed into the room where his lady, whose zeal had enlisted him in the fatal cause, sat singing at her needlework, and failing other means of concealment, was indebted to her prompt invention. As she quietly raised her hooped gown, the affianced lover quickly disappeared beneath its ample contour, where, thanks to her cool demeanour and unfaltering notes, he lay undetected while the Uncle and baffled soldiery ransacked the house."

Sir Thomas, the Chief Justice, was married at the Fort church in October, 1806, to Miss Louisa Burroughs, youngest daughter of Sir William Burroughs. The register book is signed by B.W. Bentinck and James Strange. Their eldest son, Thomas William Lumisden Strange, was baptised in 1808 at the Fort, and there have been Lumisden Stranges connected with Madras throughout the whole of the century. Sir Thomas did not live in the Fort; he rented Brodie Castle at the Adyar, between Madras and St. Thomé, from a merchant named James Brodie who was its builder and owner.

In 1685 the scare concerning a siege by the Moghul subsided, and the English set themselves to their trading without troubling further about the Hindu and Mahomedan world that raged in war and treachery outside the confines of the Company's territory. In 1689 the Prince and Princess of Orange were proclaimed King and Queen of England; and following close in the train of this event came an alliance with the Dutch. Hitherto, whether the two nations were at war or at peace in Europe, the Dutch and English merchants had been bitter rivals in the great mart of the East, and often at open hostility with each other. All this was changed and not only were the Dutch friendly, but they were forming alliances with the English by marriage. The weddings took place at the English church in the Fort and were productive of happiness and good will. There is only one instance recorded when a Dutchman became turbulent. He was named Van Luhorn, and short work was made of him when it was found that he was incorrigible; he was simply turned out of the Fort and forbidden to return under threat of dire punishment. His chief offence was quarrelsomeness.

An exchange of visits was made between the Dutch and the English representatives, which was conducted in a manner after Yale's own heart. He sent three of his Council, Nathaniel Higginson, Robert Freeman and Thomas Wavell, to Pulicat; they were courteously received by the Commissary General and the Governor, Heer Lawrence Pitt, with due ceremony and salutes. The following day the visit was returned, and the Dutch officials were met with even more ceremony than they had shown. The garrison was drawn out, guns were fired, and they were conducted to the Fort house by Sir John Biggs, John Littleton and the three men mentioned above, where Yale received them at the top of the stairs. After a sumptuous dinner, when toasts were given and healths drunk amidst the booming of cannon and the sound of trumpet and drum, the party proceeded by water to the Company's Garden House. Here another feast had been prepared, and after doing justice to it, an exchange of compliments and thanks was made, and the Dutch took their leave, well pleased with the reception Yale had given them. An alliance offensive and defensive was the outcome of it.

At this time the French were threatening the Dutch from Pondicherry where they had established themselves; and the colony at the Fort, fearing that they had designs upon Fort St. George as well, made common cause with the Dutch for protection. Shortly afterwards the Madras roads were the scene of a naval engagement.

On the 15th of August 1690, the alarm was given in the Fort, that seven ships belonging to the enemy were approaching from the South. The garrison was called out; the gates were shut; the gunners were posted at their guns, which were directed on the anchorage in the roads, and every preparation was made to defend the place. The news was sent to the Dutch Governor at Pulicat to the North of Madras, and he was also informed that one of the French fleet was a fireship. He returned a valiant reply to the effect that he was quite ready for the enemy and had no fear for himself or his ships.

The French advanced, sailing as close inland as possible, and the action was opened by a shot from the Fort. It was replied to by a sharp fire directed at the Dutch ships, and the French managed to get their fireship into close quarters with the Dutch Admiral's vessel. Fortunately, the Admiral cleared himself of his dangerous neighbour before any damage was done, and the fireship drifted harmlessly through the united fleets. The firing of the two fleets continued for three hours with the addition of the Fort guns, but no ships were sunk and no advantage was gained on either side. At the end of that time the French withdrew suddenly and retired without any apparent reason. It was reported that they had lost heavily, but there was no means of ascertaining the real facts. They were satisfied with their show of hostilities; and though every preparation was made in the Fort for a second attack, which was confidently expected, they did not appear before Madras again during the century.

Yale with the true spirit of the merchant was not slow in obtaining all that he could for his employers from the native rulers. Whenever there was a change of Government amongst the latter it was necessary to have new treaties, or firmans as they were called, drawn up. In the firman secured by Yale, three valuable villages were made over to the Company in return for a sum of money. Subsequently a number of fine garden houses were built on the new property, and to this day these houses retain their popularity with the English residents. To show how he appreciated the firman, Yale resolved to receive it in person from the Nabob himself and to make the ceremony more impressive, he dressed himself, in a rich native costume, which the Moghul had sent as a gift. The firman secured the land to the English and the usual privileges of trade; also liberty to coin rupees. This last was always included in the firman from the very beginning, allusion being made in the records to the mint as early as 1661, a little more than twenty years after the foundation of Fort St. George. The mint was also one of the subjects mentioned for enquiry when Major Puckle visited Madras. The Directors complained that they lost over the coining of bullion through mistakes which were always made on the side of the owners of the bullion, and they suspected that all was not fair and square on the part of those in charge of the mint.

The currency of India was formerly in gold, and it is said that the Portuguese swamped it by flooding the country with silver. The gold coin in use when the English appeared in India was the star pagoda. It is described as being like a pill, four-tenths of an inch in diameter, slightly flattened on each side. On one of the flat surfaces was stamped the figure of a swami and on the other a star. A story is told of some French soldiers who, at the taking of a fort, found a large bag of what they thought were peas, inside the building. As the native showed great anxiety to possess the peas, the soldiers sold them by the handful at what they thought a remarkably good price even for a first-class seed grain. Too late they discovered, to their intense disgust, that they had unwillingly parted with a sack of the precious star pagodas, which, discoloured by long storage, had not been recognised. All salaries were paid in pagodas, but it is probable that the actual coin received was in rupees. The pagoda appeared in all the Company's books, but was seldom seen in circulation; and long after it disappeared altogether the accounts were kept in pagodas and fanams.

Gold and silver were exported by the English to India; the silver was sent out in the form of bars, or in Spanish coins called reals or ryalls of eight. These were already known as the country through the

Portuguese; and the Hindu merchants were willing to accept them in payment for goods. But as they were not current they had to be coined into rupees, and the Company was not long in perceiving that it was more profitable to coin the rupees themselves than part with the reals. It is curious to note that exchange fluctuated from the earliest times. In 1614 the gold or star pagoda was worth about five shillings and eight pence. From this it rose to eight shillings. In 1675 the Directors ordered it to be priced at nine; and the rupee was reduced from two shillings and six pence to two and three pence.

The native rupees varied in price according to the alloy, the Arcot coin being reckoned the most valuable on account of its purity. There was always a certain amount of risk in sending out bullion, and the Company refused to ship silver and gold for private trade except at the owner's risk. There was no system of bills of exchange for remitting money, and every purchase necessitated cash payments in coin. At first, as has been shown, an endeavour was made to barter English goods for Indian produce, but there were many difficulties attached to this system and it was speedily abandoned for money payments. There was risk by land as well as by sea when the money was transmitted to the subordinate factories, but an armed escort was usually employed and we do not hear of many losses of treasure.

In the year 1688, Armenian merchants settled in Madras under the protection of the British, and ever since then they have formed an important and highly respected portion of the community. Their numbers are less in the present day chiefly through absorption by marriage into European families. They have proved themselves good citizens and law-abiding subjects, and by their instinctive habits of trade they have in years gone by, taken a foremost place amongst the native merchants of the town. They are especially interesting as an example of what Christianity can do for the Oriental in making a peaceful and useful citizen of him.

The nation had its origin in the country of the Euphrates and Tigris. St. George, the Illuminator, carried the story of the Gospel to them in the fourth century. They received him and his Faith favourably; and Armenia has the honour of being the first nation to recognise Christianity as its national religion. After a cruel persecution in the seventeenth century a number of them came to India and obtained through Sir John Chardin,[24] the celebrated traveller, the permission to settle in Madras. Sir John warmly espoused their cause, and represented the advantages which would accrue to the Company by establishing a colony within its territory. Wheeler in his careful search amongst the records of Fort St. George in 1861 came across a copy of the contract made between Sir Joseph Child on behalf of the Directors and Sir John Chardin and Coja Panous Kalendar, an Armenian merchant of Ispahan on behalf of the Armenian nation. The contract, dated 22nd June 1688, gave them the same privileges that were accorded to the British free merchants. It allowed them to own houses and landed property within the Company's towns and garrisons; to hold civil appointments such as were open to English-born subjects; and to trade to any of the Company's ports, making use of their ships for freight and passage on payment of the customary dues; they were also permitted to exercise the rites of their religion. A plot of ground was allotted to them on which to build a church, and a grant was made of fifty pounds a year for seven years to maintain their elected minister.

The community grew and flourished trading in precious stones and rich stuffs with Persia and other Eastern ports. They rarely meddled with politics or troubled themselves with the burning questions which at times convulsed the Hindu and Mahomedan religious world. Their only failing was a weakness for the interloper with his illicit trade which tempted them sorely. Occasionally this led to their being called before the Council, when they received a warning that their privileges would be withdrawn if they abused them; sometimes they were bound over not to offend again. They invariably expressed sorrow and promised amendment. They acquired wealth and owned some fine ships, the "Quedah" being one of them, which they officered with Englishmen and sailed under European flags. In the early days the Armenians buried their dead in the English cemetery belonging to Fort St. George, and there still remain a few tombstones bearing inscriptions in Armenian character in the compound of St. Mary's church.

1 2

JOB CHARNOCK'S VISIT TO FORT ST. GEORGE, AND THE BAPTISM OF HIS CHILDREN

It was in the time of Elihu Yale that Job Charnock or Channock as he has sometimes erroneously been called, the founder of Calcutta, visited Madras. Calcutta did not exist in those days; it was but a sandy flat by the banks of the Hugly, where each year a cotton market sprang up in the shipping season; and it went by the name of the Cotton Mart. The native name was Chuttanuttee or Sutanuti. Charnock came of a good Lancashire family, of the same standing as that of Master. He arrived in India in 1656 and entered the Company's service September 30th, 1658, on a salary of twenty pounds a year. In 1666 he became Senior Merchant, and he seems to have been always employed in the factories of the Bay, and never to have held any appointment in Madras.

When the Bay was placed under Master's supervision Charnock was brought into contact with Master, as has already been mentioned; the result was not very fortunate. Charnock at the time was busy inland at Patna, trying to obtain saltpetre for his employers. There was no obstacle in the way of purchasing it, but considerable difficulty was experienced in getting it down to Ballasore at the mouth of the Hugly, where the ships were awaiting it. If it did not arrive within a certain time they would have to sail without it, because of the monsoon. It had to go down the river in native boats, and it is easy to understand how the determined, but quick-tempered merchant must have been irritated by the senseless delays made by the boatmen. When at last he did get his saltpetre loaded and dispatched, he had the vexation of seeing the boats return after they had got halfway to their destination. He was not a man to give in to adverse fate or the stupidity of the native, and instead of obeying Master's orders he remained at Patna until he had assured himself that every boat-load would reach Ballasore. Probably it was the fear of pirates which caused the boatmen to make the delay; pirates infested the creeks of the Hugly and laid wait for boats ascending and descending the river.

In the midst of all Charnock's trouble and anxiety over the saltpetre so urgently demanded by Directors, Master made him Chief of Cassimbazaar, ordering him to appear at the factory to take charge of it, and meet the Governor and his staff who were on tour through the Bay. Charnock accepted the chiefship, but said briefly, that he was unable to come down to Cassimbazaar immediately. Master gave him a short period of grace, and then finding that he did not appear, he bestowed the appointment of another man. Although Charnock felt the slight of being superseded, he made no effort to explain matters, but merely nursed his wrath against the man who had wronged him. His uncompromising character prevented him throughout the whole course of his service from ever doing himself justice. He would not stir a finger to secure the goodwill of his fellowmen, nor even take the trouble to show his best side to the Directors. They recognised his worth and called him honest; for he was one of the very few men who abstained from private trade, and after thirty-eight years in their service died a comparatively poor man. But they found occasion to abuse him for his determination, a quality which they recognised only as obstinacy; they called him blatant and truculent, and gave him credit for contentiousness, when he was only showing his colleagues that he possessed the courage of his opinions.

In 1680 he was sent to Murshidabad. There he had to put up with much opposition from the natives, who besieged him in his factory. He escaped and went to Hugly, and in 1686 the Directors placed a force under his command to enable him to effect a settlement, which would offer strategical advantages and could be fortified. They were beginning to understand the necessity of fortifications if their trade was to be undisturbed, and were anxious to build just such a Fort in the Bay as had arisen in Madras on the Coromandel Coast. They knew very little of the geography of India, and had made up their minds that Chittagong would be the most suitable of all sites in the Bay for the new factory. To Charnock this must have appeared nothing short of madness, Chittagong being far away on the Eastern side of the Bay and the refuge of all the European outcasts of the East. It was a home for the pirate and the robber, a place to be avoided rather than sought. No man knew the Hugly better than Charnock; and he had already gauged the advantages offered by the strip of land on which the Cotton Mart stood. There was a good anchorage in the river for ships on one side, and a series of salt-lakes and swamps on the other, which would protect it from the attacks of natives. It had one disadvantage, namely its unhealthy climate, but this he thought might be overcome, and prove no worse in the end than the climate of Hugly, Cassimbazaar and other places in the Bay. But the Fates were against him; he was driven from pillar to post, up and down the river, without being able to effect his purpose, strongly opposed by the natives and discountenanced by the Directors.

In 1688 Captain Heath was sent out direct from the Court to carry a severe reproof to the truculent Charnock, and he was further enjoined to convey the unfortunate merchant with his party *nolens-volens* to Chittagong. Heath arrived, and Charnock pleaded hard for assistance and time to carry out his original scheme; but the Captain refused to listen. Chittagong was the spot selected by the Directors for the new fort, and to Chittagong Charnock should go. The disheartened man felt it was useless to oppose the will of the Court any longer, and sorrowfully he and his staff embarked. Heath set sail for his Eldorado, having, like his employers, the haziest notion of its locality. When at last he anchored before it, he found it was impossible to establish a colony there, partly on account of its lawless inhabitants and partly because of its unsuitable situation. But he was unwilling to allow Charnock to return or to listen to his "I-told-you-so"; and after sailing about the Bay for three long weary months, he landed his passengers at Madras on March 17th, 1689.

Their arrival was unexpected, and somewhat disconcerting to Yale and his Council, as Charnock's staff alone amounted to twenty-eight people,—council, factors and writers. The Bengal ships brought also his soldiers, four companies in all, with many "supernumerary officers"; and there was some difficulty in housing such a party. To make room in the garrison for the soldiers, the topasses who had refused to serve in any other place but the Fort were disbanded and dismissed; and Charnock and his party were accommodated among the English residents, being fed at the Company's expense. The enforced rest to the harassed merchant must have been beneficial, although he doubtless chafed at the inactivity of his life in the Fort, and at the temporary failure of his designs.

Here he had to remain in uncertainty until October, when a letter was received from the Nabob, Ibrahim Khan, inviting him to return to Bengal and promising him his protection. The matter was referred to Surat for decision, and on the receipt of the approval of the Governor there, Charnock and his party set sail for the Bay. On August 24th, 1690, he once more anchored before Cotton Mart; and landing with a guard of only thirty soldiers, he set himself to his self-appointed task of founding a fortified factory on the river. The few buildings he had erected in 1688 had been destroyed, but, nothing daunted, he began to rebuild and fortify with all his old dogged determination and indomitable spirit, laying the foundation of a city whose future greatness he could never know, nor in his most ambitious moments even dream of. He and his people had to be content with mud huts and native boats for their habitations; the palaces were for posterity.

Charnock's visit to Madras is not only interesting on account of his having sailed thence to found the City of Palaces, but also because there is positive proof that he brought his family with him on that occasion. He was never married, but formed an alliance with a caste Hindu lady who claimed his protection under romantic circumstances.

The story, as originally told, came from the pen of Captain Alexander Hamilton.

It is as follows: In the early days of his residence in Bengal before the Moghul war, Charnock wished to see the ceremony of Suttee in which Hindu widows were burnt alive with their deceased husbands. It was common enough in those days, but difficult of belief to the foreigner and the stranger. He accordingly attended the burning-ground on one occasion when the ghastly ceremony was to be performed, accompanied by a bodyguard of soldiers. When the young widow was brought to the pile he was much touched by her beauty; it seemed so iniquitous a thing that she should be sacrificed to the memory of a dead man, that he ordered his troops to rescue her. They carried her away by force, and she was sheltered in his own house. The natural consequences ensued, she being full of gratitude towards the preserver of her life, and his heart being softened with pity. If once he set himself to obtain a thing, Charnock was not the man to be bulked of his wishes. Probably the conquest was easy in this case; for a return to her people was impossible. She was an outcaste for ever in their eyes; and her fate in their hands would have been worse than death. She accepted Charnock's offer of a home with him, and she became the mother of his children. She bore him three little girls, who accompanied him to Madras, and she lived with him until her death, and was ever his faithful companion. Hamilton avers that at her request Charnock embraced Hinduism, but he admits that he gave her decent burial, "the only part of Christianity that was remarkable in him" continues the sharp-tongued historian. "He built a tomb over her, where all his life after her death he kept the anniversary day of her death by sacrificing a cock on her tomb after the Pagan manner; this was and is the common report, and I have been credibly informed, both by Christians and Pagans who lived at Calcutta under his Agency, that the story was really matter of fact."

There is an entry in the baptismal register book of St. Mary's church which rebuts the accusation of Paganism on the part of Charnock. It is as follows: "August 19th, 1689, Charnock, Mary, Elizabeth and Katherine, daughters of Job Charnock, baptised by J. Evans. Francis Ellis, Godfather, Ann Seaton and Margery Heathfield, Godmothers."[25]

The absence of all mention of the mother's name points to the improbability of there ever having been any form of marriage ceremony between the parents. In all the other entries made of baptisms where the children are legitimate, care is observed to give the mother's name. The entry clears the memory of Charnock from the imputations of heathenism, and testifies to his Christianity; for otherwise he surely never would have brought his children to the font in the beautiful church of St. Mary's.

Hamilton gives Charnock a character for harshness and cruelty towards the natives, and speaks scornfully of his choice of a site for the new colony. Considering the treatment Charnock met with from the natives, and the infamous conduct of Ibrahim Khan's predecessor, who caused the Englishman to be severely flogged, it is possible that defaulters met with swift and unflinching retribution at his hands and that he did not spare the treacherous. But there is nothing to substantiate Hamilton's accusation of cruelty, and it seems to be as unfounded as the other charge of heathenism.

Evans, the Chaplain who baptised the little girls, was a Welshman; he had been attached to Charnock's party for some time; he was with him in his troubles at Hugly and was one of the party carried away by Heath and landed in Madras. He might, of course, at any time, have performed the ceremony at Hugly or Cassimbazaar, although there was no church at either place. But the worries and anxieties of life were sufficient to prevent Charnock from paying any attention to domestic matters, and it was not till he reached the Fort that he had leisure to think about such things; even then it is more than probable that Yale, who so frequently interested himself in such affairs, suggested the ceremony. Ellis, who stood sponsor, was an old friend of Charnock's and a member of his Council; he intended returning to the Bay with his chief, and consequently would be near his godchildren.

When the site of Calcutta was chosen and the foundations of Fort William were preparing to be laid, the new settlement ranked only as one of the minor Agencies; Charnock was its first Agent or Chief, and he with two old friends, Francis Ellis and Jeremiah Peachie, formed the first Council of Calcutta. The Council held its first consultation on August 24th, 1690, the day of their landing from Madras, just half a century after the foundation of Fort St. George. The three men who stood on the bare unhealthy strip of land at Chuttanuttee and talked over the new fort, all passed away within a short period of each other. Peachie died in Madras, in 1702, Charnock in Calcutta in 1692, and Ellis in 1704. They may well be called the three fathers of Fort William and its wonderful city.

The Directors knowing how great an interest Yale took in church matters and philanthropic works, commissioned him to see to the building of a church for "the Protestant black people and Portuguese and slaves which serve them". Also to make some arrangement for the systematic relief of the poor; both of which schemes, be it noted, were to be carried out through private subscriptions from the residents in the Fort.

Historians usually claim the first missionary efforts made in India on behalf of Protestant Christianity for the Danish agents of the Lutheran Mission, they being the first professed missionaries in the field. It is only fair to the Company, however, to recognise the endeavours they made to promote Christianity among their Eastern dependents. It is true that they did not make it their primary business to proselytise generally, but they cannot be accused of neglecting the cause; and considering the smallness of the field and the number of difficulties, it does the old merchants credit that an attempt to proselytise was made at all. But that it was made may be gathered from the records. In the year 1674 there is mention of a "Christian Protestant convert." 'He was a Moor who had been baptised by the name of John Lawrence and had married a Christian wife. A fellow-countryman who had not embraced the Faith, asked Lawrence for his daughter and offered him a sum of money. The girl must have appealed to the authorities for protection, as an order records that, the Moor intending to carry out the contract, the person of John Lawrence was secured to prevent further trouble. In 1678 a "Popish priest" named Padre Pasquall, was accused of tampering with a convert, a Caffre or African slave, belonging to one of the Company's servants, whom he tried to seduce "from the Protestant religions in which he was educated and doth constantly profess". If the accusation were proved true, the Padre was to be turned out of the place by the Justices of the Choultry. In the same year a Portuguese

Padre got into trouble through baptising a slave belonging to the English, and was ordered to leave the town.

In a letter sent to Surat in 1679—a copy of which was received by the Governor and Council of Madras—there was the following clause which speaks of Missionary effort on the party of the Directors. "As to the buying of 100 black servants, if you can procure such as are willing to serve we shall approve thereof. But to order that you shall cause them to be instructed by our Chaplain in the Christian religion, and for their encouragement let them know that if they shall attain to such a competent knowledge therein, as to qualify them for Holy Sacrament of Baptism, that after three years as Christians, and being of good conversation, they shall be admitted freemen."

Beyond directing the schoolmaster and Chaplain to instruct servants and slaves in the principles of the "Protestant religion", by which the Directors meant the religion of the Church of England, no distinct effort at special missionary work was made until Yale was asked to see to the building of the church. Following upon that came a gift of prayer books in the Portuguese vernacular, at that time commonly in use amongst the Eurasian population, and two Ministers were sent out "who have applied themselves to the learning of the Portuguese language, we designing them to be Ministers for the new Portuguese church which we have desired you to cause to be built." The services were inaugurated, but there is no evidence to show that a church was built. Had Yale remained in power for any length of time he would undoubtedly have carried out the directions of the Court regarding it. But the Directors called upon him to retire in the following year, and on his departure from office the interest in mission work appears to have flagged, although the Portuguese services were performed and baptisms continued to take place, showing that efforts on the part of the Chaplain and private individuals were still being made. The Portuguese services were discontinued in 1851, when they were no longer thought necessary, the descendants of those for whom they were instituted having been absorbed into the Eurasian population which had adopted the English language.

Twenty years later, in 1711, religious matters appear to have been very slack in the Fort; for on August 2nd in that year the factors and writers were called before the Council to receive a reprimand for their non-attendance at Divine service; and they were warned that a repetition of the offence would ensure fining, the money to go to the poor. In the following year, 1712, mission matters once again revived. The Society for Promoting Christian Knowledge approached the Directors on the subject, and asked for permission to establish schools in Madras under the Danish Missionaries of Tranquebar. It also asked for free passages for a schoolmaster and two printers for the Mission, which were granted.

It was not the custom of the Company to allow of separate or independent organisation to carry on work that might be deemed necessary for the good of their servants and their dependents. When a thing had to be done, whether it was soldiering or doctoring, trading or preaching, the Directors deputed one of their own servants to do it. So now there was a desire on the part of the Court to take up the mission work themselves and employ their own chosen men. And to effect this, they at once issued an order that all their ministers sent to reside in India should learn the Portuguese language and the vernacular, "the better to enable them to instruct the Gentus that shall be servants or slaves of the Company or of their Agents, in the

Protestant religion," by which they meant, as before, the religion of the Church of England. The letter containing this order is dated the 2nd February 1712.

The work of the Danish missionaries had not altogether pleased the authorities, and in their reply the Governor and Council expressed a hope that if the S.P.C.K. intended sending any agents to Madras (for independent work) it would choose Englishmen. As, however, the Society was unable to secure the services of any Englishmen for the purpose, an offer from the Tranquebar Mission was accepted, and in 1717 the Danish Missionary, Ziegenbald, in conjunction with the Fort Chaplain, opened two schools in Madras,—one for the Portuguese in the English town, and one for the Malabars in Blacktown. It was not until 1728, a little more than half a century after the name of John Lawrence, the Christian Moor, is mentioned, that Benjamin Schultz, the first Agent of the S.P.C.K. arrived. With his advent the Society took up the work, and thus relieved the Company of all further responsibility in the matter of missionary effort amongst the natives and the Portuguese.

Besides the laudable attempt on the part of the Company to provide for the spiritual needs of its dependants, there was a great deal of private charity which was more generous than wise. The result was the creation of a begging nuisance within the Fort walls, which became intolerable. Every morning gangs of beggars thronged the streets, bringing disease with them and impeding the traffic. Yale was asked by the Directors, to whom the state of affairs was reported, to institute some system of relief. Overseers were appointed, and the doles of the charitably disposed were administered at the Choultry, through the hands of these "Fathers of the Poor" as they were called.

Provision was also made for the orphans of poor Europeans by the St. Mary's Vestry, as has already been described, which resulted in the foundation of St. Mary's School in the Fort.

The St. Mary's School still exists, though it is no longer situated in the Fort. In 1872 it was removed to Egmore, and amalgamated with the Civil Orphan Asylum, another charitable institution for destitute children. The boys of the Asylum still sing in the choir of St. Mary's church, and claim the services and supervision of the Fort Chaplain.

13

FIFTY YEARS OF MERCHANT GOVERNORS: HIGGINSON, PITT, ADDISON, FRASER, HARRISON, COLLET AND MILTON'S DESCENDANTS

Yale and his Council fell out during the latter portion of his governorship. It was the old story of private trade, jealousy on the part of his fellow-merchants, and suspicion and distrust at home as his wealth accumulated. Thomas Yale, Elihu's brother, was the immediate cause of the trouble in consequence of his irregularities in the China trade. Elihu Yale defended his actions, and as was then accused of being a partaker in the plunder. In the mutual recriminations that followed, the Council declared that the Governor had helped himself from the Company's funds. He indignantly denied it, and drew the Council's attention to the fact that at the time he had £175,000 lying in his name. Yale's enemies then altered their tale, and endeavoured to smirch his good name by mixing it up with that of a friend and neighbour, Mrs. Catherine Nicks, whose dealings with the Company's goods appear to have been of a doubtful nature, and whose husband, John Nicks, had been dismissed from the Company's service. The result of the quarrelling and backbiting was the removal of Yale from office, and the appointment of Nathaniel Higginson in his place. Yale remained on in the Fort some years after his supersession; by the time he had realized his fortune and adjusted his differences with the Council, his name was cleared of all scandal. He returned to England in 1699, and was subsequently made Governor of New York, when he endowed the College in Connecticut now so well known by his name.

In consequence of the trouble in the Council at the end of Yale's term of office, the Directors once more sent out a Commissary-General to enquire into affairs, and to settle them on the spot in the name of the Court. They chose Sir John Goldsborough, and he arrived in December 1692. Like Major Puckle, Sir John did not live to carry out his work; he succumbed to the climate at Chuttanuttee on the Hugly, the year after his arrival, during one of his journeys up the coast. His widow, who was living at the Fort, remained there, and in 1695 she married for her second husband, Roger Braddyll, who in 1688 was serving in the Bay. She died in 1698 and on her death the silver flagon and font-basin were presented in her name to St. Mary's Church.

Higgison[26] became Governor in 1692. From his time until the year 1746 (when the Fort was rendered up to the French), the records are full of the details of native intrigue within and without the walls; of industrious and ever increasing trade; and of the gradual and almost unconscious growth of the political power of the Company in the Presidency. But though that power was slowly and surely consolidating and increasing, the Directors only recognised it as an engine of commerce. The daring conception of administering the country for the sake of its revenues had not yet taken place in their minds. All things were subservient to trade, and whilst the keenest desire was shown on the part of the Directors to grasp every advantage to develop that trade, they shrank, as in the early days, from taking upon themselves too much territorial power. But India was much the same then as it is now, inherent with a motive power of its own, which swept ruler and ruled along a pathway of fate not always of their own choice; and whether the Englishmen willed it to be so or otherwise, British influence increased politically as well as commercially, until the time came when the crown of the ruling monarch was forced upon the brow of the merchant.

During the half century that elapsed between Higginson's time and the rendition of the Fort to the French, the records teem with interesting matter ably detailed by Talboys Wheeler in his History of Madras. Fourteen men stood in turn at the head of the government, every one of them having two definite objects in view, one being the advancement of the Company's mercantile affairs; and the other, the accumulation of a private fortune. The Directors were learning that their servants could grow wealthy in their service and yet advance the Company's interests. The old accusation against a man of enriching himself at his employer's expense appeared less frequently: greater liberality and goodwill was shown to retiring Anglo-Indians on their return to England with their fortunes; and it was understood that there was room in the broad fields of India for all.

Something of this liberality must have been extended to the renowned "Pirate Pitt", the man who proved such a red rag to Hedges in Bengal, and whom the Directors designated as a desperate fellow, and one that, we fear, will not stick at "doing any mischief that lies in his power". The Court made Thomas Pitt Governor of Fort St. George in 1698, by which time they seemed to have lost all their former jealousy of his mercantile successes and to have reposed the utmost confidence in him. He was forty-five years old at the time, and had a son named Robert, who was already starting in trade for himself in Madras. This son Robert was the father of William, the famous Lord Chatham.

Thomas Pitt lived as much as possible in the Company's garden houses. There were two, one (the erection of which was sanctioned in 1678) on the banks of the Cooum, and the other near St. Thomas' Mount. The latter is now called Guindy, and it is to this day greatly preferred as a residence by the Governors to the palace by the Cooum.[27] Pitt was fond of gardening, and at Guindy he had great scope for his hobby. But he was not left in peace to enjoy it. Dawood Khan, the Nabob of the Carnatic, assumed a hostile attitude to the English, and made it so unpleasant for them that it was not considered safe to remain outside the walls of the Fort. They were advised to come in from their garden houses and from St. Thomas' Mount, where one or two had ventured to establish themselves with their families. In 1702 Dawood Khan fulfilled the worst fears expressed concerning him, and blockaded the Fort. The outlying villages which had been bought by the Company were plundered, and there was a panic amongst the peaceful inhabitants, who had been enjoying the comfort of regular government. The native population of Blacktown took fright as well and fled. The blockade lasted three months. At the end of that time Pitt and his Council succeeded in making terms with the Nabob. Dawood Khan received a sum of money in cash, in return for which he undertook to restore the trade, to give up the villages he had seized, and to compensate the inhabitants for the loss of their property. This was the usual way of dealing with the blackmailing Prince under the merchant Governors; it required a Clive to administer a dose of cold steel in place of the silver salve supplied by Pitt; but Clive was not yet born.

Whilst Pitt was Governor of Madras, a gem merchant named Jamchund brought a Kistna diamond of great size for sale. He asked £30,000 for it in the rough. It should of course have been bought on behalf of the Company, but Pitt, seeing money in it, could not resist the temptation of making a private bargain. He became the possessor of the stone for the sum of £20,400; and he was quite satisfied that he had behaved honourably when he paid the man, who on his part was also content. But the diamond was known to be worth more than Jamchund had received, and the transaction gave rise to a good deal of gossip, which was in no way decreased when later on Pitt had the stone cut in England, and sold it to the Regent of France for £135,000. Even that enormous sum did not represent its true value. The stone was set in the Royal Crown of France where it still remains, and it is valued in the present day at £480,000, close upon half a million sterling. It weighed 410 carats in the rough, but the cutting reduced it to 136 carats.

During Pitt's time there were frequent caste troubles in Blacktown which resulted in faction fights. They rose to such a pitch that trade was disorganized and the English residents suffered the utmost inconvenience. The workpeople engaged in preparing the calicoes for export, joined with the petty traders and domestic slaves in the rioting, and left their work to take care of itself. They armed themselves as best they could, and set themselves to break heads over the route that should be taken by their religious processions in Blacktown. When one party was successful, the other fled to the outlying villages to gather their forces and recommence the strife. These caste disputes are an ever-present trouble all over India to this day; and in spite of police supervision and the binding over of the headmen to keep the peace, they often end in rioting and bloodshed. In the South of India one cause of disputes is the claim of one party to take its religious processions down certain street inhabited by members of the opposition faction. As the procession passes the opposition place of worship, it is greeted with a shower of stones, and a free fight is the immediate result. There is not much doctrine involved between the disputants, but there is a little. The one side may be said broadly to hold the doctrine of predestination, and the other that of free will. The caste marks differ slightly, but the difference is scarcely perceptible to the uninitiated. The quarrels were going on in Aaron Baker's governorship within thirteen years of the founding of Fort St. George, and even in those early days legislation was necessary to keep the peace. Baker's endeavour was to make a fair division of the native town, confining one sect to one half and the other sect to the other half. He gave his ruling in the vernacular in writing, and the document was preserved down to Pitt's time when it was produced as evidence in support of the rights of one of the factions. The troubles were greatly increased by the matter becoming a party affair with the servants of the Company. Pitt championed one side and William Fraser the other. Fraser had served the Directors for some years past and had already proved himself contentious by his antagonism to Higginson. He now transferred his enmity to Pitt and his Council, and warmly espoused the cause of those who fell under the condemnation of the government. Pitt and his Council were neither to be browbeaten nor overridden, and on one occasion when a communication from Fraser was particularly offensive, they ordered it to be burnt by the Marshal under the gallows.

The Directors were far from satisfied with the state of affairs. It appeared to them that the Governor failed in his government when he allowed the caste disputes to assume such dimensions; and, moreover, they had heard of the diamond transaction. The result was that orders were sent out for the removal of Pitt, who was told to handover the reins to Gulstone Addison. Having made a large fortune, Pitt was quite ready to retire at their bidding. He returned to England where he became a member of Parliament. He died in 1720 at the age of seventy-three, and was buried at Blandford in Dorsetshire, the town of his birth.

At his retirement the Company bought his plate for the use of the public table which was still maintained for the Company's servants. There was a small quantity of plate already in existence; but it was battered and worn with the rough usage of the native servants. In these days it would still have been deemed valuable, and would have been prized for its antiquity; but then it was looked upon only as so much bullion in useless form, and it was melted down, its value being reckoned at a hundred pounds sterling as metal. Pitt's plate, which was new, was valued at seven hundred and sixty-five pounds. It included, besides other articles, sixty-six silver plates and twelve dishes. There were forks, spoons, salvers, bowls, candlesticks, an aster and chelmger which weighed a hundred and fifty-five ounces; and five cuspidores weighing forty-two ounces; also a Monteith (a scalloped basin for cooling glasses). Thirty years later this plate was so much damaged by ill usage, that more than half of it had to be melted down, and the metal given in exchange for new plate.

Gulstone Addison, who had been living some years in Fort St. George was very much out of health when he received charge from Pitt. He was only able to attend half a dozen council meetings, and he died a month after. He was succeeded by William Fraser. Addison was born in 1673. He was the son of the Reverend Lancelot Addison, Dean of Lichfield, and of Jane, daughter of the Right Reverend William Gulstone, Bishop of Bristol. He was much respected by his fellowmen and was always spoken of as a man of irreproachable character. He was married to Mary Brook in St. Mary's church in 1701. She died in February 1709 and her husband followed her to the grave in October of the same year. A third member of the family and brother of the Governor, named Lancelot Addison, fellow of Magdalen College, Oxford, was also laid in the Fort cemetery in August of the following year. He came out to India to visit his brother and succumbed to the ill effects of the climate. As Gulstone left no children, his brother Joseph, the essayist, inherited all his wealth. Wheeler says that it came at an opportune moment and enabled Joseph to marry the Countess of Warwick with whom he had fallen in love.

In Pitt's time there arrived in Madras Caleb Clarke, a grandson of the poet Milton. He occupied the position of clerk to St. Mary's church, to which that of schoolmaster appears to have been sometimes joined. Caleb Clarke had three children by his wife Mary; Abraham, baptised at the Fort church in 1703; Mary, baptised in 1707; and Isaac, in 1711. The two Marys, mother and daughter, died in 1716 and Caleb in 1719. There is no further mention of Isaac in the register books, but Abraham married Anna Clark in 1725, and he had a daughter baptised by the name of Mary in 1727. There is an entry of the burial of an Abraham Clarke, a soldier, in 1743, but there is nothing to identify him with the great-grandson of Milton. On the contrary, it seems more probable that this man was a soldier of that name serving in Cuddalore, at Fort St. David, in Captain Viver's Company, in 1711, when the other Abraham was only eight years old. In the margin of the register book is the following note, adjoining the entry of the burial of Mary, Caleb's daughter: "Deborah, third Daughter of Milton, the Poet, by his first wife, was married to Abraham Clarke, weaver in Spitalfields, by whom she had issue the above Caleb Clarke of this Parish, anno 1717; born unto him sons and daughters as testified in this Register."

The Edinburgh Review for 1815 says: "Milton's direct descendants can only exist, if they exist at all, among the posterity of his youngest and favourite daughter Deborah, afterwards Mrs. Clarke, a woman of cultivated understanding, and not unpleasing manners, known to Richardson and Professor Ward, and patronised by Addison, who intended to have procured a permanent provision for her, and presented her with fifty guineas from Queen Caroline. Her affecting exclamation is well known, on seeing her father's portrait for the first time more than thirty years after his death: "Oh, my father, my dear father!" She spoke of him, says Richardson, with great tenderness; she said he was delightful company, the life of the conversation, not only by a flow of subject, but by unaffected cheerfulness and civility. This is the character of him whom Dr. Johnson represents as a morose tyrant, drawn by one of the supposed victims of his domestic oppression. Her daughter, Mrs. Foster, for whose benefit Dr. Newton and Dr. Birch procured *Comus* to be acted, survived all her children. The only child of Deborah Milton of whom we have any account besides Mrs. Foster, was Caleb Clarke, who went to Madras in the first years of the eighteenth century, and who then vanishes from the view of the biographers of Milton."

Addison being a friend of the family was without doubt instrumental in sending Caleb Clarke out to Madras where Gulstone Addison was able to forward his interests, even though Caleb held the somewhat humble post of church clerk. There is little or no hope of tracing the family further, or of identifying it with any family of that name now to be found in the Eurasian community. There were no other register books kept in the Presidency at that time excepting those of St. Mary's, and all burials, marriages and baptisms at outstations, if recorded at all, were sent to be entered in the St. Mary's books. The registers kept by Schwartz, the Danish missionary, and his successors, who served as garrison chaplains at Trichinopoly during the latter half of the eighteenth century, have been examined, but without throwing any further light on the subject. When Fort St. George was rendered up to the French by treaty in 1746 all the English inhabitants were turned adrift. The bulk of them went to Fort St. David at Cuddalore; but there were many families who threw themselves on the kindness of the Dutch at Pulicat and Negapatam, and the Clarke family, consisting of Abraham and his wife and daughter, and possibly his brother Isaac, may have migrated there. The climate of India is destructive to all records in the shape of books and papers; moreover, family tradition is not venerated amongst the country-born Anglo-Indians and Eurasians as it is in England. Even if Milton's descendants still exist, it is to be feared that they are of mixed blood, and having lost all record and tradition in their wanderings, they are totally unaware of their relationship to the illustrious poet. Caleb Clarke's name appears in the records of the St. Mary's Vestry proceedings, but it throws no light on the fate of his descendants. At his death money was deposited in the Church Fund for the benefit of his family. In the cash books, there is a record of three payments "of small sums made to Isaac Clarke on account of Caleb's estate," two in 1737 and one in 1739. There may have been more later, but the books for 1740 and onwards have not been preserved. In 1767, the estate, through an error, was said at a Vestry meeting to have been charged as a debt on the books. The error was pointed out, and it was proposed that as there had been no payments, debit or credit, since 1754 the estate should be considered as a donation to the Church Fund and be administered for the benefit of the charity.

Fraser was removed from power as suddenly as his predecessor, after holding office for eighteen months. He was succeeded by Edward Harrison in 1711. During Harrison's time there were troubles at Cuddalore in the Government of Fort St. David; but within the walls of Fort St. George all was going on with tolerable smoothness, excepting for native intrigue, from which the Europeans were never free; and a few irregularities amongst the English such as might be expected in any community like that of the Fort. The curious part of it is, that these peccadilloes should have been thought of sufficient consequence to occupy the valuable time of the Governor and Council, and figure in the records at all.

The following is one of the trivial matters which exercised the minds of the rulers of the Fort. Henry Dobbyns, the son of William Dobbyns, Esq. of Lincoln's Inn, London, came out as a free merchant to Fort St. George at the beginning of the eighteenth century. He was not in the Company's service, yet it was thought necessary to enquire into the fact of his private life. Report said that he had been married to a Mrs. Rachel Baker by a Roman Catholic priest. The rules made by Master against such marriages were still in force, and Dobbyns was sent for and examined by the Governor and Council. He resented their conduct and at first refused to give any information, but thinking better of it he produced two witnesses, Mr. John Sewell and Mrs. Anne Masters, who testified to the validity of the marriage. He refused to give the name of the officiating priest, however, and it was solemnly ruled that he should not be allowed to live with his wife. The marriage register book of St. Mary's tells the sequel of the story by recording the union of Henry Dobbyns with Rachel Baker according to the Anglican rites, and later on the name appears in the baptismal register. But Dobbyns did not long enjoy his conjugal bliss; he died a few years after his marriage, and his widow took a third husband named Thomas Curgenven. Curgenven died in Bengal, and his widow once more occupied the minds of the Governor and his Council by resisting her brother-in-law's attempts to seize her late husband's property, and by appealing to the authorities for protection and justice.

Another case was that of a man named John Mitchell, who went out of India as a soldier, and electrified the community by declaring himself to be a clergyman in Holy Orders. His tale was plausible; he said that he had been a chaplain in H.M. fleet, but that he forfeited his position by contracting a debt on behalf of a brother; he had fled to

India to escape his creditors. He had no credentials or letters to support his story, nevertheless the confiding inhabitants of the Fort accepted it and allowed themselves to be beguiled into the belief that he was a veritable clergyman. The post of Chaplain was fortunately filled at the time, and Mitchell was made schoolmaster of the St. Mary's Charity School, for which he received a good salary. After a time suspicions were aroused by his irregularities. Finally he made love to the daughter of a Captain and married her without her father's consent, performing the marriage ceremony himself. The indignant father prosecuted him in the Mayor's Court, and the marriage was ruled to be null and void. He was forced to resume his military duties, and had to give security for his good behaviour under threat of being shipped home by the next vessel.

In 1717 Harrison gave up the reins to Joseph Collet, who remained in office three years, and seems to have been a man of courage and decision. Five villages had lately been granted to the Company by the Moghul, and Collet went in state to take possession of two of them and to set up the Company's flag. The Nabob who ruled the country under the Moghul demanded a sum of money as a douceur, threatening to blockade the trade of Madras if his demand were not complied with. It was thought best to give him the thousand pagodas he asked for, and it was accordingly promised. The apparently easy acquiescence of the English in this blackmailing encouraged the Nabob's officers to try to obtain the same thing for themselves. Diaram, the head renter or revenue collector, demanded a thousand pagodas. He was refused; and gathering a force of a thousand men, he proceeded to Trivatore, one of the villages, and cut down the Company's flagstaff. He invested the place with his men and sent a message to say that he would not retire unless the English sent him the money. It is refreshing to read of the firm and decided attitude taken by Collet and his Council. The commercial worm turned at last; the tearing down of the Company's flag, they wisely agreed, was an affront which could not be endured; the enemy must be driven out by force; and other course would only court further insult and trouble. A council of military men was called by the Governor, and Lieutenant John Roach was entrusted with the expedition. Roach and Lieutenant Fullerton advanced on Trivatore with two hundred and fifty men of the garrison, and after an action, which lasted six hours, they succeeded in driving out the enemy with considerable loss and putting them to flight. Only one soldier and three native peons were wounded on the side of the English. Diaram's son, who was commanding, was shot through the shoulder, and a panic seized his followers, who refused to remain in the neighbourhood of the English lest they should be pursued and again attacked. It was a complete victory, and did much towards establishing the prestige of the English with the Nabob and his people. Collet and his Council were lavish of their praise of Roach's valour, and he was made "Major of all the Honourable Company's forces on the Coast of Coromandel and in the Island of Sumatra." For his Brigadiership, he was to receive the rather inadequate salary of twenty pagodas a month; but a gold medal was also awarded. It was set with diamonds and inscribed with the date and the occasion, and was valued at three hundred pagodas. Collet might very suitably have received a medal also. He richly deserved one for daring to show his teeth instead of meekly submitting to blackmail. The event had an admirable effect on the native mind; the Nabob received his douceur like a lamb; his people gave no further trouble, and the Company entered into quiet possession of its new territories.

14

FIFTY YEARS OF MERCHANT GOVERNORS (*CONTINUED*)

Joseph Collet returned to England early in 1720, leaving Francis Hastings, who had been in the Company's service twenty years, at the head of affairs. It is not known exactly how Hastings was related to the noble family of that name, but there is no doubt that he was a scion of it. Elizabeth, Lady Moira, daughter of Theophilus Hastings, ninth Earl of Huntingdon and mother of the Marquis of Hastings, Governor General of India in 1813, says in a letter dated 18th April 1803, that this Francis of Madras was the grandson of Sir Edward Hastings and Barbara Devereux, and the great-grandson of Hastings, second Earl of Huntingdon. She describes him as being "stationed in some government in the East Indies; and there is now in the family a writing-box of cedar, inlaid with ivory and ebony, with the family arms, which was sent over to my aunt, Lady Elizabeth Hastings, in the beginning of the last century, from such a person ; and I was once in company (fifty years ago) with a person, who mentioned having been at the place where he (Francis) was stationed to govern; and though he had been long dead, his memory there still remained idolized for worth, humanity, and every virtue a mortal could possess."

Hastings' term of office was short and unfortunate, lasting only a little more than a year. He quarrelled violently with Nathaniel Elwick, one of the members of his Council, who certainly gave him great provocation, and opposed him unnecessarily in his ruling of a native case. Hastings demanded Elwick's suspension and refused to sit in Council with him. The matter was discussed by the members, who took the part of Hastings and agreed that Elwick had been negligent of his duty towards the Company, and disrespectful to the Governor. He was accordingly suspended, and an account of the affair was laid before the Directors. Elwick must have had powerful friends on the Directorate. The reply of the Court came as a bombshell upon the Council. Hastings, without a word of explanation, was directed to handover charge to Elwick, who was appointed Governor in his stead. The letters directing this change arrived on the afternoon of Sunday, October 15th, 1721. The Council was summoned, and the two packets, which were addressed to the Honourable Nathaniel Elwick, Esq., President and Governor, William Jennings, Nathaniel Turner, Richard Benyon, Catesby Oadham, John Emmerson, Randal Fowke, James Hubbard, and George Drake, were opened in the presence of all except Jennings.

Elwick at once took his seat in the presidential chair, and by virtue of his new powers, then and there called for the cash book, although it was Sunday and the meeting extraordinary. The Secretary dared not do otherwise than comply, and the book was brought for examination. It showed that no entries had been made since the last day of September and that there ought to be a large sum in the cash-chest; it was therefore sealed and locked securely in the silver room, the key being given to Elwick. On the following day the Council met and the cash-chest was solemnly opened in their presence. Except for a few papers and a small coin or two, it was empty. The cash-keeper, Thomas Cooke, was questioned, and he said that he had sold the silver at the direction of Hastings. He was told that as he had sold it without the authority of the Council he would be held responsible for the amount. Elwick sent for Hastings, to whom all this must have been gall and wormwood, and he gave his word to the new Governor that the cash should be repaid in a few days.

It is easy to imagine the consternation and gossip that ensued, and the triumph of Elwick over his enemy. But the Council were not sympathetic with their new chief, nor were they inclined to adopt harsh measures. They gave Hastings the time he asked for without putting him under arrest, and they kept their eye on Cooke. On the very day that the money was to be paid in, Hastings was taken dangerously ill. A calculation had been made, and it was found that he owed the Company something over seventy-two thousand pagodas. As the money was not forthcoming the Council put Cooke under arrest. Measures were also taken to arrest the unfortunate Hastings if he should recover sufficiently to attempt to escape. But this was not necessary as on the following day he paid in a part of the money; two days later he deposited diamonds of considerable value, and in less than a week, he had completed the security for the sum in full. There was no longer any necessity to put restraint on his actions, and he was allowed to live in peace in his garden house. His health was completely shattered, and two months after the incident of the cash-chest he applied for passages home for himself and his English servant. His request was granted, but he did not live long enough to avail himself of it. He died on December 15th, 1721, and was buried in the Fort church at the West end under the tower. His grave is marked by the plain slab, inscribed simply with the letters "M.S.", under which is his name "Fran: Hastings." There is no date and his age is not given.[28]

Elwick was married in St.Mary's church in 1722 to Mrs. Diana Robinson, and he had a daughter baptised there just before leaving India. His Governorship only lasted three years, and was not remarkable for anything beyond the usual incidents of trade, the warehousing of country produce, the sale of European goods, and the arrival and dispatch of the Company's ships as each monsoon came round. In January 1725, Elwick left India for England, and James Macrae took his place, being next on the list of promotion.

Macrae may be called the prince of the merchant Governors, although his descent was anything but princely. Wheeler went to some trouble to obtain an account of his personal history, which he gives in detail in his book, "Madras in the Olden Time". He describes him as being a Scotchman from Ayr. His parents were of the labouring class, and when his father died his worthy mother supported herself by laundry work. Macrae went to sea when he was a boy and found his way in to Indian waters, where in course of time he commanded a ship. In that capacity he was able to render service to the Company's servants in Sumatra, and in return they gave him a lucrative post in the service. His work was most satisfactory, and the Company's affairs prospered in his hands. At the same time he was able to put by a private fortune without raising a breath of scandal against himself. Finally he rose to be Deputy Governor of Fort St. David, which was the stepping-stone to the governorship of Madras.

Macrae was as canny a Scot as ever lived, and the trade of Fort St. George, increased and flourished under his rule as it had never done before. He possessed the art of taking pains, and had a keen eye for detail. He looked closely after the interests of his employers, never hesitating to examine personally the merchandise purchased on their behalf, and to superintend in buying and selling, where supervision was necessary. He may even have gone as far as Thomas Pitt, who told the Directors that in their interests he had beaten a native clerk with his own hand. At the same time Macrae managed to keep an eye on his personal interests, and took care not to fall foul of the interests of others. So long as his subordinates did not act unfairly towards their employers he gave them a free hand, and encouraged rather than discountenanced free trade; although it was in a somewhat arbitrary fashion, for he knew very little of the principles of free trade. The natives found him severe, but just, and his justice commanded their respect. For fifteen years he stood firmly and judiciously at the head of affairs in Fort St. George; and though he and his subordinates amassed large fortunes, not a word of complaint was raised, either in India or at home, against him and his staff.

His dubash or native headclerk, was not so fortunate. Macrae's retirement was the signal for an outcry against the clerk and the man's methods of shaking the pagoda tree. Judging by what is known of the native character in the present day, it is probable that more than half the charges made against the dubash were false. But it is more than probable that he accepted every bribe and present offered, and that he traded on his supposed influence with his master. Such things exist still, and the Englishman can only wonder at the credulity and the marvellous ignorance of the Hindu who can be so easily imposed upon. The dubash was heavily fined and made to disgorge some of his ill-gotten wealth, but his master was in no way implicated in the man's irregularities.

In 1728 the Chaplain of the Fort, William Leeke, died; and as it would be some months before another could be sent out, it was decided in Council that the services of the church should be performed by two laymen, Randall Fowke and George Torriano,[29] and that they should receive fifty pounds a year each as salary. Their names figure frequently in the burial register as officiating at funerals; but the baptisms and marriages were performed by Schultz, the Danish Missionary, who had by this time established a mission amongst the natives outside the Fort. In the following year the Revd. Thomas Consett arrived to take Leeke's place, and the services of the laymen were dispensed with.

Major Roach of Trivatore fame got himself into trouble about this time through sheltering a young woman of Portuguese descent. She left her guardian's protection at St. Thomé, and arrived at midnight at Major Roach's house where she was received. She remained under his roof for a month, and then, in consequence of a petition from the girl's guardian and the Roman Catholic padres, the Council was obliged to interfere. Roach was ordered to send her back, on the ground that she had come into the Fort without permission and had no right to be there. He was also asked for an explanation of his conduct; and he had excused himself on the plea of being a justice of the peace, in duty bound to give protection to anyone in distress. But this excuse did not save him; he was fined three hundred pagodas for aiding and abetting a young woman to run away from her lawful guardians. History does not explain his motive. As Roach was a married man and his wife was then living at the Fort there was nothing scandalous in his action. He was married in 1717 to Miss Adeodata Wheatly. He may have been helping a friend, but if so, he kept his friend's name secret from the Council. Major Roach sailed for England in January 1735, having made provision through the St. Mary's Vestry for his wife, who remained in the Fort.

In May 1730 Macrae was superseded by George Morton Pitt, and seven months later, sailed for England, worth, it was said, a hundred thousand pounds. He had been absent from Scotland forty years and during that time he held no communication with his family. Wheeler gives a full account of his last years and how he made amends for past neglect.

"On Mr. Macrae's arrival in England, his first object appears to have been to enquire about the fortunes of his family. It seems that his mother had been dead some years, and that his sister, who was still living at Ayr, had married a man named Macguire, who gained a livelihood partly as a carpenter, and partly as a fiddler at kirns and weddings. Mr. Macrae accordingly wrote to his sister at Ayr, enclosing a large sum of money, and engaging to provide handsomely for herself and family. The surprise of Mr. and Mrs. Macguire was of course unbounded; and they are said to have given way to their delight by indulging in a luxury which will serve to illustrate both their ideas of happiness and the state of poverty in which they were living. They procured a loaf of sugar and a bottle of brandy, and scooping out a hole in the sugar loaf, they poured in the brandy, and supped up the sweetened spirit with spoons, until the excess of felicity compelled them to close their eyes in peaceful slumber.

"The grand object which Mr. Macrae appears to have had in view during the remaining years of his life, was the elevation of his sister's family, the four daughters of Mr. and Mrs. Macguire. (The information here given has been derived from descendants or connections of the family who are still living.) The eldest married Mr. Charles Dalrymple, who was Sheriff Clerk of Ayr, and received the estate of Orangefield .The tradition is still preserved of a large box of tea, a great rarity in that time, having been presented to Mrs. Dalrymple by Governor Macrae; this box proved so large that the doors at Orangefield would not admit it, and it became necessary to haul it up on the outside for admission at a large window. This box strongly bound with brass is still in existence, and is used as a corn-chest by Dr. Whitehouse of Ayr. The second daughter married Mr. James Erskine, who received the estate of Alva; and was afterwards elevated to the Bench under the title of Lord Alva. The third daughter married William, the thirteenth Earl of Glencairn. In this match Governor Macrae took the liveliest interest, but it did not come off till the year 1744; and the old Nabob was so seriously ill that the doctor could not assure him of living until the solemnization of the nuptials. On this occasion Governor Macrae gave his niece as 'tocher' the barony of Ochiltree, which had cost him £25,000, as well as diamonds to the value of £45,000. But the marriage did not prove a happy one, for the Earl had no real affection for his wife, however much he may have respected her wealth. The Earl, however, was not inclined to submit to any taunting allusions to his wife's family, for when Lord Cassilis reproached him at a ball with having so far forgotten his rank as to marry a fiddler's daughter, he at once replied, 'Yes, my Lord, and one of my father-in-law's favourite airs was,' "The Gipseys came to Lord Cassilis yett," referring to the elopement of a Countess of Cassilis and the Gipseys, celebrated in the old song of 'Johnny Faa.' The second son of this Earl of Glencairn, by the niece of Governor Macrae, succeeded to his father's title as James, fourteenth Earl of Glencairn, and is known as a benefactor of the Poet Burns. This Earl died in 1791, when Burns wrote his 'Lament for James, Earl of Glencairn,' concluding with the following pathetic lines:

> *'The bridegroom may forget the bride*
> *Was made his wedded wife yestreen;*
> *The Monarch may forget the crown*
> *That on his head an hour has been;*
> *The mither may forget the bairn*
> *That smiles sae sweetly on her knee;*
> *But I'll remember thee, Glencairn,*
> *And a' that thou hast done for me.'*

"The fourth daughter of the Macguires married a young gentleman of suspicious origin, who went by the name of James Macrae. This young man was said to be the nephew of the old Governor, but he is generally supposed to have been a natural son. The barony of Houston was conferred upon the pair, but the subsequent career of this branch of the family was far from fortunate. A son known as Captain Macrae, became a reputed bully and profussed duellist at Edinburgh; and is represented in one of the caricatures of the time as practising with a pistol at a barber's block. Captain Macrae fought a celebrated duel with Sir George Ramsay in which the latter was mortally wounded. It seems that whilst both gentlemen were escorting some ladies out to the Theatre in Edinburgh, their servants quarrelled as to whose carriage should be drawn up at the door. Each of the gentlemen took his servant's part, and the result was the duel, which occasioned the death of Sir George Ramsay, and the exile and outlawry of Captain Macrae.

"In conclusion we must notice the very few recorded events which are still preserved of the last years of Governor Macrae. The old Anglo-Indian appears to have passed some fifteen years in his native country prior to his death in 1746. In 1733 he was admitted as a burgess of the old town of Ayr, when his name was entered as "James Macrae, late Governor of Madras." In 1734 he presented the citizens of Glasgow with the metallic equestrian statue of King William which still adorns that city. How he employed himself during the latter years of his life is nowhere dated, beyond the bare fact that he lived and died at Orangefield. We can easily, however, imagine the old man busy in promoting the advancement of his nieces, and in superintending the estates which he purchased from time to time. One of his last recorded acts occurred in December 1745, when he lent £5000 to the community of Glasgow, to meet the sum which had been levied from them by Prince Charles. He died somewhere about the year 1746, and was buried in Prestwich churchyard. Such is the eventful story of Governor Macrae, the son of a washerwoman at Ayr."

George Morton Pitt, who became Governor in 1730, was born in Fort St. George and baptised in St. Mary's church in 1693. He was the son of John Pitt and Sarah Wavell who were married at St. Mary's, and he was a distant cousin of Thomas Pitt the earlier Governor. He remained in power till 1735, when he left India for England, and the appointment devolved upon Richard Benyon, who ruled till 1744. Benyon was twice married during his residence in Madras, first to Mary Fleetwood, daughter of Edward and Mary Fleetwood, in 1724; secondly to Mrs. Frances Davis in 1738. These fourteen years saw very little change within the Fort. The community life with its common table in the Fort House had been given up in 1722, and a subsistence allowance was added to the salary of each servant instead, according to his rank. The large handsome garden houses, which are still an ornamental feature of Madras, had greatly increased in number, and they were naturally much preferred to the less roomy residences in the Fort. But the Fort houses were by no means abandoned by their owners; they were held in readiness for any emergency that might arise, and many continued to be occupied by the junior servants of the Company and the less wealthy free-traders.

Besides the Fort the English possessed at this time Blacktown and a few villages in its vicinity. The entire revenue from all sources, including rents and customs, did not amount to more than thirty thousand pounds sterling a year. The wealth of the place was in its trade and to this alone the Directors looked for their dividends.

Towards the end of Benyon's time there were great political changes in the native governments of South India. The Mahrattas were once again coming Southward, plundering, pillaging, and seizing on town and country alike. The people were panic-stricken and paralysed with fear. They dared not ply their trades, nor carry their goods to the markets, lest they should be robbed and beaten; and though the English were careful to preserve a strict neutrality with the Mahratta leaders, they began to feel the evil effects of their presence. At length the marauders ventured into the confines of Fort St. David and seized some goods; they were driven off by the guns of the Fort, but not without difficulty; and the Governor and Council of Fort St. George began to fear lest, in spite of treaty and neutrality, the horde of robbers should attack Madras. As usual there was a hasty examination of the defences which were reported to be weak on the West, the side whence an attack was expected. Food and water were ordered to be stored; the guns on the bastions were looked to, and arms and accoutrements counted over. Added to the Mahratta trouble there was friction with the French over trade rights. The French power had been growing at Pondicherry; and a good deal of jealousy was exhibited on both sides. But nothing was feared from the French at present, and the anxiety of the Governor was only to put the Fort into a state fit to resist a siege by native troops.

At this time the place was very much as Edward Fowle had designed it, and nothing like the fort of the present day. It was oblong in shape, as has already been described, but somewhat broader at one end than the other. At each point or corner there was a bastion, and between each bastion a curtain. This was nothing more than an ordinary wall of a few feet in thickness, the width of that on the sea face being only four feet. The distance of the surf from the sea wall was between twenty and thirty yards; and the area enclosed by the walls was about fifteen acres. There was no moat but the dry ditch or trench which had been dug before the sea wall. On the South the swamps and quagmires of the Cooum, which were not drained as in the present day, formed a protection. And on the West there was the arm of the river, which in 1744 was only two feet deep, and fordable

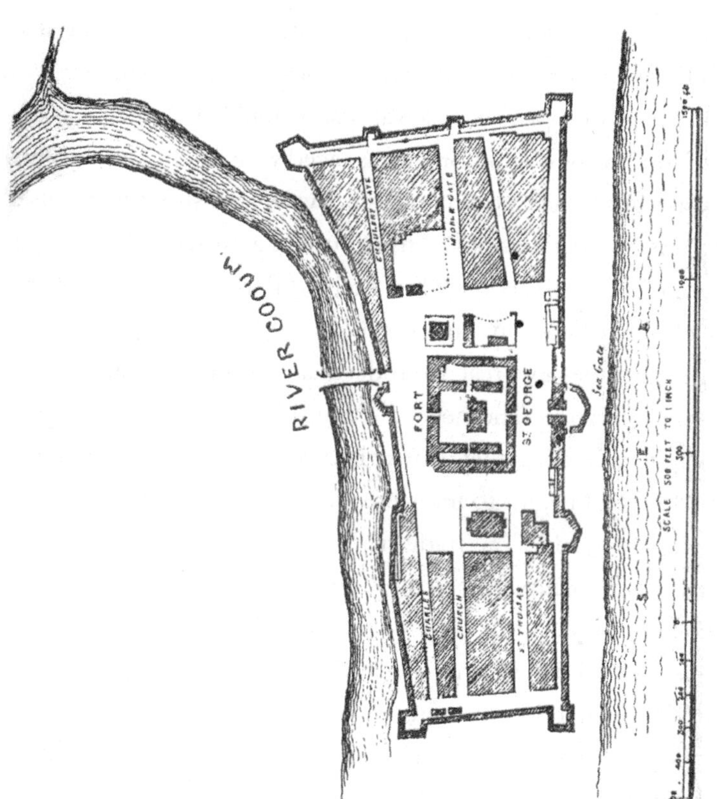

Fort St. George in 1733

everywhere. On the North the native houses had encroached from Blacktown till they reached the very gates, and it would have been impossible to get the guns on the bastions to play upon any force advancing under cover of the buildings. In 1743 two of the Company's engineers, Major Charles Knipe and a Mr. Joseph Smith, the father of Colonel Joseph Smith of subsequent military fame in South India, made plans for the enlargement of the Fort on the West or land side. By his plan its area was nearly doubled. A ditch was dug to mark out the new addition; it was faced with bricks and supplied with water from the Cooum; but as no walls or bastions were raised above this moat, it was not of much use as a protection. Such was the state of Fort St. George when Richard Benyon gave over charge to Nicholas Morse in January 1744 and sailed for England. In September the news reached India that King George had declared war against France. The news did not disturb the Governor and Council. Their fears in that quarter had not been raised even though the French had begun to interfere with their own weavers and to endeavour to deflect the trade from Madras to Pondicherry. The Mahrattas still occupied their attention; and between them and the difficulty of procuring goods for the next shipping season, Morse and his subordinates were too fully occupied to dream of the catastrophe which was looming in the distance. Had the suspicions of the Governor been raised they would have been allayed by Dupleix, who wrote to ask that peaceful relations might be preserved between the French and English trading Companies. He went so far as to suggest that a mutual agreement should be signed not to allow the war to interfere with the commercial affairs of the two nations in India.

1 5

CLIVE, DUPLEIX, THE CAPITULATION OF FORT ST. GEORGE TO THE FRENCH, 1746, AND ITS SIEGE BY LALLY IN 1758

At the south-east end of the Fort, close to St. Mary's church there is a block of buildings facing the sea, which now provides the younger officers of the garrison with quarters. Within this century the block has been partly demolished and the house at the north end has been rebuilt.[30] Several of the original houses in the row are intact; they are interesting because it was in Writer's Buildings, as the block was called, that Clive was first lodged when he arrived in Madras, May 31st, 1744.

Street Doorway in Writers' buildings

Robert Clive was the descendant of an old Shropshire family which traced its ancestry back to the times of Henry II. His father, Richard Clive, lived at Moreton Say, near Market Drayton, and married Rebecca, daughter of Nathaniel Gaskell of Manchester. Robert was his eldest son and he was born in 1725. He was brought up by his maternal aunt, Mrs. Bayley of Hope Hall, Manchester; and he seems from all accounts to have been a regular "broth of a boy." He could not have been more than seven when his uncle described his temper as fierce and imperious, and the child as "out of measure addicted to fighting".

He was sent to school at Market Drayton, and here he fully maintained the reputation his uncle has given him. But with all his mad and adventurous escapades he was always a gentleman. There was no spite nor malice about him; it was pure mischief. On one occasion the inhabitants of the town were horrified at seeing young Clive astride the water spout of the church tower. At another he was damming up a flowing gutter with his own body to cause an overflow into the shops.

He left England in 1743 and an unfortunate and perilous voyage to India. The ship was driven out of its course to the coast of Brazil, and Clive was obliged to remain there some months. He utilised the time by learning Portuguese, which he found extremely useful in India when he was dealing with the native troops, Portuguese being much more commonly spoken then than now.

He arrived in the roads in the hottest month of the year; and it is easy to imagine the disgust and depression which overcame him as he looked over the bulwarks of the ship at the dreary waste of sand, the glaring sea and the dazzling haze of the heat. He landed in a surf-boat and was put down on the beach with his personal baggage according to the custom of the day. There he was instantly surrounded by a noisy gang of coolies clamouring to be employed as porters and seizing his goods without ceremony. To this day the European finds it difficult to keep his temper when first setting his foot on India's coral strand, although the arrangements for landing have been vastly improved since Clive's time.

Clive had not far to walk; he waded ankle-deep over a belt of sand, and passing through the sea gate found himself within Fort St. George. The sentry at the gate could point out his new home, which was not fifty yards distant. His rooms faced the sea, but the Fort wall shut out the view as effectually as any prison wall; and the high-spirited, adventurous lad must have felt his heart sink deeper still as he contemplated the dreary prospect. There was the dull monotonous roar of the surf outside and the hoarse croaking of the carrion crows about his window, a brick wall as a view, and a fierce tropical sun overhead which he was already beginning to feel insupportable. The friend who was to have welcomed and received him, had left for England, and the disheartened lad was dependent on strangers.

He was at once told off to his duties, which were bookkeeping and office work. He loathed the desk and hated the confinement of the office. The monotony, the discipline and the heat affected his temper, and before long he fell out with the secretary under whose immediate control he came. His insubordination was reported to the Governor, and Clive had to apologise. The secretary was a good-natured man, and he felt sorry for the lonely homesick lad.

He accepted the apology and followed it up with an invitation to dinner. Still smarting under the apology which had been forced from him, Clive refused the invitation, adding that "the Governor did not command me to dine with you." It was in Writers Buildings that Clive, according to his own account, attempted to commit suicide. One of his young companions looked him up in his room and found him sitting in gloomy contemplation. Clive pointed to a pistol which lay on the table and asked his friend to fire it out of the window. He did so, and on its discharge Clive jumped up, exclaiming, "Well, I am reserved for something. That pistol I have twice snapped at my own head." In spite of his peppery temper Clive was very grateful for kindness shown to him, and it is probable that when he came to know some of his neighbours in the Fort his life grew brighter and the homesickness wore off.

Clive had arrived at the beginning of stirring times. The declaration of war with the French was followed by the appearance of British and French men-of-war off the Coromandel Coast. In 1745 the Governor of Pondicherry appealed to the Nabob of the Carnatic to enforce peace; but a year later when the French fleet had been augmented by the arrival of more war vessels, the French were no longer so anxious that the native ruler should restrain foreign powers from coming to blows within his jurisdiction. They themselves took the initiative, and a naval engagement of Negapatam was the result. The English hearing that preparations were being made to attack their settlements, called upon Nabob in their turn to restrain the French and maintain peace. But their appeal was to no purpose.

On August 18th, 1746, the French fleet appeared off Madras and cannonaded the Fort to the great terror of the inhabitants.

No harm was done, however, and the authorities looked confidently to the advent of the English ships to disperse their enemies. A fleet had been sent out for the express purpose of protecting the Company's ports. But it failed to appear. For reasons best known to himself, Commander Peyton sailed northwards to Bengal and left Madras to take care of itself.

Three weeks later the French fleet again made its appearance, this time commanded by De la Bourdonnais. An army, consisting of eleven hundred Europeans and eight hundred native troops with some heavy pieces of ordnance, was landed a few miles South of Madras to make an attack by land; whilst De la Bourdonnais proceeded with his ships to the roads. A bombardment was begun from the West and South which lasted a whole day. At the end of that time two English deputies were sent to treat with the French Commander. On September 10th, 1746, it was agreed that the Fort should be given up at once, Governor Morse and his Council being of the opinion that they could not withstand a general assault; and De la Bourdonnais promised faithfully, by a treaty which he signed a month later, that is should be restored in three months time for a ransom of £440,000. Orme says: "The capitulation was signed in the afternoon, when M. De la Bourdonnais, at the head of a large body of troops, marched to the gates, where he received the keys from the Governor. The French colours were immediately displayed; and at the same time, the English ship belonging to the East India Company, which lay in the roads, was taken possession of without resistance by the boats of the French squadron. There was not a man killed in the French camp during the siege; four or five Englishmen were killed in the town by explosion of the bombs, which likewise destroyed two or three houses."

The keys mentioned here are still at Pondicherry. When the French settlement was captured some years later by the English, the keys of Pondicherry were brought to Fort St. George, where they were retained until recent times. On the occasion of a visit made by one of the French Governors to Madras, he was shown the keys of Pondicherry. The Governor smiled as he looked at them, and quietly replied, "Ah! we, too, have the keys of Fort St.George at Pondicherry."

After the capitulation the French removed the merchandise, bullion, stores, ordnance and ammunition to Pondicherry to the value of nearly £200,000. (Some of the ordnance was recovered when the Fort of Chingleput was taken a few years later.) On De la Bourdonnais' departure Dupleix sent orders for the inhabitants of the Fort to be called together, and a manifesto was publicly read, repudiating the French Commander's treaty, and declaring it null and void. Those who were willing to take the oath of allegiance to the French King were told to leave the Fort in four day's time; and those who refused to swear allegiance were to be sent prisoners to Pondicherry. Amongst the latter were most of the military men, together with Clive and his friend Edmund Maskelyn. These two escaped from the Fort, disguised as Mahomedans, and found their way in safety to Fort St.David. Morse and some of his Council were sent to Pondicherry, where they were made to pass through the streets in a kind of procession which was felt to be unnecessarily humiliating. The French then plundered the houses in the Fort and behaved with great harshness and severity towards Europeans and natives alike. A great many of the English women and children had already been sent to Negapatam, where they were received kindly by the Dutch Governor; but most of the refugees found their way to Fort St. David at Cuddalore, which now became the seat of government on the Coromandel Coast;

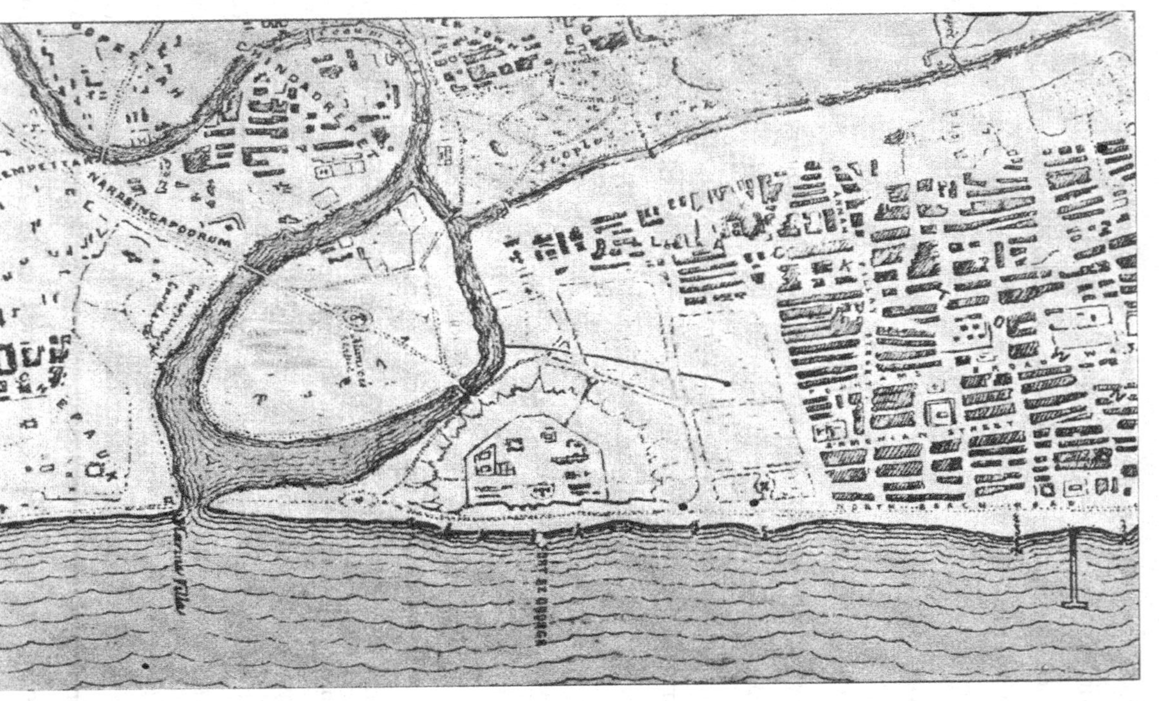

The Island, the Fort and Black Town

and there Morse arrived in due course of time with the remnant of the Company's servants; having been exchanged for French prisoners of war.

The French seem to have contemplated retaining Fort St. George permanently; for they set about its reconstruction at once. The native houses clustering near the North side and belonging chiefly to the Armenian merchants, were demolished, and a glacis was formed with the debris. The bastions and walls were enlarged and strengthened; and the place, though nothing like what it subsequently became, was stronger than it had ever been before. The interior of the Fort was left intact; and the records and books were fortunately preserved. At the restoration of Madras nearly all the records were returned to the English, but the gold plate on which was engraved the first treaty made by Francis Day with the Rajah of Chandragheri was missing. Amongst the records were the register books of St.Mary's, in all of which there is a gap of three years, from 1746 to 1749. The last burial took place in October 1746, and immediately following the entry is this note: "From this time Fort St. George, contrary to the articles of capitulation and agreement, was under the Government of the French, till the 21st of August, 1749, when it was restored by the articles of peace signed at Aix la Chapelle the latter end of the preceding year, and the Honourable Edward Boscawen, Rear Admiral of the White Squadron, General and Commander-in-Chief, on an expedition to the East Indies, took possession of this town and its dependencies the said 21st day of August 1749."

Morse was called to England to see the Directors during the French occupation. He returned to Madras after its restoration, but not to his former power, as the seat of government was still kept at

Cuddalore. He seems to have had an affection for the place, having been married at St. Mary's and had six of his children baptised there. He died in 1772, aged seventy-two, and was buried in the present St.Mary's cemetery on the island, which was opened in 1763 and which is still in use. A large monument marks his last resting-place.

In 1749, as the note above says, Admiral Boscawen[31] formally received the Fort back from the French and replaced the French flag with the Union Jack. It must have been rather a sad affair. The community was dispersed beyond recall, and property gone beyond recovery. The place was needed more as an asylum for sick sailors and a military depot than as a trading centre, and it took months to reform its constitution and restore order. The country was unsettled with war, and trade thoroughly dislocated.

On Clive's arrival at Cuddalore he was given a commission as Ensign and sent to serve his first military apprenticeship under Colonel Stringer Lawrence. Fighting was far more to his taste than bookkeeping, and it must have been with many regrets when at the conclusion of the war, he turned his back on field service and found himself once more within the walls of Fort St. George at its restoration. He relieved the monotony of garrison life by fighting with his fellow-officers, and soon after his return to Madras was the hero of a duel. He quarrelled over a game of cards in which he detected his companions in cheating. He refused to pay what he had lost and openly gave his reason. One of the young men sent him a challenge, which he accepted. They met without any seconds and Clive fired, missing his man. His antagonist, coming close up to him, held the pistol to his head and bade him beg for his life. Clive, quite unmoved, did so; he then demanded a retraction of the accusation which had led to the duel; this Clive refused, he then threatened to fire.

"Fire and be d-d to you," said Clive; "I said you cheated, and I say so still, and I will never pay you."

His antagonist threw down his pistol, exclaiming that Clive was mad, and so the affair ended.

He did not remain long in the Fort. His health, which was never good, had suffered in the campaign he had been through with Lawrence in the South, so the authorities sent him on a voyage to Bengal, and at the end of it he rejoined Lawrence to win fresh laurels at Trichinopoly. In 1752 he was again in Madras, and during this visit he was married in the Fort church to Miss Margaret Maskelyn, the sister of Edmund Maskelyn, his friend and companion in arms. After the marriage they are said to have lived in one of the houses opposite to Writers Buildings, but it was only for a short time as Clive's health was so undermined by all he had gone through, that he was obliged to take a voyage to England. Mrs. Clive made the best of wives and his marriage proved a lasting happiness.

In December 1749 Richard Prince became Deputy Governor of Fort St. Goerge and it was not till 1752, that the place was made the supreme seat of Government on the Coromandel Coast. Thomas Saunders was then appointed Governor. He had a difficult task before him both within and without. Within the Fort everything had to be reconstituted and reorganized, property claims had to be settled where deeds were lost, and justice administered. Without, everything was in the hands of the military, and in spite of the peace which had been made Dupliex was still struggling for the ascendancy, using as his cat's-paws the native rulers, and fighting in their names. In 1754 he claimed to have a letter of authority from the Moghul for settling the vexed question of trade and territory. Saunders was only too glad of the chance of putting an end to the unsatisfactory state of affairs, and nominated two deputies, Robert Palk[32] and Henry Vansittart, to meet a French deputation at Sadras. But in the middle of the proceedings it was discovered that the papers upon which Dupleix was acting were forged, consequently the meeting was broken up and negotiations were abruptly terminated. Saunders then wrote home to the Directors, saying that it was hopeless to attempt any settlement in India, and asking if it could not be managed by the Court. The result of his appeal was that M. Godeheu was sent out with power to negotiate, and Dupleix was recalled.

Godeheu was one of the Directors of the French East India Company and he lost no time in showing his friendliness to Saunders. His first act was to send back to Madras a Company of Swiss mercenaries who had been made prisoners by Dupleix; and this was followed by a correspondence between the two Governors, which ended in the signing of a provisional treaty establishing peace. By the articles of the treaty neither nation was to build forts, although places already fortified might be repaired. It was probably on this account that nothing was done to carry out Smith's and Knipe's plan of enlarging Fort St. George and adding new bastions. On the completion of the treaty, Saunders left for England, and the authority devolved upon George Pigot, a man of courage and resolution, who had already done good service for the Company.

In 1756 Pigot and his Council received an urgent appeal from Calcutta for troops to assist the English against the aggression of

Surajah Dowlah. The importance of the Bengal settlements was fully understood; to lose them would mean ruin to the Company. Pigot therefore sent Clive, who had returned to India as Governor of Fort St. David, with a portion of the Madras troops to Bengal. A few weeks after their departure news was received of the probability of war breaking out again with France, and of the dispatch of French troops for Pondicherry. Having barely recovered from their last trouble with the French, this news was not reassuring to the inhabitants of the Fort, and Pigot began at once to look to his fortifications. The plan of enlargement made by Smith and Knipe in 1743 was adopted, and four thousand coolies were engaged to execute the work without delay. The old riverbed flanking the West wall was filled in on the South West; the new wall was built and three new bastions were made. The largest of these was called the Royal Bastion from its superior size, a name it retains to this day. The Vauban system was introduced into the plan, and a glance at the maps will show that practically a new fort was erected, enclosing the old one.

It was anticipated that an attack, if made, would come from the West as before. Pigot therefore worked from the South along the West front towards the North, building wall and bastion, digging the moat, and pushing on night and day to get the fortifications into something like serviceable order. The improvements made in the time of the French were utilised, but the glacis they had formed was removed further out, to give more room for wall and bastion, and it was intended to make mines under the glacis had there been time.

In 1759, whilst the English were still hard at work at their building and construction, the news came that Lally had landed with his troops at Pondicherry, and that he had marched on Fort St. David and taken that place. It seemed therefore a mere matter of time before he would appear in front of the gates of Fort St. George. In November the fears of the English were realized, and they heard that he was advancing towards St.Thomas' Mount. Colonel Lawrence, who had already distinguished himself in the South with Clive, was in command of the Company's troops at the Mount. He fell back towards the Fort, feeling that he was not strong enough to contend with the superior number of the enemy. Lally followed him, but was not successful in bringing about a general engagement, and Lawrence with his men reached the Fort in safety, and slipped in on December 12th, 1759.

The gates were closed and a Council of War was called, for the siege had practically begun. Lally with his troops entered Blacktown and found quarters for themselves in some of the best native houses near the beach on the North side of the Fort. The unfortunate natives were terror-stricken. They came begging for admittance to the Fort, saying that the French troops were sacking and plundering their houses, and that they had discovered the arrack stores and were drinking themselves into madness. As the lives of the natives were not in jeopardy the authorities refused them admission, the Fort being already crowded; the Nabob of the Carnatic with his followers having sought an asylum there. The news of the disorder and drunkenness prevailing amongst Lally's troops induced the Governor to order a sally to be made, hoping the enemy might be dislodged and driven off. Some troops under Colonel Draper advanced upon the French. There was a sharp action in which the loss was about equal on both sides, and the English were obliged to return to the Fort without having affected their purpose.

The Nabob and his retinue, consisting of four hundred men and two hundred horses, were ill at ease in the besieged Fort; their quarters were necessarily cramped and rations were limited. The seaboard was still open to the English, and when the Governor offered to send the Nabob to Negapatam by a Dutch boat, he readily agreed to it. Under cover of night his embarkation was safely effected, and he was accompanied by a member of the Council. The Governor was very glad to get rid of this heavy charge on the commissariat of the Fort; he could not tell how long the siege would last, nor how long the sea would be open to the friendly shipping; at any moment the Fort might be blockaded by the French ships.

The fortifications on the North side of the Fort were incomplete on the arrival of the French. The moment they appeared the coolies ran away, and operations came to an abrupt termination. Whether it was on account of the works being unfinished on that side, or on account of the cover afforded by the houses of Blacktown, the French determined to attack the Fort from the North; and they set about building two batteries, one near the beach, the other further inland to the West, from which they intended to bombard the place. Whilst they were thus busy the English made some fruitless sallies which affected nothing and only brought loss of valuable lives.

On January 2nd, 1759, their batteries being completed, the French opened fire by throwing volleys of shells over the walls. They fell in the middle of the Fort, doing considerable damage to the buildings, and two went through the roof of the Fort House. The fire of the enemy was returned with vigour from the bastions, the English shells having good effect upon the new batteries. On the night of the 2nd several ladies and children were sent away from the Fort for safety, amongst them were Mrs. Morse and her daughter, Mrs. Henry Vansittart. Under cover of the darkness they were embarked in country surf-boats which were to carry them to Sadras, where they were confident that the friendly Dutch would give them an asylum till the troubles at the Fort were over. Two hours after their departure the news came that Sadras had fallen into the hands of the French. Arrived at their destination, the ladies landed, totally unaware of the change that had taken place in the fortunes of Sadras. The boats were immediately seized and loaded with gunpowder and military stores, and they were dispatched with the same boatmen to Blacktown, under guard of French soldiers. The ladies were not allowed to return with them, but were kept prisoners in Sadras, where they were treated with scant courtesy by their captors. At four o'clock the next morning the boats arrived off the Fort. The soldiers in charge of them were asleep, and the boatmen, whose language was not understood, freely discussed the situation amongst themselves. It was agreed to pour water into the firelocks of the troops and then seize the men and carry them round into the Fort. This was successfully accomplished, and the boats landed at the seagate. The boatmen were amply rewarded for their fidelity, but much anxiety was felt for the unfortunate women detained at Sadras.

Every morning the bombardment commenced regularly at daybreak, the shells being directed against the houses rather than the walls. The fire was always returned, and sallies were also made as well; but nothing was effected on either side beyond casualties amongst the troops. The damage done to the walls and bastions by day was repaired at night, and disabled guns and mortars were replaced from the arsenal. There was no sign of the English giving in, and Lally was beginning to lose his temper. Finding the bombardment ineffectual, he tried what mining would do, but with no better success. In the dead of night his workpeople were heard, and the English were prepared with their guns when the mine was sprung. The finances and commissariat of the Fort were still amply supplied; and in spite of the daily casualties amongst the troops from cannonballs and the bursting of shells, the courage and good spirits of the garrison were maintained. Pigot visited the works every day and did much towards keeping up their spirits by his brave martial bearing, and he did not spare himself; he also went on board the ship that lay in the roads, where he was slightly wounded by the bursting of one of the enemy's shells. He had Col. S. Lawrence and Col. Draper to advise and help him in his councils of war; and never once did he dream of submitting.

Lally was far from being at ease himself. His exchequer was low and the treasury at Pondicherry was empty. His officers, many of whom were Irishmen like himself, and men were dissatisfied, and alienated by his violent temper. His ammunition was getting short and would have to be replenished before he could assault the Fort or hope to take it. His unpopularity amongst the sepoys was even greater than with the Europeans; his overbearing manner towards them made them thoroughly disaffected. On February 15th news was brought that a body of sepoys at Tripasore Fort had mutinied and were plundering the country. The provisions of the French army came through Tripasore, and on the receipt of the information there was a general demand from Lally's subordinates to abandon the siege. He refused to listen, and the following morning the bombardment was renewed as severely as before. In the evening of that day six English ships were seen making for the roads. There could be no doubt what those ships brought. With provisions cut off, ammunition running short and the enemy reinforced, he recognised at last that it was useless to continue the siege.

At daybreak on February 17th, the glorious news spread through the Fort that the whole of the French army was moving southwards in the direction of St. Thomas' Mount. By noon the ships had landed their troops, and all fears for the safety of the Fort were at an end. The siege was over and the excitement and joy were intense. The gates were opened and the brave little community that had so valorously withstood the enemy, answering shot for shot, and patiently repairing each breach as it was made, issued through the gates on sightseeing intent, free to come and go once more as it chose. Quite a crowd of sightseers visited the batteries which had so lately been pouring forth shot and shell at them. The cannon still remained scarcely cool from use; and ammunition laid strewn about, left behind for want of means of transport. The saddest sight of all was the hospital. Here they found forty-four French soldiers who were left to the mercy of the long-suffering enemy. A letter from Lally to the English Governor commended them to the care of the latter, a trust Pigot did not betray.

The Fort was a sad wreck to look upon; the joy of the besieged at their emancipation must have been damped by the sight of its ruin. There was scarcely a house on the North and North East side of the place which was not unroofed and a mere shell; and all the old buildings erected by the earliest settlers were destroyed beyond repair. The church of St. Mary's was fortunately not seriously injured, it being (except the magazine) almost the only bombproof building in the place. It had been used as a barrack during the siege, with the consent of the Vestry. From its steeple, which was struck more than once by shot, an outlook had been kept over the surrounding country during the siege; the watchers had had the mortification of seeing the Government House near the Cooum partly demolished, and the village of Chepank close by destroyed by fire. But in spite of the destruction wrought by the enemy, the prevailing feeling was one of joy at the happy termination of the affair. Henry Vansittart, one of the Council, thus describes it in a letter sent to Clive in March 1759.

"I am very glad to begin with acquainting you that the siege of Madras is raised. Certainly it was an undertaking too great for M. Lally's force, and it was undoubtedly a want of men that obliged him to confine his approaches to so narrow a front. I will send you a plan of them as soon as I can find one of our engineers at leisure. The trenches are the weakest that ever were seen, and yet they pushed them close up under our nose. Three or four times small detachments sallied and took possession of the head of their sap almost without resistance. Our people retired after destroying a little of the work, and then the enemy returned and worked on. Their grand battery, the first that they opened, tore our works a good deal, but our men were active and got them repaired in the night. This continued for a few days, but our fire was not decreased. The enemy then lost patience, and advanced with all our defences in good order; when they got to the foot of the glacis, they erected a battery against the east face of the north ravelin, but they could never stand there for an hour together, as we had a heavy fire both on their flank and front. In three or four days they abandoned that, but still kept pushing on their sap, and presently got up to the crest of the glacis, where they erected another battery close to the north-east angle of the covered way. This cost them very dear, and they well deserved to suffer; for all our defences were yet perfect, nay, we had more guns than we had at first.

"For six mornings running they opened this battery at daybreak, and were obliged in an hour or two to shut up their embrasures. Their loss must have been very great; for it was raked from one end to the other by the flank of the Royal bastion, had a front fire from the north-east bastion, and was overlooked by the demi-bastion so with musketry that it was impossible for a man to live. At the end of six days they gave it up, and at the same time, I believe, gave up all hopes of success. It is true they had opened a narrow passage through the counterscarp of the ditch by a mine, and had beat down so much clay from the face of the demi-bastion, that there was a slope that a nimble man might run up, and that is what M. Lally calls a breach; but his people were wiser than he, if he proposed to assault it, and they refused. That letter of M. Lally's is a most curious piece. I am glad it was intercepted, that he may not say the arrival of the ships obliged him to raise the siege, and that the officers and men of the garrison may have the honour they deserve. Their duty was really severe, and what was yet worse, they had not a safe place to rest in when off duty; for there is not a bombproof lodgement in garrison, except the grand magazine, and the casemates under the Nabob's bastion, where the sick and wounded lay. Nevertheless there was a universal cheerfulness from the beginning to the end; and (what M. Lally so much expected) a capitulation never entered, I believe, into the head of any one man of the garrison.

"I believe I shall be obliged to apply to you to lay hands on some of the Chandanagore ladies, in order to exchange against Mrs. Morse, Mrs. Vansittart, and some others, whom we sent away in a boat to Sadras, just at the time that M. Lally borrowed that settlement from the Dutch. They were received by the French officer, and told that they were prisoners. They have been kept there ever since; and two days after the siege was raised I wrote to M. Lally, desiring he would let me know his resolution concerning my family; he sent back the peon without an answer, nor have I got one yet. All this I could excuse if they had but been treated with politeness; but it has been far otherwise, as you will see by a letter I lately received from Mrs. Vansittart, and which I send enclosed. I beg you will let Carnac explain it to the French ladies at Bengal, that they may see, with thankfulness, the different usage they have met with."

Lally was an Irishman by birth, of an excitable and violent disposition. He had attached himself to the Stuart cause and he took service under the French. He gained his laurels at Fontenoy, and seemed at one time likely to add to them in India. But after the siege misfortune dogged his footsteps. When Pondicherry was taken by the English in 1761 Lally was made prisoner and sent to England. From there he found his way to France, where he was arrested, tried for mismanagement of the campaign in India, and beheaded in 1766.[33]

16

PIGOT, CORNWALLIS, MUNRO, AND OTHERS

The story of Fort St. George from this period is no longer that of a fortified trading-station on a foreign shore; it is the history of a garrison and a military centre. The peace-at-any-price merchant was disappearing; and in his place was springing up the warrior and the politician. As the victorious arms of the English gathered district after district and town after town under the rule of the Honourable East India Company during the next half century, the entire aspect of affairs altered throughout the length and breadth of British India. The Company still traded, but parts of its princely revenues were now derived from its lands.

As the new Fort rose upon the old with its enlarged area, its barracks in place of private houses, its offices, its strong walls and bastions, so a new administration arose on the old, and a political power reigned instead of a commercial power. The same change

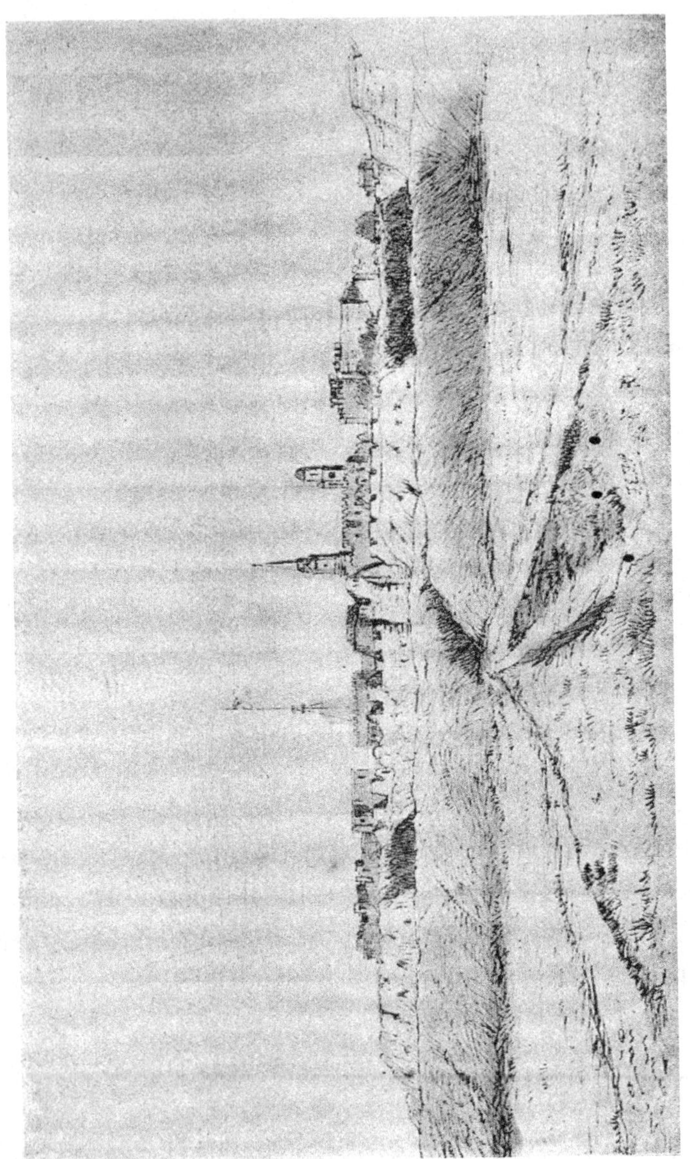

Fort St. George as it appeared after the Siege, 1759

was going on in the other Presidencies. It was not done in a year, nor was a new Fort St. George built in a day, but matters were none the less surely progressing towards that end. The story of the Fort therefore from this period is virtually the history of the Presidency, which has still to be written. In the Record Room, once the banqueting hall—built at this period and adorned with the porphyry pillars taken from Dupleix's palace at Pondicherry—there are hundreds of volumes of matter which the student will one day sift for materials for such a book. There he will find the details of the early growth and development of the political administration of Madras. There, too, he will find a host of names which are scarcely known to fame, because the clash of the sword did not ring above their heads. Yet the men who bore them added their quota to the Empire—making every whit as much as the warrior, whose deeds of valour shine through the pages of history. Many of them, like the pioneers of Company, sacrificed their lives to the climate and rest in graves within sight of the Fort.

On the departure of the French, Pigot set about the restoration of the place with vigour. Barracks were built where the old houses formerly stood; many of the merchants retired to Blacktown, or to the garden houses, which were once more safe as residences. The Fort House had to be rebuilt as well as the banqueting hall; during the rebuilding the Council held its sittings in the large room on the first floor of the Exchange, now occupied by the Regiment as a Mess house. Government House on the Cooum was restored and added to; but its banqueting hall was not erected until the end of the century. The house which today is the General Hospital, near to the Central Station, was built as a storehouse for the Company's goods some time during the latter part of the eighteenth century. The work of restoration was placed in the hands of Paul Benfield, a man who was fully qualified to do it as far as the building was concerned, and who was not limited in the matter of expense. The books show that enormous sums were paid to him without his rendering any account of how he was spending the money; but posterity can see that the work was done effectually, whatever might have been the price paid for it.

On the departure of the inhabitants to their garden houses the Fort was filled with soldiers, sailor, and sepoys. The register books give an idea as to their numbers. St. Mary's was still the only church in Madras. The marriages and baptisms continued much the same in number; but the burials were augmented to four times the usual amount. Each year that passed they increased, till in August 1781 the total for the month reached seventy-two, and the total of interments for that year was five hundred and twenty-six. In the following year, 1782, the total reached six hundred and fifty-seven, the largest number of burials in one day being ten. They were mostly soldiers and seamen. The latter were landed as invalids from the ships cruising upon the coast, carrying troops and assisting in the military operations which were progressing on land. Seamen were subject to scurvy and epidemics in those days, due to bad food and water, and probably a want of sanitation. Besides the Europeans of the garrison there were also sepoys quartered in Fort, and every casemate beneath the ramparts that could be spared was utilized as a barrack-room. The crowding of the Fort with so large a garrison and all the attendant followers did not conduce to its healthiness, and the troops suffered as well as the seamen. The greatest enemy to the Europeans was the sun, aided by the intoxicating arrack of the country. Beside the poison contained in the spirit, its deadly effect on the brain deprived its victim of all

View from Government Road, Chepauk Park

prudence, and he fell by the roadside in drunken sleep; the pitiless Indian sun completing the deadly work the arrack had begun.

Pigot remained on as Governor until the year 1763, and was instrumental in the creation of the Madras Army. In conjunction with such warriors as Lawrence, Clive, Calliaud, Joseph Smith, Coote and others, he laboured to lay its foundation, knowing that the safety of the Company's property and territory depended upon such a body. He prided himself on his military knowledge after conducting the successful defence of the Fort during the siege, and considered himself half a soldier. His contemporaries speak of him as an able and honest man; he was the personal friend of Clive. In 1765 he returned to England, taking with him a fortune of £400,000 which he had accumulated in his long service in India. With a portion of it he purchased an Irish peerage and became Lord Pigot.

On Pigot's departure there was a succession of Governors who, under the old conditions, would probably have fulfilled their duties as effectively as their merchant predecessors. But circumstances demanded something more than the man of the bureau. The English rule, as has been said, was passing through a transition state in India, which was sufficient to turn the heads of the Directors at home, and to throw every man in India who was not a "Heaven-born General" like Clive, or a politician like Cornwallis, off his balance. Even Clive found it difficult to guide and control. Less able men were unable to control at all; they too often ranged themselves on the other side, and joined in the tide of plunder and corruption. The abuses which crept in were different from those of the old days, and money was made in all sorts of ways unknown before. Military men raised regiments by contract; civilians took contracts for building; appointments were

Government house from the Glacis

bought and sold, and everywhere the hand was open to receive present and perquisite. Wherever money passed there some of it stuck, until it became a crying scandal throughout the British possessions. Pigot had seen the beginning of it, and his successors found themselves in the thick of it.

In 1763 Robert Palk, who was in Deacon's Orders and came out as a chaplain to the Fort, but afterwards dropped his Holy Orders for the more lucrative service of the Company, became Governor. His name occurs frequently in the St. Mary's registers, performing baptisms, marriages and burials soon after the restoration of the Fort to Admiral Boscawen. He was succeeded by Charles Bourchier in 1767, Josias Du Pré in 1770 and Alexander Wynch in 1773. All these men found the work of governing beyond their strength; they were imbued with the notion that native princes must be subsidised with troops as well as money, and the consequence was that the Company soon became involved in war. In Dupre's time Hyder Ally dictated terms of peace at St. Thomas' Mount to the Governor and Council, who placed themselves at his mercy. And in Wynch's time Tanjore was unblushingly handed over by the Company's troops to the Nabob. The Directors thought it was time to interfere; and they recalled Wynch. Remembering the good service done by Pigot, they turned in their perplexity to their old servant, and asked him to stand once more at the helm. Twelve years had passed since he left the country and he was no longer a young man. But the brave spirit did not quail; he accepted the appointment and set sail for the East.

He could scarcely have realised the many changes which had taken place, nor the corruptions that had crept in during his absence, or he would never have undertaken the task. His military brothers-in-arms who had stood by him in the old days were gone. Joseph Smith, now General, had retired full of honours; Lawrence had just died in England; and a stranger, Sir Robert Fletcher, ruled with a high hand as Commander-in-Chief. By this time there were a good many of the King's troops in the country besides those belonging to the Company, and friction had already sprung up between them and the civil authorities. The Company considered that the King's troops, lent to them and in their pay, were under their command, but the King's officers took a different view, and chose to ignore the authority of the Governor and Council in the conduct of military affairs. Sir Robert Fletcher was a man of the contentious disposition; from his earliest days he had given trouble by his insubordination, "and as a Lieutenant he had been dismissed, but he was reinstated through the kind offices of Eyre Coote who recognised the soldier in him. On Pigot's arrival Fletcher assumed to himself the power of acting independently of the Council as Commander-in-Chief, and drew up certain instructions for one of his officers to carry out at Tanjore. He requested the Governor in Council to consider these instructions; Lord Pigot, feeling that he was being dictated to, refused to do it, and he followed up his refusal by ordering the arrest of Sir Robert Fletcher and two of the Council. At the same time Benfield laid a claim against the revenues of Tanjore, and demanded the enormous sum of twenty-three lacs of rupees (£230000) for money lent to the Nabob, though how he became possessed of such a sum he did not say. Pigot refused to allow it as he considered it fraudulent; but several of the members of Council, being personally interested in the claim, supported Benfield, and procured a majority in his favour. The majority took action on behalf of Sir Robert Fletcher, and arranged for Pigot's arrest. As the Governor was returning from the Council Chamber in the Fort to Government House, his carriage was stopped by the Adjutant-General, Lieutenant Colonel Edington, and Captain Lysaght. Colonel Stuart, who was sitting by the side of Pigot, and of whom the Governor entertained no suspicions, stepped out of the carriage and asked Captain Lysaght to take his place. Pigot was then driven straight to St.Thomas' Mount where he was left in the custody of Mathew Horne, Major of the Artillery, and commanding the station. The trouble into which the brave old Governor had fallen preyed upon his spirits; and with excitement and infirmity his health failed. The surgeon at the Mount ordered his removal back to Government House on the Cooum. Pigot seemed unable to rally, and in May, 1777, he died there. He was buried in a nameless grave inside St. Mary's Church. A plain slab engraved with a cross and the words "In Memoriam" is the inadequate and only memorial to mark the last resting-place of a man who saw Fort St. George through a crisis in its existence, and who helped to lay the foundation of that bulwark of the Presidency, the Madras Army. His name was cleared of all imputations; and the charges made by his enemies against him of enriching himself fraudulently were amply refuted. It was in his endeavours to suppress the very fault he was charged with that he made himself enemies.

Pigot came out to India as a Writer in 1736; he was taken prisoner with Morse in 1746 by the French. He was the last of the old style of merchant Governors, of whom Master and Yale were amongst the first of any importance. He was excellent in his time, and nothing better was needed so long as the Fort was merely a trading centre. But when he returned as Governor the second time, he was out of date and a consequent failure, as were the few insignificant men who attempted to hold the reins of government during the next five years. It is impossible to put back the hands of the clock even for Governors. Pigot's reputation was high and safe till he was tempted to plunge into politics a second time, and contend with younger men and with younger ideas. His fall is pathetic, his death from chagrin most sad; for in spite of his failure to rule new men and new ideas, he was distinctly in the middle of the century a capable and high-spirited Governor.

At the death of Pigot the Directors prohibited all mercantile dealings on the part of their servants in India and raised their salaries to compensate them for the loss occasioned by such a rule; but it was not till Cornwallis, time that the rule was vigorously enforced throughout the country.

Pigot was succeeded by Sir Thomas Rumbold who arrived in 1778; and Whitehill held the reins in the interval. Rumbold did his best, but he was not strong enough for such troublous times. All kinds of accusations were levelled against him, which further investigation proved to be false; he was weak rather than unfaithful in his trust; unwise but not dishonest. Hastings, who was Governor General, lost all patience with him, however, and he was dismissed in 1781. Lord Macartney succeeded him. In his time Sir Eyre Coote died in Madras. The brave old warrior was buried there, and his burial is entered in the St. Mary's register book. A little later his body was sent to England to find a resting-place amongst his ancestors.

Early in 1786 Lord Cornwallis was made Governor General, and from this date order was evolved out of chaos. Clive and Hastings had done their part in adding territory to territory and Lord Cornwallis brought the whole under an orderly administration. Marshman says:

"To the task of reform Lord Cornwallis applied himself with the greatest assiduity. He hunted out frauds in every department, and abolished jobbing agencies, and contracts and sinecures. His greatest difficulty arose from the importunity of men of power and influence in England, who had been in the habit of quartering their friends and kindred, and even their victims of the gaming-table, on the revenues of India. But the Governor General was inexorable, and he had the courage to decline the recommendations of the Prince of Wales himself, afterwards George the Fourth, who, as he remarked, "was always pressing some infamous and unjustifiable job on him". These reforms, however, were not consummated till he had convinced the Court of Directors of the truth, which Clive and Hastings had in vain pressed on them, that 'it was not good economy to put men into places of great confidence, where they have it in their power to make their fortunes in a few months, without giving them adequate salaries". The Court parted with the traditional policy of two centuries with great reluctance; but Lord Cornwallis at length succeeded in annexing liberal salaries to these offices; and in giving gentlemen a prospect of acquiring by economy a moderate fortune from the saving of their allowances".

At the end of 1790 Cornwallis went down from Bengal to Madras to superintend the war against Tippoo, and one of his first successes was the capture of Bangalore, when Colonel Joseph Moorhouse was killed. Moorhouse is said to have risen from the ranks; he was as gallant a soldier as ever stepped. He was married at the Fort Church; and there is a monument to his memory in St. Mary's describing how he fell in the moment of victory at the gates of the town. The capture of Seringapatam followed that of Bangalore, and Tippoo's power was broken; Cornwallis made peace on his own terms and returned to Bengal to continue his work. He settled the land revenue and reformed the civil and criminal courts; one of his ablest coadjutors was Sir George Barlow, Governor of Madras, who afterwards became Governor General.

A statue of Cornwallis by Thomas Banks, London, 1799, stands in the barrack square under a canopy in front of the Secretariat. It is larger than life, and the head is uncovered. Round its base are four panels, one of which contains the following inscription:- "This statue is erected by a general vote, at the joint expense of the principal inhabitants of Madras, and of the Civil and Military Servants of the East India Company, belonging to the Presidency of Fort St. George, as a grateful testimony of the high sense they entertain of the conduct and actions of the Most Noble the Marquis Cornwallis during the time he held the high offices of Governor General and Commander-in-Chief of all the forces in India." On two others, there are single figures of Britannia and the Angel of Victory. On the fourth there is a scene in bas-relief representing the giving up of the young Mysore Princess to Cornwallis. A group of British officers stand behind the Marquis, one of them being a civilian and another a particularly good figure of an officer of the Madras Artillery.

In a semicircle before the statue are five guns, one taken at Seringapatam, two of Portuguese make and two Danish. The Seringapatam gun is highly ornamental, the muzzle representing the open mouth of a tiger. The Portuguese guns have the Royal Coat of Arms of Portugal on the breach near the touchhole.

In 1785 Sir John Burgoyne died in Madras and was buried in St. Mary's church. He was an officer in the King's service; like

Sir Robert Fletcher and several others in a similar position, he refused to acknowledge the authority of the Company, and endeavoured to act independently of the Governor and Council. The consequence was a rupture and the recall of Burgoyne, who, however, did not live to return to England.

It is impossible to mention all the able men whose names were associated during the 19th century with Madras. The chiefest amongst them is Sir Thomas Munro, whose remains lie in the church. The story of his life and work has been ably told by Dr. John Bradshaw, late of the Educational Department, Madras, in the "Rulers of India" series, and it is not necessary to recapitulate Munro's deeds. He was born in 1761, and was the son of a Glasgow merchant who traded with America. He combined the politician with the warrior in his person, and was the ablest man of all those who stood at the head of affairs in the Madras Presidency. In his early days he knew what it was to rough it up-country, as the following extract from one of his letters to his sister, dated 1788, will show:

"I have often wished that you were transported for a few hours into my room, to be cured of your Western notions of Eastern luxury, to witness the forlorn condition of old bachelor Indian officers, and to give them also some comfort in a consolatory fragment. You seem to think that they live like those satraps that you have read of in plays; and that I in particular hold my state in prodigious splendour and magnificence... that I never go abroad unless upon an elephant, surrounded with a crowd of slaves... that I am arrayed in silken robes, and that most of my time is spent in reclining on a sofa, listening to soft music while I am fanned by my officious pages; or in dreams, like Richard, under a canopy of state. But while you rejoice in my imaginary greatness, I am most likely stretched out on a mat instead of my regal couch; or walking in an old coat and a ragged shirt in the noonday sun, instead of looking down from my elephant invested in my royal garments.

"You may believe me when I tell you that I never experienced hunger or thirst, fatigue or poverty, till I came to India,—that since then, I have frequently met with the first three, and that the last has been my constant companion. If you wish for proofs, here they are. I was three years in India before I was master of any other pillow than a book or a cartridge pouch. My bed was a piece of canvas stretched on four sticks, whose only ornament was the great coat that I brought from England, which, by a lucky invention, I turned into a blanket in the cold weather by thrusting my legs into the sleeves, and drawing the skirts over my head. In this situation I lay like Falstaff in the basket, hilt to point, and very comfortable, I assure you, all but my feet; for the tailor, not having foreseen the various uses to which this piece of dress would be applied, had cut the cloth so short, that I never could, with all my ingenuity, bring both ends under cover; whatever I gained by drawing up my legs, I lost by exposing my neck; and I generally chose rather to cool my heels than my head. This bed served me till Alexander went last to Bengal, when he gave me a Europe camp-couch. On this great occasion, I bought a pillow and a carpet to lay under me, but the unfortunate curtains were condemned to make pillowcases and towels; and now for the first time in India I laid my head on a pillow.

"But this was too much good fortune to bear with moderation; I began to grow proud, and resolved to live in great style: for this purpose I bought two tablespoons and two teaspoons, and another chair,—for I had but one before—a table and two tablecloths. But my prosperity was of short duration, for in less than three months I lost three of my spoons, and one of my chairs was broken by one of John Napier's companions. This great blow reduced me to my original obscurity from which all my attempts to emerge have hitherto proved in vain.

"My dress has not been more splendid than my furniture, I have never been able to keep it all of a piece; it grows tattered in one quarter while I am establishing funds to repair it in another; and my coat is in danger of losing the sleeves whilst I am pulling it off to try on a new waistcoat.

"My travelling expeditions have never been performed with much grandeur or ease. My only conveyance is an old horse, who is now so weak that in all my journeys I am obliged to walk two-thirds of the way; and if he were to die, I would give my kingdom for another and find nobody to accept my offer. Till I came here I hardly knew what walking was. I have often walked from sunrise to sunset, without any other refreshment than a drink of water; and I have traversed on foot in different directions almost every part of the country between Vizagapatam and Madura, a distance of eight hundred miles".

Munro retained many of his old habits contracted from the life described above until his death. He was always partial to old clothes, and the cue of his wig was often tied with a piece of red tape. One of his favourite amusements was throwing stones, a trick he learnt as a schoolboy. In 1827 he was anxious to get home as the climate was telling upon him. He was tempted to pay a farewell visit to the Ceded

Districts where he had ruled, as Collector in 1800. Cholera was rife and it seized him at Putticondah. He was buried at Gooty and his body was afterwards removed to the Fort, where it was interred in a vault inside the church in 1831, with military honours. The Bishop of Calcutta read the service. Heber, who knew him personally, described him as a fine dignified old soldier. By a curious fate his historian, Dr. Bradshaw, who visited Putticondah and Gooty to verify his historical facts, was seized with the very disease which proved so fatal to Munro, and died on his return to Madras.

In 1814, on Christmas day; Vice Admiral Sir Samuel Hood, Commander-in-Chief of H.M. fleet in the East Indies, was buried in the centre aisle of St. Mary's Church. He distinguished himself by the bloodless capture of the Island of St. Lucia, which was held by the French in 1803. The French Fleet was occupying the Bay; Hood, like the Irish peasant, trailed the tail of his coat before the Frenchmen so effectively that he tempted the fleet to come out for the purpose of giving him battle. Having got the enemy clear of the Bay, he slipped in behind them, and they dared not follow. He was thus left master of the island, which relied entirely on its naval defence for protection, and its possession was confirmed to England in 1814.

Lord Cornwallis had set himself to reform abuses which he found rife in the Government of the country, but there were other evils yearly increasing which he could not grapple with even had he been so minded. Society was lax enough in England in the Georgian era, but in a foreign country, which possessed no moral public opinion at all, matters became much worse, and Englishmen allowed themselves an unbounded licence as a kind of compensation for their life of exile. There was a certain percentage of men who did not follow in the stream of pleasure; who married wives and lived decently. But English women were not plentiful, and many men found it easier to form liaisons with native and Eurasian women than to procure a suitable wife of their own class. These unions resulted in a large increase to the Eurasian population. A great many children were brought to the font and their baptisms were recorded under names to which they had no legal right.

Such a state of affairs was distressing to the Clergy. Schwartz and Pohle worked indefatigably amongst the garrison of Trichinopoly, persuading the soldiers to marry, baptising their heathen consorts and providing means of educating their children. The Clergy of Madras also did what they could to improve matters, but the task has ever been found difficult. Frequently the mothers and their children were deserted or else left destitute through the misfortunes of war. In such cases, the orphanages, supported by the charitable, provided a home and education for the waifs. In the case of the wealthy suitable provision was usually made by the father.

The Revd. Richard Hall Kerr, who was Chaplain at Fort St. George at the end of the eighteenth century, laboured hard amongst the growing Eurasian population, hunting up the children, bringing them in batches to be baptised, and seeing that those who were old enough to attend school were sent. He came out to India like Robert Palk and Benjamin Millingchamp, two former Chaplains, in Deacons' Orders; and he received his appointment from Sir Charles Oakley, the Governor, which was an irregular proceeding. When there was a prospect of his being in sole charge of the Fort Church many people objected to his appointment. He solved the difficulty by returning to England where he received Priests' Orders,

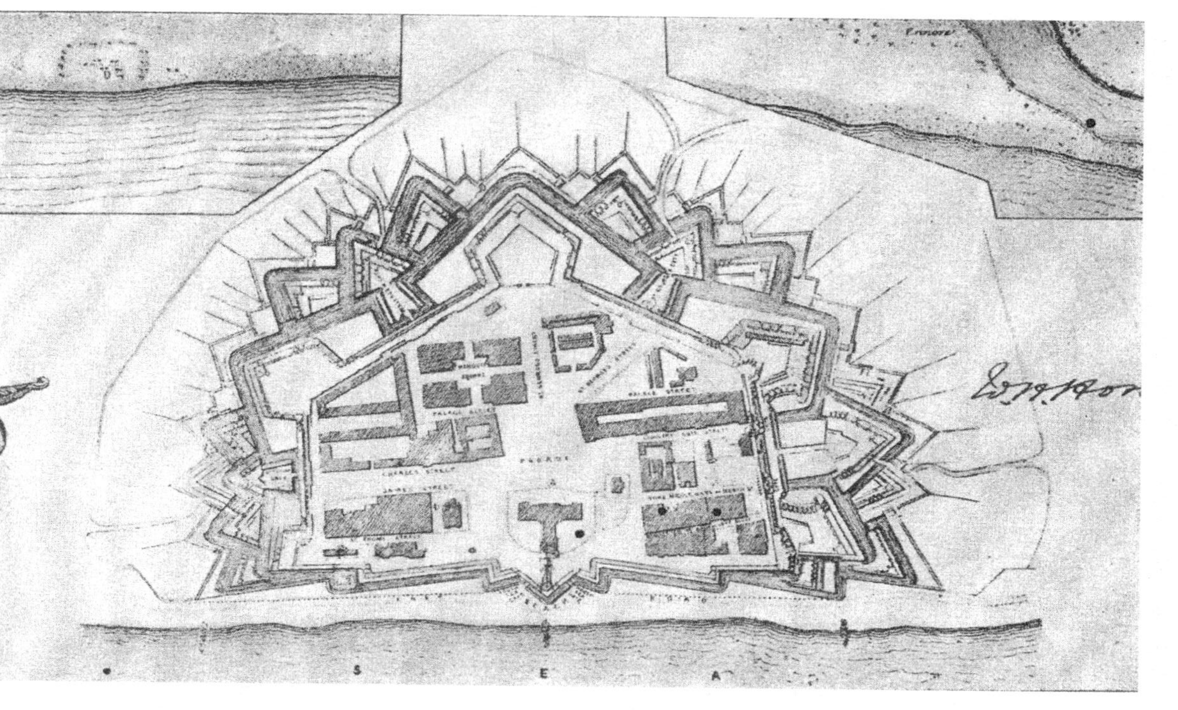

Fort St. George in 1862

and got his appointment confirmed by the Directors. He came back to the Fort and preached a crusade against the evils of the day, sparing neither rich nor poor.

Amongst his many good works was the superintendence of the Male Asylum. It had been the custom to apprentice the boys as a means of providing them with a trade. Kerr was not satisfied with the result, and he was anxious to add an industrial department to the School. The Government gave him no encouragement; he therefore embarked his own capital in setting up a printing press. In 1799 he was able to present the sum of one thousand pagodas to the School out of the profits. This was the foundation of the Lawrence Asylum Printing Press where all the Government papers are printed. Kerr was instrumental in building a chapel of ease in Blacktown for the use of Eurasians. It was the second Anglican church for English service which was raised in Madras. It was opened in 1800, and its founder was laid to rest within its walls in 1808 at the age of thirty-nine.

Kerr urged the Directors in view of the laxity of morals to increase the number of Chaplains, and through his exertions may be said to have been initiated the Ecclesiastical Establishment of Madras. His preaching was not without effect on the English community; and he was held in the highest esteem by Sir Charles Oakley and his successor, Lord William Bentinck, and also by Sir Thomas Strange, the Chief Justice.

17

FORT ST. GEORGE IN THE PRESENT DAY

Fort St. George as it now appears at the end of the nineteenth century is entirely different from the original Fort projected by Francis Day in 1640. The walls, bastions, and gates have all been rebuilt, and the houses on the North and North West side, where the first settlers lived, have disappeared entirely. So also has the Roman Catholic church which was served by the two French Capuchin friars in the early days. During the siege of 1750 the Roman Catholics were discovered to have signalled to the French from their church tower, and directly after the siege the church was levelled to the ground, and the Roman priests were dismissed. The church of St. Mary's and the substantial houses to the South of it, built nearly half a century after the foundation of the Fort, are the oldest existing buildings in the place. The Mess houses near the Council chamber, and the adjacent bombproof storeroom come next. The latter was once used as a theatre, and still contains the stage with its trapdoor and its orchestra pit. There is not

St. Thomé Gate

a window in the room, and when filled with an audience it must have been little short of the Black Hole of Calcutta.

Many of the private dwellings have been turned into public offices, which are busy during the day with the scribbling shaven-headed native clerks, and are wrapped in silence at night. Amongst the officers permitted to live in the Fort are those serving with the troops quartered in the barracks; the Surgeon, the Chaplain, and the Assistant Adjutant General. The A.A.G. has a fine house near the Wallajah Gate, which was formerly occupied by the Town Major, an important individual in his day. The office of Town Major was created in the year 1755, and his duties corresponded with those of the A.A.G. in the present day. Captain Timothy Bridges was the First Town Major. The appointment was abolished in 1860 when the command of the garrison of the Fort was given up by Sir Charles Trevelyan, the Governor, to Sir Patrick Grand, the Commander-in-Chief.

The handsome barracks to the right on entering St. George's Gate have been built in recent years; they replaced some low wretched buildings utterly inadequate to the requirements of troops, if they were to be kept healthy and free from disease. The basement of the old barracks was below the level of the ground, and the rooms were small and airless. Up to the middle of this century the Battery of Artillery was quartered in the casemates near St.George's Gate; these were, if anything, worse than the old barracks, being shut off entirely from the sea breeze.

The Fort is entered by six gates. The Sea Gate is on the East, where in the earliest times all business was transacted between the servants of the Company and the natives. On the bastion above it

St. George's Inner Gate

stands the flagstaff which signals each ship as she comes into harbour; the office of signaller is hereditary. The St. Thomé Gate is in the South Wall and it leads to the new garrison hospital. The Wallajah and St. George's Gates are on the West, where formerly there was only one, the Fort Gate, which was in the old Fort wall—done away with at the enlargement. On the North are the Choultry Gate—bricked up and no longer used, and Middle Gate; the latter is now called the North Gate. At each gate there is a drawbridge over the moat, a terror to the inexperienced horse when his ears are assailed by the thunder of his iron-shod hoofs on the wooden platform as he crosses to enter the low, deep gateway.

Life in the Fort is curiously unlike the usual experience of the Anglo-Indian. The houses open on to the streets as in an English town, and are without garden or compound. The bugle sounds in the barrack square, and groups of Englishmen move hither and thither on duty or pleasure intent. Towards sunset the voices of soldiers' children, sturdy boys and girls, pale-faced, but British to the backbone, are heard as they run from the married quarters by St. George's Gate to play on the sands outside the Sea Gate. Yet English as the scene is, India cannot be forgotten, for at the magazines stand the sepoy sentries supplied from the native Regiment quartered three miles away near Perambore; at the heels of the English children follow ayahs instead of the nurse-girl; and moving in a stream Westward to the turbaned clerks from the offices. The Fort frequently re-echoes with the tramp of the mounted Bodyguard and the clatter of wheels as his Excellency the Governor drives down from Government House to the Council Chamber; and long after dark the lights in the Secretariat testify to the diligence of the hard-worked Under Secretaries, who are helping to govern an Empire on the spot, where two centuries ago their merchant

Sea Gate

forebears thought of nothing else but the dispatch of cargoes, and the pacification of blackmailing native princes.

On the broad width of the walls and bastions where the big guns lie wrapped in their tarpaulin covers, the grass springs up green and feathery after the welcome rain; and a beautiful sea convolvulus with pale mauve blossoms throws its green mantle at the feet of the cruel implements of war. Tiny pimpernels and wind-blown mouse-ear push their heads through the grass towards the sun, to add their mite to the beautifying of the walls. There are trees within the Fort, chiefly banyan and margosa, which give the landscape of street and wall and sky another welcome splash of green. Minas and sparrows chatter amongst the branches, and the coppersmith barbet, hidden deep in the glossy foliage, tink-tinks the whole day long in absolute security. On roof and wall the rooks and carrion-crows caw and croak incessantly, telling news in the morning, as the natives say, and clamouring for food after gunfire at noon. They are vulgar familiar birds, always conversing in loud coarse notes, when they are not employed in foraging in the dustbins or gulping down a land crab. Occasionally the soft hooh-hooe of the hoopoe is heard as he searches in the crannies of the masonry with his long curved bill for a morning meal. He disdains to be seen on the same side of the street with the quarrelsome mina and the impudent sparrow, but he does not object to the small grey squirrel, to whom nothing comes amiss, from a white ant to a nut. The glossy chestnut plumage, the beautiful black crest and the mottled wings of the hoopoe give him the palm for beauty amongst all the birds of the Fort. After rain the dainty little black robin with his mouse-coloured mate deigns to honour the ramparts with his presence; but he is shy and nervous. Even the sheltering body of the great machine gun does not give him confidence, and he never ventures on a song. He is a fastidious bird and he reserves himself for the concert platform of the Eucharis lilies and roses in the gardens inland where he has his home. The most charming of all the birds of the Fort is the wagtail. They build in the chinks and crevices of the brick walls of the moat, where the water-plants spring up to hide the nest. The proud bird pours forth his song, half lark and half canary in sound, to the rising and setting sun. His family cares come upon his graceful shoulders twice a year, and his song is never ending, sweeter than the call of the bugle, sweeter than the strains of the organ in the church close by, or the band as it plays on the Island, the sweetest thing within the Fort. High above wall and bastion hover the kites and fishing birds of prey; now and then a long-legged paddy-bird or a gull crosses the sky in its flight, but none of these are to be seen lingering on the ramparts; they are mere passers-by. So are the butterflies, which, tempted by the blossom of the grass and convolvulus, flutter over the walls in the midday sunshine, making momentary colour-patches on the grey cement. They come and go on the sea breeze which wafts them inland with the robins to the shelter of the gardens.

Outside the Fort there is always the sea in all its varying moods and shades; deep indigo under the stiff sea breeze, green-grey under the lowering sky of the North East monsoon, and intense azure blue in a morning calm, when the monsoon, has spent its fury and emptied its water-laden clouds. At night the long line of breaking surf is marked in phosphorescent light; by day it is a dazzling white as it beats upon the long stretch of sandy beach. The black hulls of the steamers plough their way, rough or smooth, through the waves to the harbour, and the sound of their siren call for the pilot mingles with the caw of the rooks, the call of the bugles and the song of the wagtails. In old days when the white wings of the sailing vessels were seen instead of the black smoke of the funnel, a gun announced the arrival of a ship as it dropped its anchor in the roads. There was no harbour then, nor even a pier, or apology for a breakwater. The ships tossed at anchor in the open roads, and discharged passengers and cargo into the rough surf-boats of the country.

The earliest scheme for a pier was formulated by Captain Lennon in 1803, and an attempt was made to deepen the mouth of the Cooum so as to bring the ships up the river; but it was found impossible from the rapid silting of the sand and the absence of any stream from the Cooum. The Military Board did not encourage the scheme; the reason given was that any pier or harbour would facilitate the landing of an enemy and destroy one of the best defences of Fort St. George. The Board of Trade put forward a still more frivolous objection; they said that the boatmen would be deprived of the means of existence if anything of the kind were built. The matter was dropped until 1835, when Captain Cotton, (Sir Arthur,) designed a breakwater which was partly carried out, but had to be abandoned in the face of such a surf as the North East monsoon produced. In 1875 the present harbour was planned, and built on laterite with concrete blocks made in Madras. There were many difficulties to contend with, and the work was partially destroyed by a cyclone during the course of its construction. It took years to complete, but success crowned its promoters' efforts at last, and it has proved an immense saving in time, expense, and damage to goods by seawater.

As a place abounding in historical interest the Fort, which can no longer be called impregnable, is full of charms—only as yet half explored—to the student of the Honourable East India Company's story.

18

THE MONUMENTS OF THE OLD CEMETERY

The old cemetery of St. Mary's lies outside the Fort on the North, beyond the glacis, where the Law Courts now stand. The Monuments, which with three exceptions no longer exist, were large cenotaphs of brick and mortar with nothing architecturally beautiful to recommend them. There was no limit then to size, and no Government regulations to insure the order, which marks the Anglo-Indian burial ground of today. Masonry was cheap, and it seemed as though the mourner endeavoured to show the magnitude of his grief by the dimensions of the monument. In consequence, many of the erections partook more of the nature of small temples than tombs, and they became the haunts of all kinds of men and animals. The burial ground was open to the public, and there idlers, beggars and vendors of fruit and sweet-meats congregated to loaf and sleep and eat, sheltering themselves in the tombs from the sun by day and the dews by night. Even herdsmen with their goats and buffaloes joined the throng.

Sewage farm on the beach, looking inland from the Marina

Bridge over the Cooum near Government House

Cooum river, looking toward the sea from
Government road, Chepauk

At last it became a disgrace to the English community, and efforts were made to do away with the abuse. In 1758 Lally, the French General, made use of the monuments as a cover when he was attacking the Fort. On his departure they were all levelled with the exception of the three already mentioned, one of them containing the memorial slab erected by Elihu Yale to his only son David. Many of the stones were broken by the shot fired from the Fort at the French, but those which were worthy of preservation were placed as a pavement on the North side of St. Mary's church, where they may still be seen. The earliest were roughly engraved with incised lettering without any ornamentation; but at the end of the seventeenth century, the Dutch method of raised letters was adopted. Handsome floral borders were carved in relief round the edge of the stones, and an attempt was made to reproduce the arms and crests of the families, with rich floral embellishment. The stone used was a grey-black granite or gneiss, which was at first brought from the Island of Johanna, on the coast of Africa. It was afterwards found in South India, and quarried near Madras. When rough-hewn it is a cool grey, but it assumes a marble blackness under the polisher's tool, which makes it preferable to ordinary granite for ornamental work. The following is a list of the names on the stones.

AISLABIE, JOHN; son of William Aislabie, Esq. General of India and grandson of John and Carolina Burniston. (There is no date, but the Burial Register gives the date of burial as June 9th, 1708.)

ALFORD; (A fragment of a stone to the memory of the first and second wives of Henry Alford, one of the Company's Servants. He married Elizabeth Mellish in Nov: 1681; she died in Feb: 1682, and in Feb: 1683 he married Elizabeth Lott. She died in Aug:1687.

Richard Browne, Esq.

Noah Casamayor

In 1688 he married a third wife, Elizabeth Brereton. Henry Adolf died in May 1692 and his widow married Mathew Empson the following year.)

ALVERGARIA, MARIA SOARES DE; daughter of Anto: Soares de Alvergeria and Francesca Ribiera. She died Jan: 12th, 1712, aged forty years and three months.

ATKINSON, ROBERT; Gunner of the Garrison for many years. He died Aug: 27th, 1711, in his forty-seventh year. (He married Elizabeth Holt in 1693, and secondly, Elizabeth Goodman in 1706.)

ATKINSON, CHARLES; son of Robert, who died Dec: 22nd, 1714, aged about seventeen years.

AUBONE, THOMAS; Commander of the "James and Mary," died Aug: 19th, 1725, in his forty-ninth year. (In 1683 the name occurs in the Records and it is spelt Aubonee; he is there called an Interloper.)

BAKER, ELIZABETH; wife of Aaron Baker, President of the English Company of Merchants. She died Aug: 5th, 1652. (Baker was the first President and Governor of Fort St. George; he arrived by the "Roebuck" Sep: 1st, 1652.)

BARKER, JOHN; he died Dec: 4th, 1707. Also Robert; Mary; Fran; John; Francis; Timothy; Nathaniel; Anne and Benjamin. Also John and Francis his grandchildren. (*See* Ribiera. John Barker succeeded Ralph Ord as Schoolmaster in 1682. The stone bears no dates except the one given, and no ages.)

BARRY, STEPHEN; died Sep: 8th, 1719, about twenty-four years old. (He is entered in the Burial Register as Stephen Berry, Merchant.)

BETT, FRANCIS; Merchant; he died Dec: 14th, 1701. (He was a Writer in the Company's service in 1685 and was stationed at Masulipatam).

BOONE, JANE; daughter of Daniel Chardin and wife of Charles Boone. She died in childbirth Nov: 28th, 1710. (She was baptised at St. Mary's in Nov: 1687. She married first Joseph Lister in March 1704, and secondly Charles Boone in June 1709.)

BRABOURN, JOHN; the son of John Brabourn, Esq., deceased; he died May 13th, 1710.

BRABOURN, DEBORAH; the daughter of the above John; she died May 15th, 1708. (John Brabourn married Ann Bright in June 1705, and their son John was baptised in Nov: 1706. Brabourn was Chief at Anjengo. When Burniston of the Bombay Council died in 1704. Brabourn was called upto take his place; but not being satisfied with his prospective colleagues he declined the promotion and came to Madras from which place he returned to Anjengo.)

BROOKS, EDWARD; died Nov: 19th, 1722, in his fifty-fourth year.

BROOKE, WILLIAM; Captain. March 20th, 1700–1. (The Burial Register styles him mariner.)

BROWN, SAMUEL; died Dec: 21st, 1698. (He was one of the Company's Surgeons. In 1693 he accidentally poisoned, to his great distress, James Wheeler, a Member of Council, by preparing a medicine of powdered pearl in a mortar where arsenic had been pounded. He married Ann Baker in June 1688. In 1700 Mrs. Brown married John Foquet, a Member of Council.)

BROWN, SAMUEL; son of the above Samuel and Ann, and brother of Elizabeth, Mrs. Charles Long. He died July 5th, 1695.

BROWN, RICHARD; Chief of Vizagapatam, Esq., died Jan: 26th 1690–1. (The Register calls him merchant.)

BULKLEY, EDWARD; Surgeon in the Company's service; he died in Aug: 1714.

BURNISTON, CAROLINA; relict of John Burniston, deceased, Deputy Governor of the Island of Bombay. She died July 11th, 1708. (Her name is entered in the Register as Buriston. *See* Aislabie and Scattergood, her grandsons.)

CARVALHO, JOHN; The Father of widows and orphans and Defender of the Poor. He died Jan: 13th, 1733. (There is no entry in the Burial Register.)

CASAMAJOR, NOAH; died Sep: 4th, 1746, aged forty-five years. (He married Rebecca Powney in June 1736, and is entered in the Burial Register as Factor and Registrar of the Mayor's Court. His eldest son, James Henry, was baptised in St. Mary's church. *See* Church Monuments; Russell. Mrs. Casamajor was the daughter of Captain John Powney and his wife Mary Heron, and she was baptised in Sep: 1715.)

CHARDIN, DANIEL; merchant and inhabitant of this place, and a native of France. He died Sep: 7th, 1709. (He was the brother of Sir John Chardin and the father of Jane Boone. Mary Lovise (of Louise) Chardin married Henry Devonport, (sometimes written Davenport,) in Feb: 1707 and died in Dec: 1712. She was buried in the old cemetery although her name is not inscribed on the Chardin Tombstone.

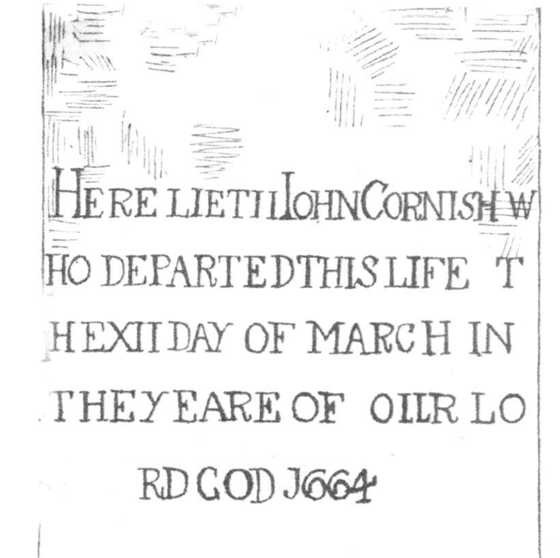

Stone removed from the old cemetery to church compound

Thomas Clarke, who called himself one of the first inhabitants of the Fort came from Masulipatam. The stone was probably broken by a cannon-ball when standing in its original position in the old cemetery.

Daniel's wife was a French woman; she survived her husband and sailed for England in Jan: 1714, in company with Devonport, Boone and Brabourn. She was styled Madame Chardin in the list of passengers, and she took her "family" with her, probably her grandchildren.

CLARKE, THOMAS; son of Thomas Clarke, Agent to the English Company of Merchants at Masulipatam. He died Oct: 6th, 1683. (He was Interpreter to the Company. There is no entry of his burial in the Register.)

COOKE, MR. FRANCIS; he served the Company for twelve years as Merchant and Assay-Master; he died Feb: 1711–12, aged thirty-nine years.

CORNISH, JOHN; died March 12th, 1664. (No age mentioned.)

COTERELL, JOHN; died Dec: 19th, 1724, aged fifty-one years. (His name is entered in the Burial Register as John Cothel; he is called Cotterell and Cottrell in the Records.)

COYLE DE BARNEVAL, ANTHONY; he was of good birth and was born in the County of Clare in Ireland. He belonged to "the Catholic Religion"; and died in the year 1724.

CRADOCK, THOMAS; son of Christopher and Florentina Cradock; he died Aug: 13th, 1712, in his fourth year. (Christopher Cradock married Florentina Charleton in April, 1707. Their son Christopher was baptised in 1710 and he married Grace Cook in 1736. *See* Warre and Wynch. In 1735, Christopher Cradock commanded the Royal George, one of the Company's ships.)

CRAWFORD, HENRY; Merchant, died Jan: 26th, 1741, aged fifty-three. (He is entered in the Burial Register as a free-merchant. He married Ann Plumb or Plumbe, in 1730.)

DE TORRES, PETER; a native of Homscot in Belgium; died in Aug: 1694, aged sixty-three. (His estate was administered by a Dutchman in the service of the Dutch East India Company.)

ELLIS, FRANCIS, ESQ.; He served the Company many years in Bengal, and died Second in Council at Madras on March 6th, 1703–4.

ENGLISH, RICHARD; he died Sep: 1st, 1729 in his twenty-seventh year. (His name is on the same stone as that of Oadham, to whom he was related by marriage. He was in the Company's service and married Rebecca Fullagar in May 1729.)

FLEETWOOD, EDWARD; a merchant of good family. He died Feb: 16th, 1711–12, aged forty-four.

FLEETWOOD, MARGERY; died Aug: 3rd, 1711, aged three years. (*See* Poirier. Edward Fleetwood married Mary Caryl in March 1694, and their daughter Mary, baptised May 22nd, 1703, married Richard Benyon in October 1724; Benyon afterwards became Governor of Madras.)

FOQUET, ANN; She was the widow of Samuel Brown, and married John Foquet or Focquett; she died Sep: 2nd, 1715.

FORD, EDMUND: Captain; died May 21st, 1711, aged thirty-nine years. (His name is on the same stone as that of John Lawrence. Edmund Ford married Elizabeth Lux in June 1700.)

Antonius Coyle de Barnaval

Note—The legend on the de Barnaval coat of arms is *superius vires mea.* The imapaled coat is an engrailed shield of ermine.

Edward Fleetwood

Arms of Lady Goldsborough engraved on large silver bason fitting into the Font.

Also on the silver flagon.

FOWKE, ANNE; wife of Randall Fowke. She lived twenty-one years with her husband and died Aug: 3rd, 1734, aged fifty years.

FOWKE, RANDALL; he was forty years in the service of the Company and many years in the Council. He died Oct: 2nd, 1745, aged seventy-two. (He married Anne May in Dec: 1713. *See* Walsh.)

FOXCROFT, NATHANIEL; son of George Foxcroft, Agent and Governor of Fort St. George. He was born Sep: 6th, 1635, and died Oct: 26th, 1670. (His name is not in the Burial Register which begins only in 1680.)

FULLAGAR, JOHN; he died May 10th, 1727, in his twenty-seventh year. (He was in the Company's service and he married Rebecca Floyer in April 1724. *See* English.)

FULLERTON, ALEXANDER; Captain. He was born in Argyleshire in 1683, and he died March 11th, 1723. (He was Captain of a Company of Foot in 1709.)

FREEMAN, ROBERT; Merchant in the Company's service and sometime Chief of Metchlepatam (Masulipatam.) He was afterwards in the Council of Fort St. George. He died Feb: 7th, 1688. (The stone is a fragment, but intelligible with the assistance of the Burial Register.)

GOODWIN, MARY; wife of Cornelius Goodwin and daughter of Captain John Bowney. She died Nov: 19th, 1742, aged twenty-three years and seven months. (She was baptised at the Fort May 12th, 1718, and she was married Oct: 24th, 1741. Her monument remains in its original position over the vault or grave, and stands in what is now the compound of the High Court Buildings.)

GOULDING, JOHN; he was a native of London and in the Company's service. He died June 28th, 1738, aged forty-two years. (The stone bears a long and laudatory inscription in Latin, setting forth his many virtues, and his utility to the two Governors under whom he served— George Morton Pitt and Richard Benyon. The Burial Register describes him simply as "Gunner of this place.")

GRAY, MR. THOMAS; Junior. One of the Council. He died Aug: 6th, 1692, in the twenty-third year of his age. (Thomas Gray married Frances English at St. Thomas' Mount, July 1690.)

GREENHILL, HENRY; he belonged to the English Company of Merchants and died in 1658. (The name occurs in the Register and Records later on, and a Henry Greenhill was buried in June 1691.)

GRIFFIN, MARY; wife of William Griffin. She died in childbirth June 26th, 1720, aged thirty-nine.

GRIFFIN, WILLIAM; Cooper of Madras. He died Sep: 30th, 1722, aged forty-two. (Master Cooper of the Company was one of the lesser appointments, as also were Master Carpenter and Master Bricklayer.)

HAINES, JOB; the son of John Haines and Mary, his wife; born Dec: 30th, 168—and died April 16th, 1687. (The stone is a fragment. Haynes died at Fort St. David, and in 1712 his estate was administered for the benefit of his children by Mr. Heriot, his son-in-law. Robert Heriod married Elizabeth Hayns, June 29th, 1710.)

HASTINGS, FRANCIS. (The stone contains nothing but the name and the letters M.S.; there is no date. It is supposed to cover a vault where the body actually rests. Hastings was serving the Company in 1701 and he died in 1720.)

Mr. Thomas Gray, Junior

Henry Greenhill

David Murray, late of Edinburgh—arms worn
away by footsteps

HEATON, SAMUEL; Captain. He died Dec: 21st, 1708, in his thirty-eighth year.

HEATON, JANE; wife of Samuel Heaton. She died in childbirth April 25th, 1701, aged twenty-one years. (Samuel Heaton married (1) Jane Gibson, June 20th, 1700. (2) Judith Paine, Aug: 1704.)

HENRIQUES, MARIA; daughter of Emmanuele Henriques and Felippa Botelha.

HERON, GEORGE; Captain: born July 1646 and died May 2nd, 1727, aged eighty-one years. (His name is amongst the earliest mentioned in the Records of Fort St.George. He commanded one of the Company's ships, the "Arrival", in 1676, and he was one of the first pilots of the Hugly.).

HIGGINSON, RICHARD; son of Nathaniel Higginson, Esq., formerly Governor of Fort St. George; he died in the thirty-second year of his age, being then seventh in Council, June 7th, 1726. (Nathaniel Higginson married Elizabeth Richardson in May 1692, and their son Richard was baptised in may 1695. He is entered in the Burial Register as Mr. Higginson, a Councillor.)

HOPKINS, CHARLES; he died March 5th, 1711, aged fifty-three. The monument was erected by his son in 1739.

HYNMERS, JOSEPH; he served the Company several years and died Second in Council, May 28th, 1680. (His widow married Elihu Yale, and two of his children, Benjamin and Elford Hynmers, were sent to England on Captain Goldsborough's ship in Oct: 1685. Joseph Hynmers, Junior, was in the Company's service, and he left it in 1698 to trade as a free merchant. He died at Fort St. David in 1703.)

Isaac; an Armenian Merchant. (No date.)

Jennings, Elizabeth; wife of William Jennings, Esq., Second in Council. She died in childbirth Feb: 7th, 1718–19, aged thirty. She left issue one son by her former husband, Mr. Robert Wrighte; and two sons and two daughters by the said William Jennings, Esq., [William Jennings married (1) Elizabeth Wrighte in 1711, and (2) Deborah Higginson in July 1724.]

King, Robert; third son of Robert King, Esq. of Blackberry End in the county of Hertford. He was in the Company's service and died April 15th, 1723, aged twenty years.

Lawrence, John; died Jan: 17th, 1720–1. (He married Martha Owen in May 1717. The name is spelt Lawrence in the Register. *See* Ford.)

Large, Mr. Peter; Merchant. He lived thirty-nine years in India and died March 29th, 1694, in his seventieth year. (Peter Large was living in the Fort as a freeman in 1684 with his wife, who was an Englishwoman.)

Legg, Hannah; the wife of John Legg, Esq., one of the Council and Mayor of Madras. She died in childbirth July 27th, 1717, in the twenty-third year of her age. She was the daughter of Francis Seaton by his wife Hannah Mackrith. She was baptised July 1695, and was married Feb: 1713. *See* Seaton.)

Lewis, Louisa; (A fragment with the Latin inscription to the memory of the wife of George Lewis, who was Chaplain of Fort St. George. She died July 16th, 1707. George Lewis married Lovise Poirier, July 14th, 1702. Her name is entered in the Burial Register as Lovise Lewis. Lewis returned to England in Jan: 1714.)

Lister Joseph; he was in the Company's service, but asked to be allowed to leave it and trade as a free merchant. He is described simply as merchant on his monument. He died March 14th, 1706–7, in his thirty-eighth year. (He married Jane Chardin. *See* Boone.)

Long, Charles; son of Charles and Elizabeth Long; he died June 5th, 1730. (The Revd. Charles Long was Chaplain of the Fort in 1715. *See* Brown)

Lucas, Dorothy; the wife of Thomas Lucas. She died April 8th, 1685. Also in memory of her two children by her former husband Charles Proby, Catherine and Elizabeth Proby. Also to her two children by her second husband, Thomas Lucas, Jane and Thomas Lucas. (No dates nor ages given. Thomas Lucas commanded the Company's troops at the proclamation of King James II. He was afterwards a member of Council.)

Maubert, John; diamond merchant. He was in Madras eleven years and intended returning to England in 1722. He died Oct: 15th, 1721, aged about thirty-seven. (Maubert resigned the Company's service in 1715)

Marques, Francysco; died Aug: 23rd, 1687.

Marshall, Thomas; died May 28th, 1701, aged twenty-eight years. (There is no entry of his burial in the Register; he was married at the Fort Church in October 1698, to Dorothy Ward, and a Dorothy Marshall was buried May 19th, 1701.)

Melique, Frances; daughter of Louis Melique de Antonia Pestanha. She died Jan: 16th, 1720, aged seventeen years.

MEVERELL, ANN; wife of Samuel Meverell. She died April 18th, 1689.

MEVERELL, MARY; daughter of Samuel and Ann Meverell. (She was baptised and buried on the same day, April 18th, 1689).

MICHELL, EDWARD; He was the son of—Michell of Chiltern in the county of Wilts, Esq.; and was nine years in the Company's service. He died June 6th, 1741, in the twenty-eighth year of his age.

MIDON, BERNARD; a native of Witsen in Germany. He married D.M. Sequeira, and died Dec: 28th, 1689.

MURIELL, LUCY; wife of Mr. Francis Muriell, free merchant. She died July 22nd, 1755, in the twientieth year of her age. (Her name is entered in the Burial Register as Murrell.)

MURRAY, DAVID; late of Edinburgh. He was chief Gunner of the Garrisson and died Oct: 22nd, 1732, in the forty-fifth year of his age.

OADHAM, CATESBY; Fourth in Council, Mayor and Assay-Master of Fort St. George. He died March 5th, 1722–3, in the thirty-sixth year of his age. (Catesby Oadham married Mary English in Oct: 1717.)

OADHAM, MATHEW; he died June 22nd, 1725, in the twenty-sixth year of his age.

OATES, TITUS; son of Samuel and Mary Oates of Yarmouth. Pilot of the Bengal river. He died June 3rd, 1723, in the forty-fifth year of his age. (He is entered in the Register as Captain Titus Oates. buried May 29th.)

PARHAM, MARY; relict of Captain John Parham, mariner; and eldest daughter of Stephen Poirier, Esq., Governor of the Island of St. Helena. She died Jan: 8th, 1700–1. (She was married in Nov: 1698.)

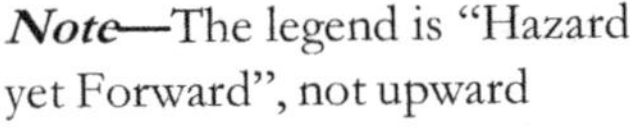

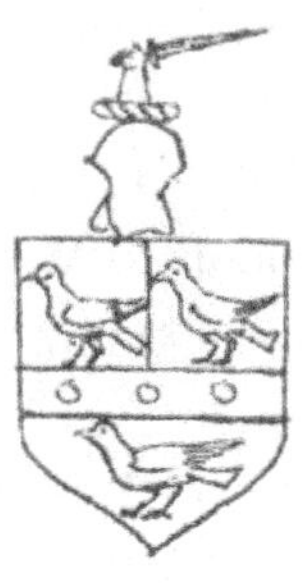

Titus Oates

Ann wife of Francis Seaton Captn. of the Grenadiers

Note—The legend is "Hazard yet Forward", not upward

Joseph Walsh

Martha Skingle

Curious design in relief on stone to the memory of Diana daughter of John and Elizabeth Styleman

PARAO, NARCIZA IGNACIA; daughter of Ioao Paroa. She died Dec: 10th, 1742, aged fourteen years.

PEARSON, BATTSON; he died Nov: 22nd, 1697. (The Burial Register states that he was drowned, and the Records say that his body was recovered at Covelong, on the coast, and was brought into Madras for burial.)

PLUMB, THOMAS; Merchant, died March 17th, 1711–12, aged fifty years.

PLUMB, VIOLANTE; wife of Thomas Plumb. She died Jan: 16th, 1713–14, aged forty-two.

PLUMB, ANN; daughter of William and Ann Plumb. She died Oct: 12th, 1739, aged twelve years. (Henry Crawford's name is on the same stone as that of the Plumb family.)

POIRIER, GABRIEL; Captain. He served the Company seventeen years in military employment and died July 1716, in the forty-sixth year of his age. (*See* Parham.)

POIRIER, LUCY; wife of Gabriel Poirier, and daughter of Robert Fleetwood, formerly Chief of Masulipatam. She died Oct: 20th, 1712, aged forty-eight years. [She married (1) John Field, (2) George Croke, Sep: 25th, 1689, and (3) Gabriel Poirier in June 1699. The Records state that she claimed the property of her husbands, John Field and George Croke.]

POWNEY, JOHN; Captain ; died Sep: 10th, 1740, aged fifty-seven years. (He was in the Company's service, in command of one of their ships, in 1717, and he married Mary Heron, Feb: 15th, 1706.)

POWNEY, JOSEPH; died April 15th, 1725, aged ten years and ten months.

POWNEY, GEORGE; eldest brother of Joseph Powney. He died Dec: 8th, 1732, aged twenty-five years. (He was the son of John and Mary Powney and was baptised Jan: 7th 1708.)

POWNEY, JAMES; born June 30th, 1734, and died July 6th in the same year. (He was the son of Captain John Powney and Mary his wife, and was baptised on the day of his death. The Powney inscriptions are on a tomb in the High Court enclosure where the bodies lie.)

PYE, ELEANOR; relict of Captain John Pye. She died Jan: 1st 1743, aged forty-eight years. (She is entered in the Burial Register as School Mistress, and her signature is to be found in the Vestry cash book, attached to the receipt for the salary of the Mistress of the St. Mary's Charity School. Ann Pye married Foss Westcott, a merchant, in May 1743, and her jointure was administered by the St. Mary's Vestry.)

RIBEIRA, DOMINGAS; legitimate daughter of Antonio Ribeira and Sebastian Roiz, widow of John Barker. She died Sep: 18th, 1719, aged sixty-nine. (*See* Barker. Her name is not in the Burial Register.)

ROBSON, THOMAS; he was chief surgeon of Fort St. George for eleven years. He died May 6th, 1720. (He married Diana Bridges in Feb: 1709, and in 1718 he received the estate of the late Richard Bridges, who married Diana Baggs May 13th, 1693.)

ROBSON, CHRISTOPHER; son of Thomas and Diana. He died in Oct: 1720. (He is entered in the Burial Register as Robertson, Oct: 29th, but is called Robson in the records.)

RUSH, FRANCIS; late Ensign. (He married Mary Johnson in 1722, and she married for her second husband, John Holme, in Jan: 1731.)

SABAN, PETER LUDER; he died August 8th, 1719, aged twenty-one. (He is entered in the Burial Register as Peter Lubee, the Governor's servant.)

SCARLETT, KATHERINE; the daughter of Mr. John Scarlett, merchant in London. She died April 23rd, 1685, in the seventeenth year of her age.

SCATTERGOOD, JOHN; son of John Scattergood, Merchant. He died an infant about 1708. (John, son of John and Arabella Scattergood and baptised June 15th, 1709, and was buried Oct: 10th of the same year. John married Arabella Forbe in August 1706.)

SEATON, HANNAH; wife of Captain Francis Seaton. She died Feb: 3rd, 1709–10. (There are some verses on her memorial stone, the initial letters of each line form her name. Francis Seaton married Hannah Mackrith as his second wife in Feb: 1693.)

SEATON, ANNE; wife of Francis Seaton, Chaplain of the Grenadiers of the Garrison. She died May 16th, 1691.

SEATON, ELIHU; son of Francis and Anne. He died May 3rd, 1691.

SEATON, FRANCIS; son of Francis and Anne. He died May 1st, 1692.

SKINGLE, MARTHA; and her daughter Sarah, "of whom she died in childbed", August 29th, 1711, aged thirty-one. (Martha was the wife of Richard Skingle, a Factor in the Company's service.)

SMART, JOSEPH; Merchant in the Company's service in several stations and Fifth in Council. He died Dec: 13th, 1715, aged about thirty years.

SMITH, RICHARD; died Oct: 23rd, 1712. (His estate was paid to his sister and her husband in England in 1717.)

SMITH, WILLIAM; Surgeon. He died Jan: 9th, 1721–22, aged about twenty-five years.

STUBS, ANNE; daughter of John Stubs of London, merchant. She died Oct: 3rd, 1701, aged sixteen years, eleven months and seventeen days. (A Thomas Stubs came out in the Company's service in 1683 and was associated with Ord in Sumatra.)

STYLEMAN, DIANA; daughter of John and Elizabeth Styleman. She died in March 1685–6, aged five months. (John Styleman was living in the Fort as a freeman in 1683; he must have joined the Company soon afterwards, for he was on the Council of Madras in 1694. His wife was an Englishwoman. He had sisters as well as children with him at the Fort, and in Feb: 1688 he gave Elizabeth Styleman in marriage to Armiger Gostling who in 1667 was commanding the Company's ship "James".)

TAINTER, CHARLES; he died Dec: 29th, 1697.

TORRIANO, GEORGE; Esq., late of Council. He died May 16th, 1741, aged forty-one.

TORRIANO, SUSANNAH CATHERINA; wife of George Torriano. She died Sep: 15th, 1741, aged thirty-seven years. (George Torriano married

Susanna Catherine de Dorpere; in April 1725. George was the son of Nathaniel Torriano. He left issue.)

TRENCHFIELD, ROBERT; (He was in the service of the Company and died Oct: 3rd, 1699.) The stone is a fragment, and on it are also the names of the following.

TRENCHFIELD, THOMAS; the son of Richard and Elizabeth Trenchfield. He was baptised July 25th, 1692, and was buried Oct: 26th, 1696.

TRENCHFIELD, JUDITH; daughter of Richard and Elizabeth Trenchfield. She was baptised Nov: 7th, 1693, and was buried Oct: 26th, 1696.

TURNER, JOHN; son of Nathaniel and Elizabeth Turner; and infant. He died Sep: 21st, 1721–2. (Nathaniel Turner married Elizabeth Farmer in July 1717. He was in the Company's service.)

TURTON, JOHN; he served the company nine years and was youngest in Council when he died, April 5th, 1720, aged about twenty-seven years.

WALSH, JOSEPH; he died June 2nd, 1731, aged thirty-seven years. He was the son of Enoch Walsh and his wife, Elizabeth Child, who were married in 1690. Joseph was baptised in Nov: 1694, and he married Elizabeth Maskelyne in Dec: 1720. His daughter Elizabeth was baptised in Sep: 1731 and married Joseph Fowke in May 1750. Enoch Walsh was in the Company's service in Bombay, but he was removed from there on account of various complaints made against him of debt and inattention to the Company's affairs. In 1702 he fought a duel with Ralph Hartley, who was severely, though not mortally, wounded. Joseph Fowke was the son of Randal and Ann Fowke. He was baptised in Oct: 1716.)

Warre, William; Armiger; he died Third in Council May 6th, 1715, aged about thirty-five years. [He married (1) Ann Nicks in May 1704, and (2) Florentia Cradock in March 1715. See Cradock. Ann Nicks was the daughter of John Nicks who married Catherine Barker, Nov: 11th, 1680. Ann was baptised April 22nd, 1689 and was buried March 27th, 1711. John Nicks was in the Company's service and went out to India in 1668. He had nine daughters and one son baptised at the Fort; the latter died in Dec: 1686. Mrs. Catherine Nicks died at Madras in Dec: 1709, and John Nicks, March 14th, 1711.]

Wendey, Francis; died in March 1725. (There were two Chaplains of this name at the Fort; the Revd. James Wendey in 1698, and the Revd. Thomas Wendey in 1719. The latter married Frances Johnson in Oct: 1724.)

Wigmore, Thomas; Merchant. He was in the Company's service several years and died May 10th, 1708, in his fortieth year. (He married Ann Maesfen in Jan: 1700.)

Williams, Anthony; Captain; a Briton. He died Nov: 8th, 1691. (A mariner.)

Williams, Richard; Captain; brother to Captain Anthony Williams. He died March 26th, 1725, in his fifty-ninth year.

Wrighte, Robert; he was the third son of Sir Nathaniel Wrighte, Knight, Lord Keeper of the Great Seal to King William III. and her present Majesty Anne, Queen of Great Britain. He died Oct: 16th, 1709. (*See* Jennings. Robert Wrighte married Elizabeth Hard in Feb: 1706, and their son Nathaniel was baptised in Dec: 1707).

WRIGHT, FRANCES; wife of Thomas Wright. She died Feb; 9th, 1703–4. [Thomas Wright married (1) Frances Lightfoot, March 9th, 1696, and (2) Mary Beard, Widow of John Beard, Esq. Beard died at St. Thomas' Mount and was buried in the Fort Cemetery, July 15th, 1705, with military honours and a salute of forty guns His wife Mary was the daughter of Edward Fowle.]

WYNCH, SOPHIA; wife of Alexander Wynch. She was one of the daughters of Edward Croke, Esq., and died June 3rd, 1754, aged twenty-five years.

WYNCH, HARRY; son of Alexander Wynch and Sophia his wife. He died Dec: 11th, 1754, aged one year and eight months. (Alexander Wynch become Governor of Madras. He married for his second wife, Florentia Cradock, in Dec: 1754. *See* Warre and Cradock.)

YALE, DAVID; son of Elihu Yale. He was born May 15th, 1684, and died Jan: 1687–8.

There is the lower half of a slab without names to the memory of two men who did business in this Presidency town for fifty-two years. One died at the age of eighty-three year; the other died Oct: 12th, 1684, at the age of eighty-five. There is no entry of any burial during the month of October 12th. The inscription is in Latin; it is therefore probably to the memory of Europeans.

All the baptism and marriages given here have been found in the Register Books of St. Mary's.

EPITAPH ON THE TOMBSTONE OF ELIHU YALE,
WREXHAM CHURCHYARD.

Eliugh Yale, Esq.,
was buried the 22nd of July, in the year
of our Lord, MDCCXXI.

Born in America, in Europe bred,
In Africa travelled, in Asia Wed,
Where long he lived and thrived; in London dead;
Much good, some ill, he did; so hope all's even,
And that his soul through mercy's gone to Heaven.
You that survive, and read this tale, take care
For this most certain exit to prepare;
Where blest in peace the actions of the just
Smell sweet, and blossom in the silent dust.

ALPHABETICAL LIST OF THE MONUMENTS OF ST. MARY'S CEMETERY DOWN TO THE END OF 1810

Amos, Mrs. Francina Cornelia; wife of Mr. James Amos, Merchant. She died July 30th, 1791, aged twenty-two years and six months.

Anderson, Robert; Esq.; late Master Attendant of Madras. He died Oct: 17th, 1800, aged fifty-nine years.

Anderson, James; M.D.; He died August 6th, 1809, aged seventy-two-years. (The Burial Register calls him Physician General. *See* Young.)

Ardley, Samuel; Member of Council; He served the H.E.I.C. twenty-two years, the last twelve of which he was Member of Council, Fort St. George. He died Feb: 9th, 1772, aged forty-four years.

Aubrey, Harriot; died Sep: 15th, 1787, aged eight months and fifteen days.

Bacon, Mary and Edward; who died infants, 1781. (Mary died in 1775.)

Baily, Mrs. Jenny; died Oct: 25th, 1808, aged thirty years.

Balmain, George; Esq.; of the Madras Civil Service; died Jan: 16th, 1807.

Birtles, Jane; wife of Mr. Thomas Birtles of Madras and daughter of Captain Crawford. She died July 28th, 1809.

Blyth, Mrs. Margarett; died Feb: 23rd, 1797, aged thirty-four years.

Bosc, Mrs. Eliza; died Dec: 8th, 1795, aged twenty-seven years.

Boswell, James Bruce; died May 21st, 1808, aged three months. (He was the son of Mr. J.B. Boswell.)

Bridges, Isabella; daughter of Captain Thomas Bridges. She died Nov: 1st, 1781, aged three years and four months.

Bridges, Catherine; daughter of Captain Thomas Bridges. She died Jan: 31st, 1782, aged two years.

Brodie, James; Esq.; of the Madras Civil Service. He died in 1802.

Bridie, James; son of James Brodie, Esq. He died August 4th, 1792, aged seven months.

Browne, Thomas Annesly; died June 18th, 1808, aged thirty-six years. The monument was erected by his widow. (In the Burial Register the name is spelt Brown.)

Brown, Robert; Lieutenant of the 73rd Regiment; he died Sep: 29th, 1792, aged twenty-two years.

Bruce, Isabella Catherine; died Feb: 4th, 1808, aged one year, and nineteen days. (She was the daughter of Mr. R.W. Bruce.)

Bullot, Colonel J.P. De Meuron; died Oct: 20th, 1803, aged sixty-three years.

Bulman, Sophia; wife of Job Bulman. She died March 22nd, 1788, aged twenty-four years and four months.

Burrows, Mrs. Mary; wife of Captain Thomas Burrows, H.E.I.C.S. She died April 19th, 1778, aged twenty-two years and seven months.

Burrows, Arnold; son of Capt. Thomas Burrows, H.E.I.C.S. He died Sep : 27th, 1779, aged one year and seven months.

Call, James; Esq.; died July 1799.

Cameron, Mr. Daniel; died May 15th, 1781, aged thirty years.

Campbell, Daniel Pasley; second son of Captain Dugald Campbell, H.E.I.C.S. He died Jan: 19th, 1780, aged four months and twenty-three days. (The Burial Register gives Donald instead of Daniel.)

Campbell, Mrs. Olympia Elizabeth; wife of Captain A. Campbell of the 71st Regiment, and sister of Sir John Morshead of Trennant Park, Cornwall. She died Dec: 24th, 1794, aged thirty-eight years. *See* Church Monuments.

Campbell, Charles; Lieut. in H.M. 74th Regiment, and second son of Colonel Donald Campbell of Glensadel; he died Oct: 24th 1790, aged twenty-three years. "A most amiable and elegant young man." The monument was erected by his friend and relative, Colonel Charles Fraser.

Campbell, John; Captain in the First Battalion of the Coast Artillery; he died Feb: 3rd 1800, aged thirty-two years. (He entered the Madras Army as Second Lieut. Nov: 6th, 1781.)

Card, Robert; died May 31st, 1799, aged twenty-five years.

Carlton, Lieut.Colonel The Hon.C; died Feb: 4th, 1806.

Cassin, Miss Mary Anne; April 1st, 1799, aged five years.

Charleton, Elizabeth Webb; wife of Captain Richard Charleton, Brigade-Major of the Coast Artillery; she died May 15th, 1799, aged twenty years. (Major Charleton entered the Artillery as Cadet, 1792, and died at Ghooty, Madras, May 12th, 1806.)

Clemons, Mary; daughter of James and Elizabeth Clemons; died Oct: 17th, 1798, aged nine years and nine months.

Coates, Master John; died Dec: 13th, 1810, aged three yeas and eight months. (The Register gives John Coats son of Major Coats.)

Collins, Edward; Major General; He served his country upwards of forty years and died April 7th, 1808, aged seventy-five years. (He entered the Madras Army as Ensign in 1765.)

Connell, James Ferrier; died Nov: 28th, 1799. (A Child.)

Connell, Ann; born Dec: 26th, 1800, died Jan: 22nd, 1802.

Coulson, Peter; a native of Clermontin in the province of Languedoc in France. He was for many years head of an eminent Commercial establishment at Pondicherry and latterly a member of the House of Francis Lautour and Co. at Madras. He was born 1747, and died May 26th, 1804.

Cox, Matilda; born April 26th, 1803, died Oct: 19th, 1804.

Cox, Joseph; born May 13th, 1804, died Jan: 17th, 1807.

Cox, Eleanor; born Dec: 17th, 1806 died Feb: 2nd, 1807.

Cox, Eliza; born March 26th, 1810, died April 3rd, 1810. The above four children were the son and daughters of Mr. James Cox and Elizabeth, his wife.

Croke, Edward: Esq.; died Feb: 12th, 1796, aged sixty-nine years.

Croke, Isabella; wife of Edward Croke, Esq.; died Oct: 4th, 1780. (Spelt Crook in the Burial Register).

Cuming, Mrs. Alice; relict of D. Cuming of Calcutta; she died May 6th, 1784, aged twenty-four years.

Cuming, George; Esq. Supercargo H.E.I.C.'s affairs, China; he died June 27th, 1799, aged forty-four years.

Daly, Mr. James; died May 24th, 1800, aged thirty-seven years.

Deckers, Mrs. Mary; died May 30th, 1810, aged twenty years, eleven months and two days. (Dickers in Burial Register.)

De Meuron, Mary; relict of the late Lieut. Colonel de Meuron; she died at St. Thomé, August 17th, 1805, aged fifty years.

Dent, Mrs. Harriet; died Sep: 18th, 1796, aged thirty years.

Dent, Mrs. Mary; died Sep: 13th, 1782, aged twenty-seven years. Her monument was erected by her surviving consort.

Dhormont, Elie; Captain of La Rochelle; died April 28th, 1785, aged thirty-six years. (Dohrmann in Burial Register.)

Dormond, Barbara; died Sep: 20th, 1764, aged nineteen years.

Drake, William Hobbs; Purser of the H.C.'s ship, "Sir Hugh Inglis", he died August 31st, 1803.

Duff, Mrs. Ann; wife of Major P. Duff, H.Cy.'s Art., Bengal; she died April 27th, 1776, aged twenty-six years.

Du Rochat, Captain De Meuron; of H.M. De Meuron Regiment; he died May 24th, 1800, aged thirty-four years.

Eidingtoun, Catherine; died June 3rd, 1788, aged sixteen years.

Fairney, Amelia; daughter of John Fairney, Merchant. She died April 13th, 1797, aged thirteen years, two months and sixteen days.

Fairney, John; Merchant; died May 29th, 1784, aged twenty-eight years.

Falconar, Alexander; L.L. and William, sons of Alexander and Eliza Falconar. One died July 1796, aged ten months; the other, Oct: 1797, aged fourteen months.

Fleming, Richard; Esq.; died Oct: 31st, 1807, aged fifty-three years; monument erected by his daughters. (His name is not entered in the Burial Register.)

Floyer, Charles Keble; son of Augustus and Jane Floyer; he died March 18th, 1801, aged seven months and fifteen days.

Forbes, Lieut. B.J., of the 74th Regiment; he died Nov: 12th, 1791, aged nineteen years.

Foulis, Captain Alexander; died May 17th, 1796, aged forty-two years. The monument was restored by his brother, Brigadier General David Foulis of the 1st Regiment of Light Cavalry, in Dec: 1834 (Alexander Foulis entered the Madras Army as Cadet in 1777.)

Franke, John De Beighling; died April 6th, 1799, aged five years and six months. (Register gives Blything instead of de Beighling.)

Frend, Miss Margaretta Juliana; died Feb: 20th, 1799, aged three years and a half. (Friend in the Burial Register.)

Gagahan, Maria; daughter of I. Gagahan, Esq., Surgeon; died Jan: 4th, 1784, aged two months and twenty-five days.

Gambier, Cornish; Esq.; died August, 19th, 1799, aged thirty-seven years.

Gardiner, Lieut. Peter; died May 17th, 1808, aged seventy-five years.

Garrow, Joseph, Esq.; Senior Merchant, H.E.I.C.S.; died August 19th, 1792, aged thirty-four years.

Gilmore, Mr. Henry Charles; of Rungpore in Bengal; died Dec: 21st, 1807, aged thirty-two years.

Goodhall, Alexander; died Dec: 17th, 1809, aged fifty-seven years.

Gordon, Major Thomas; H.E.I.C.S.; died Sep: 17th, 1798, aged forty-five years. (Entered Madras Army as Cadet in 1775.)

Gordon, William; Esq.; Head Surgeon on the Madras Establishment; died Sep: 4th, 1793, aged fifty-three years.

Graham, Mr. John, Junior; of Greigston, Fifeshire, North Britain; Cadet; died Sep: 24th, 1808, aged seventeen years.

Grant, Captain Allan; Town Major of Fort St. George; died May 3rd, 1804, aged thirty-eight years. (He entered the Madras Army as English in Oct: 1781.)

Grant, Walter; Esq.; Master in Equity in the Supreme Courts of Judicature; he died Nov: 5th, 1807, aged thirty-eight years. The monument was erected by his widow Sarah Grant.

Greenhill, Mrs. Caroline; wife of Mr. Joseph Greenhill and sister of Ensign Richard Whittall. She died Dec: 17th, 1792, aged nineteen years.

Griffin, Frances; wife of John Griffin, Mariner; died Oct: 12th, 1767, aged forty-seven years.

Griffiths, Charles; died April 25th, 1768, aged forty years. (The Register states that he was Chaplain of Fort St. George.)

Griffiths, Eliza Rebecca; born Sep: 30th, 1801, died August 22nd, 1805.

Griffiths, Martha; born April 18th, 1809 died 23rd of the same month.

Griffiths, Mary Ann; born April 27th and perished at sea on board the "Jane, Duchess of Gordon" in the month of March 1809. The above three children were the daughters of Richard Griffiths, Merchant and Elizabeth his wife.

Hall, Lieut. Colonel George; died Sep: 27th, 1797, aged forty-seven years. (He entered the Madras Artillery as Second Lieut. in 1778.)

Hardyman, Isabella Matilda; daughter of Thomas and Sancta Hardyman. She died Sep: 24th 1804, aged twenty-one years.

Harper, Lieut. Colonel Humphrey; H.E.I.C.S.; died Feb: 7th, 1785.

Harrison, Mr. William; born in County Antrim, Ireland. He was thirty years in Madras and died July 18th, 1784, aged seventy-three years

Hartwell, The Revd. Thomas Francis; Chaplain on this establishment; he died Oct: 27th, 1805, aged twenty-seven years and three months.

Henderson, Mrs. Grace; died June 8th, 1796, aged thirty-four years, five months and eight days.

Henderson, Mr. John; died Feb: 2nd, 1795, aged thirty-three years.

Henshaw, Anna Maria; daughter of Robert and Sophia Henshaw of Bombay. She died July 17th, 1800, aged thirteen months.

Hill, Thomas; Lieut. of Cavalry, H.E.I.C.S.; died Dec: 9th, 1791, aged twenty-five years. He entered the Madras Army as a Lieut. in 1785.

Hope, William; Merchant; Kezia, his wife; and Kezia, Ellen, Anna and Caroline, their four daughters and only children, who all perished at sea in the H.C.S. "Jane, Duchess of Gordon" on or about March 16th, 1809.

Houston, George; Esq.; of this Establishment; he died Sep: 10th, 1806, aged sixteen years.

Hughes, Mr. Michael; Conductor of Ordnance: died Oct: 25th, 1807, aged forty-seven years. Monument erected by his widow, Clarinda Hughes.

Hurdis, Thomas Bowyer; Esq.; Senior Merchant H.E.I.C.S., Judge of the Sudder Court; died Nov: 16th, 1808, aged thirty-seven years. The monument was erected by his widow.

Hurdis, Mrs. Catherine; wife of the late Thomas Bowyer Hurdis, Esq., of this Establishment, who was lost on her passage to England in March 1809.

Inman, Henry; Esq.; Captain in the Royal Navy; died July 15th, 1809, aged forty-six years.

Innes, Lieut. Colonel James; H.E.I.C.S.; Commandant of the 2nd Battalion of the 13th M.I.; died April 23rd, 1804, aged forty-seven years. (He entered the Madras Army as 2nd Lieut. In 1777.)

Isacke, Mrs. Sarah; died Nov: 5th, 1793, aged fifty-two years.

Jodrell, Sir Paul; M.D.; died August 6th, 1803, aged fifty-eight years.

Johns, Miss Caroline; daughter of David Jones; died May 8th, 1807, aged fifteen years and six months.

Johnson, Mrs. Joanna; died May 9th, 1810.

Jollie, Martin; Esq.; died Nov: 12th, 1810, aged twenty-two years.

Jollie, Thomas; died June 13th, 1803, aged twenty-three years.

Kelleghen, Charles John Keble; died July 22nd, 1809, aged four years. (Son of Sergeant J. Kelleghen.)

Kennedy, Sarah; wife of E. Kennedy, H.M. 73rd Regiment; died June 30th, 1793, aged thirty-three years.

Kennedy, Lieut. Colonel John; late Commandant of the H.E.I.C.'s Coast Artillery; died April 30th, 1785, aged fifty-five years.

Kerr, Alexander; died June 18th, 1800, aged four years and five months. Also Lydia and William Lewis Kerr, infants.

Kindersley, Louisa Benigna; died Feb: 21st, 1792, aged one year and four months.

Lambert, P.L. (Latin); Lieut. of the 6th Regiment M.I.; died April 12th, 1810.

Lamount, John Mackenzie; son of Captain Lamont, 73rd Regiment, died Nov: 14th, 1780, aged eleven months.

Landon, George James; died Feb: 6th 1792, aged nine months.

Lautour, Francis John; son of Francis and Ann Lautour; died Sep: 23rd, 1781, aged eight months and twenty-three days.

Lautour, Francis John; son of Francis and Ann Lautour; died Nov: 27th, 1783, aged five months and thirteen days. (The Register spells the name Latour and La Tour.)

Leatham, Mary Catherine; died Oct: 7th, 1787, aged two years and two months.

Ledsham, Mr. Thomas; died Sep: 29th, 1800, aged forty-nine years.

Leslie, Richard; M.A.; Minister of Fort St. George for more than twenty years; died June 29th, 1804, aged fifty-eight years.

Liell, Mr. Richard; died Sep: 13th, 1770, aged twenty-six years.

Lincoln, Mr. Charles; died June 10th, 1787, aged fifty years.

Little, Mr. Archibald; Surgeon, H.E.I.C.S., Madras Establishment, died August 1804. (No entry in the Burial Register on this date.

A Mr. Archibald Little, Assistant Surgeon of H.M. Ship "Belliquec" was buried Oct 2nd, 1806.)

Lucas, Colly Lyon; Esq.; Chief Surgeon, H.E.I.C.S., and Member of the Medical Board; died March 23rd, 1797, aged sixty-six years.

Macdonald, Forbes Ross; Esq.; Superintendent of the Prince of Wales Island, (Penang.) He died May 18th, 1799, aged forty-four years. (The Register calls him Major Macdonald.)

Macintosh, Mr. Angus; died May 30th, 1788, aged thirty-eight years.

Mackenzie, Crizell; wife of Daniel Mackenzie; died Sep: 20th, 1780, aged twenty-eight years.

Mackenzie, James; Major of the 73rd Foot; died August 27th, 1780, aged twenty-eight years.

Mackenzie, George; second son of the late Earl of Cromarty; Lieut. Colonel in H.M. 71st Regiment; Commandant of Walajabad. He died June 4th, 1787, aged forty-six years. The monument was erected by the Officers of the 71st Regiment, and his name-son, George Mackenzie, of 75th Regiment.

Macleod, Norman; son of Lieut. Colonel of Alexander Macleod; died Dec: 20th, 1801, aged-eight years and seventeen days.

Madge, Thomas; Esq.; died Nov: 8th, 1773, aged thiry-one years.

Malcolm, Thomas; Esq.; died Sep: 8th, 1809, aged thirty-eight years.

Mannen, Mrs. Eliza; wife of Lieut. Charles Mannen, of the 71st Regiment, and daughter of Colonel James Butler, formerly Commandant of the Artillery on this coast.

Maxtone, Charles; Esq.; Senior Merchant, H.E.I.C.S.; died March 24th, 1809, aged fifty-six years.

Mein, Nichol; Esq.; Member of the Medical Board of this Presidency. Died April 14th, 1804, aged fifty years.

Monnisse, Mr. Francis; died Nov: 8th, 1810, aged thirty-two years and twenty-nine days. The monument was erected by his widow, Margaret Monnisse.

Montgommery, Lieut. Colonel Hugh; died March 16th, 1792 aged thirty-eight years. (He entered the Madras Army as Lieut. in 1778.)

Morrison, Alexander; Surgeon, H.M. 34th Regiment; died July 17th, 1805, aged thirty-three years.

Morse, Nicholas; Esq.; Once Governor of Fort St. George; died May 28th, 1772, aged seventy-two years.

Moss, George Robert; died Feb: 20th, 1809, aged twelve years, seven months and eight days. Monument erected by his father, George Moss.

Munro, James; Merchant, died July 22nd, 1797, aged thirty-six years.

Munro, Mrs. Frances Mary; wife of Dr. Andrew Munro; died May 31st, 1771, aged fifty-three years.

Neale, Mary Ann; daughter of Daniel Neale, Esq.; died Oct: 29th, 1808, aged eighteen months and four days.

Newcome, Henry; Esq.; Post Captain in the Royal Navy and Commander of H.M.S. Orpheus. Died March 5th, 1797, aged thirty-seven years.

Nuthall, Mrs. Eleanor; died Sep: 1st, 1797, aged twenty-five years. Also her son died Nov: 28th, 1796.

Oakley, William; died Dec: 7th, 1787, aged one day.

Oakley, Emma; died Sep: 20th, 1794, aged one year.

Ogilvie, William; son of Thomas Elliot Ogilvie; died July 17th, 1785, aged eleven months and eleven days.

Oliver, Mrs. Sophia Elizabeth; died March 19th, 1810, aged twenty years.

Oram, Charles; Esq.; late Assistant Surgeon, Madras Establishment; died August 11th, 1798.

ORR, Sydenham; son of Lieut. Colonel Alexander Orr; died Nov: 5th, 1806, aged nine months.

Pasley, Susan Hannah; daughter of Gilbert Pasley; died Feb: 17th, 1782, aged five months and four days.

Pasley Gilbert, Physician; died Sep: 23rd 1781, aged forty-eight years.

Patterson, Captain Alexander; H.E.I.C.S.; died Feb: 28th, 1785, aged fifty-six years.

Patterson, Margaret Caroline; (Catherine in Burial Register) daughter of the late Lieut. Col. John Patterson, H.E.I.C.S.; died Dec: 20th, 1809.

Pepper, John Wemyss; Merchant of Madras; died Feb: 7th, 1801, aged thirty-two years. Monument erected by his widow.

Peters, Thomas (late Captain, H.E.I.C.S.); died Sep: 5th, 1798, aged forty-two years. (He entered the Madras Army as Ensign in 1780.)

Pittman, Captain Gibbon Charles George; H. Company's Engineers; died March 27th, 1798, aged twenty-four years. (He entered the M.E. as Second Lieut. in 1790.)

Ponton, Andrew; M.D.; died Nov: 4th 1795, aged twenty-nine years.

Popham, Stephen; late Solicitor to the H.E.I.C. in the Presidency of Madras. Died June 13th, 1795.

Popham, Anna; wife of Stephen Popham and daughter of Sir William Thomas, Bart. Died Dec: 25th, 1787, aged thirty-seven years.

Popham, William; son of Stephen Popham, Esq.; died Oct: 9th, 1786 aged six years.

Popham, Weekes; cousin of the above Stephen Popham; died Oct: 31st, 1787, aged twenty-five years.

Ram, George Andrew; Esq.; of the H. Company's Civil Establishment. Died Feb: 12th, 1801, aged fifty-two years.

Ranny, Mr. James; Merchant of Madras; died at sea August 3rd, 1800, aged thirty-four years.

Reily, Mr. John; died June 1st, 1810, aged forty-eight years.

Reynolds, Mrs. Elizabeth; formerly the wife of Mr. Daniel Cameron; died Feb: 23rd, 1792, aged thirty-four years.

Richardson, G.G.; died August 30th, 1805, aged thirty-eight years.

Rodgers, James; Major, H.E.I.C.S. and Military Auditor General of the Island of Ceylon. Died May 27th, 1800. (He entered the Madras Army as a Cadetin, 1778.)

Roebuck, William; Esq.; Died March 11th, 1801, aged thirty-six years. The monument was erected by his brother, Benjamin Roebuck.

Rogers, Captain William; of the "Houghton" Indiaman; died May 14th, 1763, aged thirty-two years.

Ross, Andrew; Esq.; Justice of the Peace for Madras. He arrived in 1752 and was named an Alderman for the Mayor's court in the original Charter granted that year. He died August 22nd, 1797, aged seventy-nine years.

Russell, Mr. Daniel; died Oct: 15th, 1787, aged thirty years eight months and seventeen days.

Ryley, C.D.M. (Charlotte Diana Martha); daughter of J. and C.C. Ryley; died August 6th, 1810, aged one year, one month and seventeen days.

Savage, George; Esq.; died August 10th, 1787, aged forty-four years.

Secker, Henry Elwes; died June 8th, 1792, aged twenty-three years.

Sewell, Henry; Esq.; late H.M. Naval Officer at this Port, and an Alderman of the Corporation. Died May 18th, 1800, aged thirty-nine years. The monument was erected by his widow.

Shepherd, Mrs. Joice; died June 16th, 1807, aged twenty years. (Register, Shepperd.)

Shirriff, Lieut. Colonel William; Commandant of the H.C.'s of 7th Regiment of Native Cavalry; Died April 7th, 1802 aged forty-two years. (The Register gives Sheriff.)

Simspon, William; descended from a respectable family in the County of Suffolk, England. He was for many years an Officer of the different Courts of Madras; he died Sep: 27th, 1803, aged forty-three years.

Small John; died June 11th, 1780, aged fifty years. (Captain's steward on H.C. Ship "Haleswell".)

Smart, Lieut. Colonel Charles, H.E.I.C.S.; died Oct: 3rd, 1798, aged forty-three years. (He entered the Madras Army as a Cadet in 1771.)

Smith, Captain Joshua; died Nov: 5th, 1783, aged forty-two years.

Smith, John; Esq., of the Kingdom of Ireland; late Surgeon of H.M. 94th Regiment, Scotch Brigade; died August 24th, 1807, aged fifty-one years.

Soame, Henry Z.R.; Esq.; late Lieut. in H.M. 25th Regiment of Light Dragoons; died April 26th, 1803. (The Register gives Lt. H.J.R. Soames.)

Spens, Frances; wife of Lieut. Colonel J. Spens of the 73rd Regiment. She died April 7th, 1789, aged twenty-seven years.

Spens, Frances; her daughter born and died April 3rd, 1798.

Spottiswood, Mr. Allan; died August 27th, 1808. (The Register gives Allan Spotterwood of the ship "General Stuart.")

Stevens, Mr. John; died Feb: 13th, 1808, aged thirty-seven years.

Stevenson, Elizabeth; daughter of Colonel James Stevenson; died Sep: 8th, 1798, aged two months and seventeen days.

Stoakes, Peter; Esq.; Commander of the ship "Kent"; died Sep: 30th, 1783, aged fifty-six years. (Stokes, in Register.)

Stone, John Trottore; died Feb: 13th, 1789, aged twenty-nine years.

Stringer, Mr. James; Superintendent of Public Buildings H.E.I.C.S. for twenty-four years; died March 24th, 1787, aged fifty-seven years.

Stringer, George; Lieut.; served the H.E.I.C. for twelve years; died July 12th 1804, aged forty-four years.

Stuart, John; Lieut, of Cavalry and Fort Adjutant, Fort St. George, H.E.I.C.S.; died August 11th, 1788, aged twenty-six years. (He entered the Madras Army as Cadet in 1780.)

Stuart, Miss A.E.; daughter of H.E. Lieut. General James Stuart, Commander-in-Chief of the Forces. Died March 29th, 1804, aged thirty-three years.

Sullivan, Captain Philip; sometimes called O'Sulivan as Chief of an ancient family of that name in Ireland; died Oct: 6th, 1793, aged forty years.

Sullivan, Lieut. Henry B.; died Feb: 16th, 1783, aged twenty-three years.

Sullivan, Miss Elizabeth; died August 15th, 1784, aged one year. (Register, Sulivan.)

Sullivan, Digby; died June 6th, 1794, aged seven months.

Sydenham, William; son of Captain William Sydenham, Town Major of Fort St. Geo. Died Oct: 3rd, 1780, aged two years.

Sydenham, Amelia; daughter of Captain W. Sydenham, Town Major of Fort St. George; died Sep: 5th, 1782, aged ten days.

Sydenham, William; Esq.; Major General in the H.E.I.C.S.; died June 13th, 1801, aged forty-nine years. (He entered the Madras Artillery

as Lieut. in 1768.) The monument was erected by his widow and
family.

Taylor, Thomas Rumbold; Esq.; died March 4th, 1804, aged twenty-
eight years. (The Register says Captain Thomas Rumbold Taylor
of the "Glory" Indiaman.)

Thackary, Mrs. Frances; wife of Mr. Thomas Thackary, Surgeon in
the H.E.I.C.S.; died April 16th, 1800, aged twenty-four years.
(Thackeray and Thackery in Register.)

Thewles, Lieut. Charles; died 1784, aged forty-nine years.

Thomas, Mrs. Elizabeth; died Sep: 18th, 1810, aged thirty-four years.

Turing, Robert; Major in the H.E.I.C.S.; he served twenty-three years,
and was present with the Coast Army at every battle and siege
of importance during that time. He died June 5th, 1801, aged
forty-one years. (He entered the Madras Army as Cadet in 1778.)

Upton, Harriot; died July 9th, 1782, aged three months.

Van Meirope, I.K.; Esq.; died June 21st, 1791, aged thirty three years.
(The Register records that R. Isaac Van Meirope, Esq., was buried
June 21st, 1790.)

Vaughan, Mrs. (Cecilia); wife of the Revd. Edward Vaughan, Chaplain
of Madras, and eldest daughter of Major General Edward
Collins. Died Nov: 8th, 1810, aged twenty-seven years.

Wade, William; H.M., 25th Light Dragoons; died Sep: 30th, 1801,
aged twenty-one years and eighty-two days.

Wahab, Major-General George; died Dec: 26th, 1808, aged fifty-five
years, forty of which he passed in the service of his country.
(He entered the Madras Army as Cadet in 1769.)

Wallace, Thomas; Esq.; of the H.E.I.C.S.; died April 24th, 1800, aged
twenty-five years. (Wallis in Register.)

Wallbank, Hugh Norton; Captain in the Artillery; died Nov: 5th, 1768, aged thirty-three years.

Ware, Thomas Stephen; of the H.E.I.C. Civil Service; died Nov: 5th, 1799, aged twenty-one years.

Watson, Anne; daughter of the late John Watson, Esq. Superintendent of H.C. Marine, and Member of Council, Bombay; died June 14th, 1780, aged nineteen years.

Watt, Captain James; late Commander of H.M.S. "Sultan"; died Sep: 13th, 1782.

Watts, Louisa; wife of Edward Watts; died May 12th, 1804, aged twenty-nine years.

Westcott, George; Esq.; died May 8th, 1809, aged sixty-one years.

West, James; Esq.; died Nov: 28th, 1802, aged seventy years.

Whileford, Lieut. George; the Bengal Establishment; died Oct: 11th, 1791, aged twenty-six years.

Whittall, Ensign Richard; died July 12th, 1792, aged seventeen years. (*See* Greenhill.)

Whittington, W.; Esq.; died Sep: 16th, 1806, aged twenty years.

Wood, Captain Charles; late Commander of H.M.S. Worcester; died Oct: 8th, 1782.

Wood, John; Esq.; late Colonel in the H.E.I.C.S.; died July 3rd, 1774, aged forty-eight years.

Woodall, Basil; son of Major Thomas Woodall of H.M. 19th Regiment; died Oct: 8th, 1802, aged seven months.

Woodall, Major Thomas; of H.M. 12th Regiment; died June 28th, 1802, aged thirty years.

Wooley, James; Esq.; died April 15th, 1789, aged forty-nine years.

Wynn, Martha; daughter of Captain Robert Nanny Wynn, or the Madras Establishment; died June 25th, 1807, aged fourteen years.

Young, Mrs. Ann Anderson; relict of Charles Wallace Young, free-merchant; and daughter of Dr. James Anderson, late Physician General. She died April 23rd, 1810, aged thirty-two years. The monument was erected by Andrew Berry, M.D. of the Madras Establishment, C.W. Young's cousin.

A few of the foregoing names are not to be found in the Burial Register. The following is added on account of its interest and because it records the death of Hardinge in 1808. Dawson, William; Captain of H.M.S. "La Piedmontese," to which command he had been appointed by the Board of Admiralty in reward for his brave and skillful conduct when First Lieut. of H.M. Ship "San Fiorenzo", in the three days' action near the coast of Ceylon, which terminated in the capture of the "Piedmontese" from the French, and in the fall of the "San Fiorenzo's gallant Captain, George Nicholas Hardinge, on the 8th day of March, 1808. After the battle he went to England where he met the well-earned meed of praise, and visited his Father's house, Pudsey Dawson, Esq., of Liverpool. He returned to India with impaired health but unabated ardour for the service of his King and his Country. To their loss and to the grief of all his acquaintances he died at Madras on Sunday the 29th day of September, 1811, aged twenty-eight years.

PEOPLE BURIED IN ST. MARY'S CHURCH

Burgoyne, Major General Sir John; Bart., Colonel of H.M. 23rd Light Dragoons. He died Sep: 23rd, 1785, aged forty-five years.

Campbell, Sir Alexander; Bart., K.C.B., Commander-in-Chief of the Madras Army. He died Dec: 11th, 1824, aged sixty-four years. His first wife is mentioned on the same slab, but she was buried in the present cemetery on the Island. The following is the inscription:

Campbell, Olympia; first wife of the above, and daughter of Sir John Morshead, Bart., of Trennant Park, Cornwall. She died Dec: 4th, 1794, aged thirty-eight years. The tablet was erected by their grandsons, Sir Alexander Cockburn Campbell, Bart., and Lieut. General George Alexander Malcolm, C.B.

Doveton, Lieut. General Sir John; G.C.B. of the H.E.I.C.S. He died Nov: 7th, 1847, aged seventy-seven years.

Elliot, Margaret; wife of the Right Hon. Hugh Elliot, Governor of Madras. She died March 1st, 1819.

Gwillim, Elizabeth; wife of Sir Henry Gwillim, Kt. She died Aug: 8th, 1807, aged forty-four years. (Sir Henry Gwillim was one of the first Puisne Judges of Madras. The name occurs in the Records as early as 1718, when Captain W. Gwillim, master of one of the Company's ships, was made a free merchant at his own request.)

Harris, Lieut. Colonel Michael John; of the Madras European Regiment and Town Major of Madras. He died Sep: 9th, 1830, aged forty-two years.

Hastings, Fran. (No date nor age. He was Governor of Madras in
1720, and was serving the Company in India in 1700.
See Monuments of the Old Cemetery.)

Hobart, Lord Vere Henry; Governor of Madras. Died April 27th
1875, aged fifty-six years.

Hobart, Baroness Margaretta; she died Aug: 7th, 1796.

Hobart, John; the infant son of Baroness Margaretta Hobart.
He died a few months prior to the death of his mother.

Hood, Vice Admiral Sir Samuel; Kt. of the Bath and Commander-
in-Chief of His Britannic Majesty's ships in the East Indies.
(No date is given. He was buried Dec: 25th, 1814.)

In Memoriam. (The slab is supposed to cover the remains of Lord
Pigot who died in May 1777, and was buried in St. Mary's church.
He left issue. In March 1776, Sophy Pigot married that Hon:
Edward Monckton; and in Oct: 1777, Leonora Pigot married
Claud Russell, Esq.)

Munro, Major General Sir Thomas; Bart., K.C.B., Governor of
Madras. He died July 6th, 1827, aged sixty-five years of cholera,
at Gooty. He was buried there, and afterwards disinterred that
his body might be brought to St. Mary's church.

Russell, Jane Amelia; wife of Henry Russell and second daughter of
J.H. Casamayor. She was baptised Sep: 14th, 1789; married in
Oct: 1808, and died in Dec: the same year. (The monument is by
J. Bacon, Junior, and represents a death-bed scene. James Henry
Casamayor was the eldest son of Noah Casamayor and was
baptised at the Fort, Jan: 3rd, 1746. *See* Casamayor in the list of
Old Monuments.)

Ward, Sir Henry George; Kt.; G.C.M.G.; Governor of Madras.
He died Aug: 2nd, 1860.

PERSONS TO WHOSE MEMORY MONUMENTS HAVE BEEN ERECTED IN ST. MARY'S CHURCH

Adams, Lieut. of the 3rd Light Infantry. He was killed at Sittang with Colonel Conry, Jan: 11th, 1826. His name is on Colonel Pepper's monument.

Atkinson, Lieut. Colonel W.M.; of the Madras Engineers and Colonel in the Madras Army. He died in the Red Sea on his passage to England, May 15th, 1858, in the fifty-third year of his age.

Awdry, Major Ambrose, R.E.; son of Sir John Wither Awdry, Chief Justice of Bombay. He was born April 28th, 1844, and died at Ootacamund, May 1885.

Boyton, Brevet Captain James. His name with several others placed here alphabetically, is engraved on a tablet which was put up to the memory of the officers of H.M. 63rd Regiment who died at Fort St. George whilst the Regiment was stationed there between the years 1834–7. No ages nor dates are given.

Branson, Lieut. Colonel J.H. Spring; of the Madras Artillery Volunteers. He died in London in 1897, aged fifty-six years.

Chipperfield, Surgeon William Nathan; of the I.M.D. He died May 22nd, 1873, aged fifty-one years.

Close, Major General Sir Barry; Bart. He died in England April 18th, 1813, at the age of fifty-six. The monument is fine bit of sculpture, probably by Flaxman.

Conry, Lieut. Colonel; of the 3rd Light Infantry. He was killed at Sittang in Pegu, Jan: 11th, 1826. His name is on Pepper's monument.

Conway, Adjutant General; "The solider's friend." He died May 13th, 1837. The monument consists of a large marble statue of Conway by Turnouth, and it was erected by the Army and the Public.

Coaker, Lieut. Colonel William Henry; R.E. He was born August 4th, 1834, and died in 1892.

Cursham, Captain; 1st European Regiment. He was killed at Sittang, Pegu, Jan: 11th, 1826. His name is on Pepper's monument.

Davis, Lieut.Thomas; of the Madras Engineers. He was killed at the siege of Mallegaon, May 18th, 1818. The monument is by Bacon and represents the scene of the siege with the gateway of the town in bas-relief.

Dexter, Brevet Captain Christopher; of the 63rd Regiment. *See* Boyton.

Drake, Ensign G.; of the 36th Regiment. He died on his passage to Europe, May 27th, 1856. His name with four others is on a tablet erected to the memory of the officers of the 36th Regiment M.I., who died during the service of that corps in Burmah.

Fairtlough, William Barber; Brevet Captain of H.M. 63rd Regiment. *See* Boyton.

Fenwick, Lieut. Colonel Percival; of H.M. 69th Regiment. He died at Fort St. George, March 5th, 1863.

Gericke, The Reverend Christian William; "The worthy associate of the Venerable Schwartz". He died in 1893, aged sixty-two years.

The monument is by Flaxman and represents Gerick teaching a native of high caste. The face of the catechumen is full of expression. Gericke, like Schwartz, left a large sum of money on his death to the Society for Promoting Christian Knowledge.

Harris, Michael John; Lieut. Colonel; of the European Regiment and Town Major of Madras. He died Sep: 9th, 1830, aged forty-two years.

Harris, Henry Moore; Conductor in the Ordnance Department. He died at Rangoon in 1885, aged fifty years.

Jervis, Lieut. S.; of the 36th Regiment M.I. He was lost on the transport "Lady Nugent" about May 10th, 1864. *See* Drake.

Johnson, Samuel Higgins; Ensign H.M. 63rd Regiment. *See* Boyton.

Joyce, Alfred; Captain, 36th M.I.; died at Sittang, June 14th, 1856, *See* Drake.

Keble, George Gilbert; he died August 25th, 1811, aged thirty-six years. The monument is by J. Bacon, Junior, and represents the figure of Charity with two children. Keble was a free-mason and was in the Company's service. In 1803 he was Secretary to Government.

Langley, Lionel; Major, R.E. He was killed by a tiger at Kullar in the Kistna district, in 1890, at the age of forty years.

Leslie, The Reverend Richard; M.A.; Archdeacon. He died at the Fort, June 26th, 1804, aged fifty-eight years. The monument is unsigned, but the records say that it is by Flaxman.

Macdonald, James; Assistant Surgeon of the 36th M.I. He died *en route* to Calcutta, Nov: 4th, 1854. *See* Drake.

Macpherson, Lieut. General Sir Herbert Taylor, K.C.B., K.S.I., V.C., Commander-in-Chief of the Madras Army. He died near Prome on the Irrawady, Oct: 20th, 1886, of fever contracted through exposure in Upper Burmah while commanding the forces in the field, during the third Burmese war. His remains lie in the cemetery at Rangoon. He was fifty-nine years of age.

McAlpin, Captain, W.B.; late Paymaster of H.M. 49th Regiment. He died at sea, May 14th, 1846, aged forty-eight years.

McCleverty, Anne Gildowney; wife of Lieut. General W.A. McCleverty, Commander-in-chief of the Madras Army. She died July 26th, 1868, aged forty-six years.

McCurdy, Edward Archdall; Lieut. Colonel of the 27th M.I. He died at Russel Kondah, Dec: 28th, 1842.

McNeill, Malcolm; Colonel of the Madras Light Cavalry and Brigadier General commanding the Second Brigade of the Madras troops at the capture of Pegu. He died at Rangoon, Dec: 8th, 1852, aged fifty-four years.

Mill, Charles; Lieut. Colonel of H.M. 55th Regiment. He was killed whilst gallantly leading his Regiment to the attack against the stockade of Somarpet in the territory of His Highness the Rajah of Coorg. April 3rd, 1834, aged fifty-four years.

Monteith, William Elphinstone; Son of Colonel Monteith of the Madras Engineers. He was born Oct: 15th, 1835 and died at Bangalore, Oct: 21st, 1841.

MontGomerie, Patrick; Major, R.E. He was born Oct: 26th, 1837, and died at Vizagapatnam, Jan: 8th, 1886.

Moorhouse, Joseph; Lieut. Colonel of the Coast Artillery. He was killed at the taking of Bangalore before the Pettah Gate, March 7th, 1791. The monument is by C. Peart; It represents Britannia seated on a lion, crowning a medallion head of Moorhouse with laurel. Moorhouse was married at St. Mary's church to Augusta Boisdaune in Oct: 1735.

Morant, James Law Lushington; Lieut. Colonel, R.E. He died at Melbourne in 1886.

Nattes, John William; Lieut. in the Madras Engineers. He was killed May 29th, 1818, at the siege of Mallegaon. *See* Davies.

Nicholls, Anne Lilly; wife of Henry James Nicholls of the 25th Regiment M.I. She was born Dec: 15th, 1718, and died at Negapatam, April 24th, 1842.

O'Connell, Captain Gleadowe; Commissary of Ordnance in the Arsenal of Fort St. George. He was born at Granard, County Longford, in Ireland, Oct: 25th, 1779, and died at Negapatam, April 24th, 1842.

Palliser, John Augustine; of Castlemaiden, County of Kildare. Captain H.M. 76th Regiment. He died at Fort St. George, June 30th, 1864, in the thirtieth year of his age.

Pedder, William: Captain in H.M. 63rd Regiment. *See* Boyton.

Pepper, Hercules Henry; Lieut. Colonel of the 34th Light Infantry. He died at Madras, July 25th, 1826. The monument is by G. Clarke; it is a statue of pepper, and at its base are also engraved the name of Conry, Cursham, Stedman and Adams. Pepper was forty-two years of age when he died.

Poole, Anne Jemima Clarissa; daughter of Colonel T.H.S. Conway, C.B., and wife of Lieut. Colonel of M. Poole, commanding the 5th Regiment M.I. at Vizianagram. She died May 15th, 1851, aged thirty-four years and eleven months.

Powell, The Reverend Walter Posthumus; D.C.L., of Worcester College, Oxford. Garrison Chaplain of Fort St. George. He died June 8th, 1853, aged forty-eight years.

Prendergast, Catherine Jane; wife of Guy Lushington Prendergast, M.C.S., and daughter of James Annesley, Esq., of the Madras Medical Establishment. She was born July 31st.

Raikes, Richard William; Captain of the 1st Regiment of Light Cavalry, and Commandant of the Governor's Body Guard and Major Commandant of the Madras Volunteer Cavalry Guard. He died April 1st 1859, aged forty-three years.

Richardson, James; Lieut. Colonel of the 2nd Madras European Light Infantry. He died at Penang, Sep: 15th, 1856.

Roberts, Walter Malcolm; Lieut. of the Royal Madras Engineers. He was drowned in the Godavery river, Sep: 17th, 1867, aged twenty-nine years.

Rochfort, Cowper; Captain and Brevet Major in the 27th M.I. He died at the Cape, July 9th, 1847.

Ross, Charles Robert, M.C.S. He died Nov: 26th, 1816, aged thirty-three years. The monument is by J. Bacon.

Rundall; Lieut. and Brevet Captain of the Madras Engineers, and Commandant of the Sappers and Miners. He died at Prome, Nov: 12th, 1852, aged forty years. There is a portrait medal above the inscription.

Salmon, Charles; Ensign of H.M. 43rd Light Infantry. He died at Fort St. George, March 19th, 1861, in the twenty-fourth year of his age.

Scott, C.; Captain in the Madras Engineers, and Field Engineer to General Sir Hope Grant's Column. He was killed at the attack on the Fort of Kohlee, Nov: 23rd, 1856, in the thirtieth year of his age.

Sherard, Colonel George Philip Brudenell; Judge Advocate General of the Madras Army. He died at Madras, Jan: 16th, 1880.

Shortland, T.M.V.; Lieut. and Adjutant of the 36th M.I. He was lost in the Sittang river, April 23rd, 1854. *See* Drake.

Stedman; Captain of the 34th Light Infantry. He was killed at Siatang, Jan: 11th, 1826. His name is on Pepper's monument.

Swartz, The Reverend Frederick Christian. He was employed as Protestant Missionary from the Government of Denmark, and in the same capacity by the Society for the Promotion of Christian Knowledge in England. He died Feb: 13th, 1798, in the seventy-second year of his age. The monument was erected by the M.E.I.C. in 1807; it is by J. Bacon, Junior, and represents a death-bed scene with a vision of Hope bearing the Cross.

Taylor, James Marriott; Lieut. of the 9th Regiment M.I. and Acting Interpreter to H.M. 51st K.O. Light Infantry. He was killed whilst gallantly leading a company of the 51st to the assault of a stockade in the Domben district, March 19th, 1853.

Webbe, Josiah; Chief Secretary to the Government of Madras and Resident at the Court of Scindia, where he died Nov: 9th, 1804, aged thirty-seven years. A beautiful monument by Flaxman with four figures supporting a portrait medallion; at the base is a sleeping tiger.

Whistler, Godfrey Webster; Major and Commandant of the 19th M.I. He died at Palghatcherry, of cholera, March 14th, 1843, in the forty-second year of his age.

Whittingham, Sir S.F.; Lieut. General, K.C.B., K.C.H., Colonel of the 71st Highland Light Infantry and Commander-in-Chief of the Madras Army. He died Jan: 19th, 1841, aged sixty-six years.

Wilson, William; Captain. *See* Boyton.

Wilson, Robert Scott; Captain of the 21st M.I. He died on board the "Sesostris" on his passage to the Cape, March 17th, aged forty-two years.

Young, Aretas Sutherland; Captain; *See* Boyton.

Besides these monuments, the Old Colours of H.M. 102nd Royal Madras Fusiliers are hung in the church and a tablet with the following inscription is placed beneath them.

"These Colours of Her Majesty's 102nd Royal Madras Fusiliers Regiment of Foot were presented to the Regiment, then the 1st Madras Fusiliers, on the 16th July, 1852, by Mrs. Duke, wife of Lieut. Colonel T.A. Duke, Commanding the Regiment, and were consecrated on parade by the Revd. J. Morant, Chaplain of Bellary; they bear on them 'the Royal Tiger' with the motto 'Spectamur Agendo' and the following names:—

Arcot, Plassey, Condore, Wandewash, Sholinghur, Nundydroog, Amboyna, Ternate, Pondicherry, Mahidpore, Ava, Pegu, Lucknow.

They have passed through two campaigns,—namely, the 2nd Burmese War in 1852–53, in which the following fell:— Captains Hawes, (Brevet Major,) Nicholay Geils, W.R. Brown, Tulloch and Ward. Surgeon Anderson, 2nd Lieuts. Bryce, Bower and Wing, and a hundred and eighteen non-commissioned officers, Drummers and Rank and File.

And the suppression of the Bengal Rebellion, (Indian Mutiny) in 1857–58, in which the following fell:— Brigadier General F.G.S. Stephenson, C.B., Major G.S.C. Renard, Lieuts. Croon, Arnold, Richardson, Hargood, Chisholm and Dobbs, and three hundred and fifty-two non-commissioned Officers, Drummers and Rank and File."

On each side of the Barry Close monument are The Old Colours of The 7th M.I., to which Regiment Sir Barry belonged.

Crossed over the Pepper statue are The Old Colours of The 34th M.L.I., to which Regiment he and Captain Stedman belonged.

Over the monument of Major Whistler are the Old Colours of The 19th M.I., a pair issued in 1838, and a second pair issued in 1852.

On the wall opposite the old 19th colours, at the same elevation are a pair of The 33rd M.I. and the 41st M.I., they are crossed over the monument of Lieut. Colonel McCurdy.

Over the statue of General Conway are a pair of the Old Colours of The 6th M.I.; to which Regiment he belonged.

Over the monument of the Officers of the 36th Regiment are a pair of old colours belonging to that Regiment.

There are two brass plates on the organ. The older one has the following inscription:—

> "This organ, the property of the late Captain John Hay, Mil. Sec. to the Right Hon. Lord Harris, was presented to St. Mary's Church, Fort St. George, by Sir Adam Hay, Bart., father of the deceased. Erected January 1859 in lieu of one presented by John Smith, Esquire, AD 1760."

The modern one contains:

> "This organ was erected in the year 1894 in the place of the one mentioned above, in memory of the many noble men, both Civil and Military, who have perished in the discharge of their duty to their country in this land, and especially of those whose honoured remains are buried in this church. The funds were raised principally by the Revd. A.C. Taylor, M.A., and the Revd. C.H. Pelly, M.A., Garrison Chaplains. This plate was placed here by the Revd. Frank Penny, L.L.M., Senior Chaplain, Her Majesty's Indian Service, 1897."

There is a brass plate below the Altar rails, on which is inscribed the following:

> "In memory of her friend Vere Henry, Lord Hobart ,
> this railing is placed in the House of God by the Prince
> of Tanjore, AD 1877."

The Lectern, which is of brass and adorned with a den of lilies, contains this inscription, "Thy command is exceeding broad," Presented to God and the Church by Mary Lad "Hobart, in memory of a beloved husband who rests below. On the front of the lectern is the text, "Consider the lilies."

THE CHURCH PLATE

The Church plate of St. Mary's consists of a large and handsome alms-dish of silver which was presented by Elihu Yale. It weighs 3 lbs, 2 oz. and is seventeen inches in diameter. It is engraved with Yale's coat of arms and the words "Ex dono Honorabilis Elihu Yale, Armigeri, Gubernatoris, Anno 1687."

A shallow font-basin of silver, given by Lady Mary Goldsborough. It weighs 6 lbs, 10 oz., and is twenty-three inches in diameter. It is inscribed with the words:

"Ex dono Honoratissoe Dominae

Domoe Mariae Goldsborough

Quae excessit ex hac vita

30 Die Novembris 1698."

and a coat of arms as follows:—Argent in pale a badger passant proper impaled with argent a chevron gules between three greyhounds heads.

A flagon of silver with the same inscription and coat of arms, weighing 2½ lbs; and standing eighteen and a half inches high.

A cup without any inscription, mounted apparently on the stem of an old candlestick, having the emblems of the Crucifixion round the foot. [*See* page 86.]

LIST OF CHAPLAINS OF FORT ST. GEORGE FROM THE CONSECRATION OF ST. MARY'S CHURCH DOWN TO THE BEGINNING OF THE XIX CENTURY

Name	Date	Remarks
Richard Portman	Dec. 24, 1675	Present at Consecration
Richard Elliot	1680	Died at the Fort, 1696
T. Evans	March 1689	He arrived with Charnock
George Lewis	1692	
James Wendey	1698	
Robert Jones	1710	
Charles Long	1713	Returned to England, 1721
W.M. Stevenson	1713	
Thomas Wendey	1719	Returned to England, 1727
W.M. Leeke	1721	Died at the Fort, 1728
Thomas Consett	1729	Died at the Fort, 1730
Robert Wynch	Feb. 1731	
Eden Howard	Feb. 1732	
James Feilde	1744	Died at the Fort, 1745
George Swynfen	1749	Died at the Fort, 1750
Robert Palk	1751	
Thomas Colefax	1752	Died at the Fort, 1752

(Contd.)

LIST OF CHAPLAINS OF FORT ST. GEORGE...

Name	Date	Remarks
Samuel Staveley	Aug. 30, 1753	
N. Smith	1758	
Samuel Merefield	Oct. 10, 1758	
Charles Griffiths, D.D.	1762	Died 1768
John Thomas	Nov. 11, 1765	
Benjamin W. Salmon	Sep. 3, 1769	
St. John Browne	Aug. 15, 1775	
W. Bainbrigge	July 1, 1777	Died at the Fort, 1783
John Fleming Stanley	July 1, 1778	Died in Bengal
Benj. Millingchamp	July 24, 1782	
Richd Leslie, Archdn.	Sep. 11, 1783	Died at the Fort, 1804
A. Bell, D.D.	July 15, 1789	
Richd. Hall Kerr.	Sep. 17, 1796	Died at the Fort, 1808
Charles Ball	1801	
Edward Vaughan	Apr. 23, 1805	

APPENDIX

Elihu Yale (1672) (Page 139)

Sir Henry Yule (Diary of William Hedges Vol. III; Errata and Addenda p. 13) says that Yale was born at Newhaven, New England, in 1648. "His grandfather, David Yale, belonged to a family near Wrexham, and in 1613 married Ann Morton, daughter of a Bishop of Durham. He died in 1617, and his widow in the following year married Theophilus Eaton, a London merchant, and in 1638 migrated with him and her children by Yale, to America.

Thomas was the third son of David and Ann Yale, and was the father of Elihu Yale. Eaton died in 1657, and his widow thereupon returned to England with her family, including Elihu. He was appointed to Madras in 1671.

A letter by an American, Mr. Dexter, published in the Madras Mail, Dec. 1895, says that Yale's father was one of the early settlers in America, but, disgusted with the type of Puritanism prevalent there, returned to England and sent his son to the St. Paul's School.

Of Yale's service in India there is but little account, until he became Governor, except that at the proclamation of King James II, he brought up the rear of a procession headed by the Governor. His brother Thomas was also in the Company's service, and was charged with fraud.

Elihu Yale married the widow of Joseph Hynmers (a Portuguese lady, Heronima de Paicta). On a monument on the Light House Esplanade is a monument with the following inscription:

Hic jacet, David, filius honorabilis Elihu Yale, Praesidentis et Gubernatoris Castelli Sancti Georgii et Civitatis Madrassiae. Natus fuit May 1684. Obiit Jan. 1687/8.

"Here lies interred the body of Joseph Hynmers, who served the Right Honorable English East India Company several years as second in the Council at Fort St. George, at which station he departed this life in May 1680."

Elihu Yale was a man of violent and arbitrary temper. The traveller Hamilton tells a story of his hanging his groom Cross, for taking out for exercise a horse without permission.

After his recall he remained in Madras. By his own account he was plundered, imprisoned in the Fort, and an attempt made to poison him. The next Governor reported this was entirely untrue, and that Yale's manner of living was scandalous.

He was, late in life, a great benefactor to the Connecticut College, which now bears his name.

Job Charnock (Page 153)

Very little is known of Charnock, the founder of Calcutta. There is a short account of him in the Dictionary of National Biography; and Sir Henry Yule, in Vol. 75 of the Hakluyt Society, has brought together several incidents of his career. But perhaps the best account of the man and his work is to be found in "The Thackerays in India" by Sir W. Hunter, pp. 34–54, ending in these words, "a block of rough-hewn British manhood. Not a beautiful personage perhaps for the founders of England's greatness in India were not such as wear soft raiment and dwell in King's houses, but a man who had a great and hard task to do and who did it—did it with small thought of self and with a resolute courage which no danger could daunt, nor any difficulties turn aside."

The masters who treated him so grudgingly knew his worth. He was, even in his lifetime, "Our honest Mr. Charnock," no "prowler for himself beyond what was just and modest." But the inscription on his tomb, written, let us hope, by Chaplain Evans, bishop and merchant, mutely appeals to a higher verdict than man's. He sleeps "in spe beatae resurrectionis ad Christi Judicis adventum," an exile "qui postquam in solo non suo peregrinatus, esset diu, reversus est domum suae aeternitatis." (He abides in the hope of a joyful resurrection at the coming of Christ the Judge; a wanderer who after long travel in a far country has returned to his eternal home.) Perhaps his truest epitaph is a chance line in a dispatch from the Directors a year after his death, "Always a faithful man to the Company."

John Evans (Page 159)

He was appointed Chaplain at Hoogly in 1678; and is frequently referred to in the Diary of William Hedges (Hakluyt Society, Vol. 74, passim).

In 1692, he is found at Fort St. George as Chaplain, having probably gone there with Charnock.

He had a bad reputation with the authorities, who called him the "merchant parson" and a friend of interlopers.

He left India in 1698, became Bishop of Bangor in 1702, and was transferred to Meath in 1715. He died in Dublin in 1723.

Francis Seaton (Page 159)

Succeeded James Betts as Captain of the Guard in 1692, having obtained his first commission under him four years earlier. He was a man of violent and overbearing temper. Early in his career he was tried for drunkenness and for wounding a Portuguese and was reprimanded.

In 1698 he fought a duel with a brother officer and for this was tried by court martial and cashiered, but later on he was reinstated, on apologising to Pitt.

In 1703 he fought another duel with Stratford of the Civil Service, just outside the Fort Walls. For this both were fined.

In 1704 he got into trouble with Pitt for marching his soldiers over the calico spread out to bleach on the Maidan. He was suspended and Roach succeeded him. Seaton then turned against Pitt, and started the scandalous story of the diamond, which led to Pitt's recall.

In 1708 he was ordered home by the "Heathcote" and as he refused to go was taken alongside by force. The Captain (Tolson) refused to take anyone who did not go of his own free will, and Seaton was sent on shore again.

In 1710 his wife died and he then left India for good. He was twice married; both his wives are buried in the cemetery.

Thomas Pitt (Page 170)

The fullest account of this remarkable man, the grandfather of the first Lord Chatham, and himself for many years M.P. for Old Sarum, is in Vol. 78 of the Hakluyt Society (pp.1–156). At first spoken of by the Company as "Interloping Pyt" and "Pyrott Pit", later on as "that roughling and immoral man", he became Governor of Madras, and directed affairs for nine eventful years.

He is buried at Blandford, but the church of Abbot's Ann, in the same county, was rebuilt by him after his return from Madras in 1716. There is nothing remarkable in this small redbrick church itself, though a brass and a stained window record his beneficence. The church is, however, remarkable for a curious custom still surviving. Each bride, on her marriage presents here right-hand glove, which (often with name and date) is, in due course, suspended among the rafters of the roof. There are hundreds of them there, some fresh, other grimed with the dust of ages.

As for the big diamond, which was one of the reasons for his recall, Streeter in "Precious stones and Gems" (London 1877, page 118) says, "It was said Pitt had obtained the stone at Golconda in 1702. It came from the mines of Parkal, 45 leagues S. of Golconda."

This is probably a mistake for Partiala, in the Kistna district, not far from Bezwada. There are diamond mines here, indicated in the ordnance map, and I remember when visiting them, to have been told by a Brahmin that the big "Pitt diamond" had been found in them. The mines are not deep; the diamondiferous strata crop out on the surface.

Lord Clive (Page 171)

Lord Clive died by his own hand, at his house in Belgrave Square, London.

The only notice of his death in the Annual Register for 1774 is in the Obituary. "At his residence in Belgrave Square the Right Hon. Robert Lord Clive of Plassey, in the Kingdom of Ireland, Lord Lieut. and Custos Rotulorum of the Counties of Salop and

Montgomery, K.B. and Major General in the East Indies, representative in Parliament for Shrewsbury, L, L.D. and F.R.S. Born Michaelmas Day, 1725. Married Margaret, daughter of Edmund Maskelyne of Purton in the County of Wilts."

He is buried inside the little church of Moreton Say, three miles west of Market Drayton. The old seventeenth century church is dedicated to St. Margaret. There are no aisles or transepts, only a nave and chancel, and the building would hold about 200 people. It is known that Clive is buried somewhere beneath the floor of the church, but the actual place is now forgotten and there is nothing to mark it.

A brass inside the doorway runs, "Sacred to the memory of Robert Lord Clive, K.B. Buried within the walls of this church. Born, 29 Sept. 1725. Died, 22 Nov. 1774. Primus in Indis."

Smith (Life of Bishop Heber, p. 59) says the church was rebuilt in 1788, when the part of the church where Clive is buried became the first pew to the right, facing the entrance and that his coffin was seen there not many years ago. This was not confirmed at a visit paid in 1899. Except the brass tablet, there is absolutely no memorial of Clive in the church; the vicar suggested that a window might be put in by members of the Indian Services.

"The Styche", the family house, is about three miles away, inhabited by one of the Herberts.

Moreton Say is one of the chapelries of Hodnet, six miles distant, Heber's rectory.

Lord Pigot (Page 206)

George Pigot went out to Madras in 1755, and after having risen to the position of Governor, returned to England in 1763 with a fortune of £500,000, on the strength of which he obtained an Irish Peerage.

As Lord Pigot he returned to Madras a second time as Governor, and set himself to put down the corruption he found rampant among the Company's servants. This aroused against him bitter enmity. The Nawab of Arcot had been borrowing money from the members of Council (Paul Benfield and others) at the seductive rate of 60 per cent, on the mortgage of the Kingdom of Tanjore which he had recently taken. The Council by seven to five were in favour of upholding the validity of these transactions. Lord Pigot then put two of the Council under confinement, and was in his turn arrested at their instigation.

The Directors at first supported his policy, but afterwards turned round and recalled him, but he died at Guindy before the order arrived. The members of Council were subsequently tried in England and fined £1000 each.

Sir Eyre Coote (Page 225)

Particulars of his career will be found in most Biographical Dictionaries. Macaulay's estimate of him (Essay on Warren Hastings) is well known. That of Sir Philip Francis (Junius), his contemporary, is somewhat different. "I will not content myself with saying I never knew, but upon my soul, I never heard of so abandoned a scoundrel. It is a character to which your English ideas of dirt and meanness do not reach. Nor is it to be met with even in Bengal; even here it excites execration and contempt." Sir W.W. Hunter may well ask, "Shall be accept these words as a fair portrait of the warrior statesman, before whose monument in Westminster Abbey, with its figures of victory and a conquered province, many a young soldier has paused to read a nation's record of the services of Sir Eyre Coote?"

Coote died in the Fort at Madras in 1783, two days after his arrival from Calcutta. His ship the "*Resolution*" had been chased, on her voyage by two French cruisers, and though in a weak state of health, he had unwisely remained on deck, exposed to inclement weather.

His body was eventually brought to England, and now rests in the village church of Rockburn, about six miles from Salisbury.

West Park, his family seat, still the property of the Cootes is close by, and the church contains many monuments and tablets to members of the family.

ENDNOTES

1. The first to reach the shores of Western India was said to be Thomas Stephens. He was the son of a London merchant and was educated at New College, Oxford. He sailed from Lisbon in April 1579, and arrived at Goa in October of the same year. He passed himself off as a Jesuit, and became Rector of a college near Goa.

2. The merchants, who formed the First English East India Company, held their first meeting in Founder's Hall, London, September 22nd, 1599. Each venture was subscribed for separately until 1612. From 1612 to 1661 there was a period of Joint Stocks. In 1661 a system was adopted resembling in many respects the Joint Stock Companies of the present day.

3. One of the Dutch Company's servants was an Englishman, Captain Samuel King, who helped to smooth the way.

4. Pettipoli, or Peddapalli, occupied by the English as a factory about 1613, and abandoned towards the middle of the century. Now known as Nizampatam in the Kistna District. [J.K.]

5. Towerson, however, did not die. He lived to marry the widow of Captain Hawkins, an Armenian lady, who was given to Hawkins by the Moghul. The Captain was much attached to her and carried her off under romantic circumstances. Unfortunately, he died on the journey home, and Mrs. Hawkins married Towerson.

6. George Chauncey, John Gourney and Thomas Brockedon were also pioneers on the Coromandel Coast with Floris.

7. In the museum at St. Malo, Brittany, is a large print of the surrender of Madras. It is fanciful, and it is difficult to recognize the place. I believe the Church Plate was carried off at the same time, but restored later on. [J.K]

8. In 1715 the Greenhill estate was paid to heirs in England who successfully proved their claim.

9. Hunter says that the designation "Sir" frequently met with in the old records was an abbreviation of the word "Signor" and was written Sir, a term adopted from the Portuguese.

10. The name of Foxcroft occurs in one of the early letters written to the Company (1613–14) by their Agents. Adam Denton desired certain packages sent in one of the ships might be given to Mr. George Foxcroft, Gent., of Ironmonger Lane in London.

11. In Sept. 1769 Captain Thomas Oats of the Artillery, married Ann Pelling at St. Mary's Church. George Heron also lies buried in the old cemetery, under the monument which marks his grave, and still stands in its original position in the compound of the High Court Buildings.

12. "Letters patent of 9th August, 1683, established a court of Judicature, consisting of one person learned in the civil laws and two merchants. John Gray was the first judge to preside in the Madras court."– A.T. Pringle

    Sir John Biggs was sent out in 1687 to supersede Gray, who was in office only a year and proved inefficient.

13. The first chaplain, who served the Company in the East Indies, was John Cartwright of London, Preacher. He was appointed to the first expedition on a salary of three pounds

a month. Fifteen pounds were allowed for outfit. Only half the salary was to be paid unless one of the ships returned by way of China. The first chaplain to serve on the Coromandel Coast was Edward Terry, who was on the "Globe", 1615. Until 1668 only one chaplain seems to have been appointed for the whole of the East Indies. After that date there were four, one of whom was stationed regularly at Fort St. George and visited Masulipatam at intervals.

14.   The 1st Madras Fusiliers became the 102nd Queen's, when the Hon. Company's Regiments became the Queen's Regiments. It is now known as the Royal Dublin Fusiliers. The 1st Battalion Royal Dublin Fusiliers was formerly the 102nd, and before that the Madras European Regiment. It was the very oldest Regiment, European or Native, in the Company's service, having been raised in the form of independent Companies in the various ports of the Company. These Companies were brought together, and consolidated into a Regiment in 1745. Clive rose in the Regiment, and commanded it. Malcolm, Lawrence, and Neill, who fell at Lucknow, were officers in it. In early days it was always pitted against the French under Lally. The only British Regiment that carried Wandewash on its colours. This was purely a European battle between French and English: not a Sepoy fired a shot.

Bernadotte, afterwards Marshal of France and King of Sweden, was a private in the Regiment. The Regiment landed for the first time in England in 1870, after serving in India 225 years. The second Batt. was the old Bombay European Regiment, raised in England by Charles II., and sent out to defend Bombay, which was part of his Queen's dower. The Regiment subsequently volunteered for the Company's service and remained in Bombay 200 years. [J.K.]

15. In Novemeber, 1769, "Hastings" appears amongst the names of those present at a Vestry meeting. In February 1770, the name is written in full as "Warren Hastings, Esq."; it occurs for the last time in February 1771. At this period he was living at the Mount; Mrs. Imhoff, his fellow-passenger, was his guest.

16. Father of John Arthur Roebuck M.P. for Sheffield, who was born in Madras 1801. [J.K.]

17. Further particulars about Master's career will be found in the "Diary of William Hedges," Vol.II., by Sir Henry Yule. (Hakluyt Soc.) In St. Bartholomew's Church, Smithfield, is a tablet in memory of his parents and other members of his family. Mrs. Master, his mother, daughter of Sir James Oxenden, after having had twenty children, died in 1705, circa 99 years and six months, and is buried in the church. The church of St. George the Martyr, Queen's Square, Bloomsbury, is also connected with Master. He was one of the fifteen gentlemen who were trustees for building it. It was finished in 1723, and dedicated to St. George, in compliment to Sir Streynsham Master, once Governor of Fort St. George, Madras. (Diary of Hedges, Vol.III., p.15.) [J.K.]

18. Sir Josiah Child was an Alderman and goldsmith of London, and the founder of Child's Bank at Temple Bar. He purchased Wanstead House from the Mildmays, and laid out the grounds at an immense cost. He died in 1699, and a magnificent marble monument was erected to his memory in Wanstead old church. His son, Sir Richard Child, afterwards Earl Tylney, rebuilt Wanstead House and Church.

19. Hamilton was at one period a householder in Fort St. George, and his name appears on the list of inhabitants not in the Company's service.

20. He came out in 1668 and had children baptised at the Fort. He was buried there Feb. 18th, 1695.

21. The Fleetwoods described themselves on their monument as being of good family. Robert was Chief of Masulipatam; he settled at Nursapore, near Masulipatam, where he bought property and owned a ship called the *Recovery*. He was implicated with Jearsey in contraband free trade, but nothing was proved against him. He died before 1677, in which year the Company seized the *Recovery*, and sold it in payment of a debt which was owing from the deceased man. His widow, Mrs. Margery Fleetwood, married John Heathfield, surgeon in the Company's service, who afterwards took up trade at Masulipatam. Robert Fleetwood's daughters married in the Fort. Charles and Edward Fleetwood, who were probably Robert's sons, were bringing their children for baptism at the beginning of the eighteenth century. Charles was appointed Writer in 1681. Edward's daughter, Mary, married Richard Benyon, who became Governor in 1735.

22. George Weoley was married in July 1701, to Deodate Middleton, at St. Mary's church.

23. William Gyfford was married, but his wife was in England. He had a brother, Daniel, living in the Fort, who had several children baptised there. One of them named Mary married James Berriman, a Company's servant, in 1712. Anne Gyfford, whose baptism and parentage is not recorded, married Manning Lethieullier in 1734.

24. Daniel Chardin, a brother of the Sir John Chardin who befriended the Armenians, was a resident in the Fort in Yale's time. He owned one of the largest houses and used to travel between Madras and Golconda on his own and the Company's business, though he was not in the Company's

service. Diamonds were ofcourse the object of his quest. His daughter Jane was baptised in 1689; Elihu Yale, Mrs. Gyfford and Lady Jane Biggs standing as sponsors. She married, first, Joseph Lister, one of the Company's servants, and was soon widowed. In 1709 she tried matrimony again, and chose Charles Boone who at a later date became Governor of Bombay. She died in the following year after becoming a mother. Daniel Chardin also died in Madras, and there is a stone to his memory on which he is described as a merchant and a native of France. The date of his death is September 7th, 1709. His wife's name was Mary or Marie; she is described in the baptismal register of her daughter as Mary; but the list of freemen living in the Fort in 1696 gives her name as Marie and calls her a French lady. In 1707, two years before Daniel's death, Mary Louise Chardin was married to Henry Devonport, who was afterwards Deputy Governor of Fort St. David. She was probably another daughter of the French merchant. A daughter of Henry and Mary Lucy Devonport was baptised in 1708; the godparents being Thomas Pitt, Sharington Devonport, Mary Magdalen Chardin and Jane Lister. On December 21st, 1712, Mary Louise Devonport was buried. There is no further mention of the name of Chardin in the register books, but the records state that Madame Chardin and family sailed for England in January 1714.

25.   Mrs. Seaton and Mrs. Heathfield were both Madras ladies. The latter has been already mentioned as the widow of Robert Fleetwood. The former was the wife of Captain Francis Seaton who commanded the garrison.

The three little girls grew up to womanhood and married. Mary, the eldest was the wife of Charles Eyre, who was knighted and made the first president of Fort William. She died in 1697, and her husband built the mausoleum at

Calcutta which afterwards marked the resting-place of her father. Elizabeth, the second, married William Bowridge, and she survived in Calcutta till the year 1753. Catherine, the youngest, became the wife of Jonathan White in the service of the Company. She, like her eldest sister, died young and was buried in 1701. She left a daughter, whom Mrs. Bowridge took to England with her own child after Mrs. White's death.

26. He married Elizabeth Richardson in the Fort church in that year, and like Yale brought several children to the font.

27. It has been sometimes stated that Guindy Park with a house was presented to the Company in 1695 by Chinna Vencatadry, a wealthy native merchant who was a relative of Timanna and a partner in the firm of Timanna and Viranna, the Company's brokers. But no historical proof has been found that Guindy and Chinna Vencatadry's gift are identical.

28. His estate was paid to his brother, John Hastings of Gray's Inn.

29. George Torriano was the son of Nathaniel, who came out as supercargo on the Company's ship *Hertford*. George married Susannah Catherine de Dorpere in April 1725; when he died in May 1741 he was on the Council. He left descendants in Madras; and the name figures on the list of the victims of the Black Hole tragedy. Randall Fowke served the Company for forty years, and he, too, was a member of Council before his death, which event took place in October 1745, when he was seventy-two years of ago. He married Ann May in 1713, and his son Joseph entered the Company's service. Joseph was in the Fort when it was given up to the French in 1750. His wife Elizabeth Walsh was the grand-daughter of Enoch Walsh.

30.   It is difficult to assign any exact date to the rebuilding of the Fort. For a few years after Lally's departure very little was done; but by 1770 funds were more plentiful. Building and restoration went on briskly until the end of the century. During those thirty years the present Secretariat, (without the wings,) the Banqueting Hall with its pillars from Pondicherry, the King's Barracks, the steeple of St. Mary's church, and nearly the whole of the northern portion of the Fort was built. The Exchange, the mainguard block and the houses near the Exchange were restored. Government House on the Cooum, as it now is, was also rebuilt at this period; the new Banqueting Hall commemorates the fall of Seringapatam in 1799.

31.   Boscawen handed the Fort over to Colonel Lawrence, who called the first Council-meeting in November, at which he and two others were present. Their first act was to confiscate the church and houses—seven of the latter—that belonged to the Roman Catholics, who had behaved treacherously during the siege.

32.   He came out in deacon's orders and was appointed to Fort St. David, March 31st, 1749. He was doing duty at Fort St. George in 1751. In 1752 he was associated with Lawrence in political affairs and was appointed Paymaster and Commissary in the Field. In 1754 he was successfully negotiating with the French. In 1756 the Nabob asked to see him on political matters. Palk sailed for England in October 1758. When he returned as Governor in 1763 he had dropped the title of Reverend for the more suitable one of Esquire.

33.   Henry Vansittart became Governor of Bengal in 1760. He was drowned at sea when the *Aurora* frigate was lost on her homeward voyage in 1760. He married Emilia, the

daughter of Nicholas Morse, June 1st, 1754, at St. Mary's church. She was born in Madras and baptised May 27th, 1738. She had a son named Henry baptised at St. Mary's, April 30th, 1755. Mrs. Vansittart's sister, Frances, baptised September 6th, 1736, married Charles Boddam, junior, of the Company's service. He was born in Madras and was baptised May 10th, 1718. His mother was Mary Hart, and her marriage to Charles Boddam, senior, is recorded in June 1716. Charles Boddam, senior, came out in the Company's service as a master of one of their ships, and he was permitted to trade on his own account as a free merchant. He sent his son Charles to England for education, and the young man returned to India in 1735, having received his appointment as writer from the directors. Morse was the great great-grandson of Oliver Cromwell through the Protector's daughter Bridget, who married Colonel Ireton. Bridget Ireton's grand-daughter, Jane Floyd, married a Morse and became the mother of Nicholas, Daniel, and three daughters. Daniel came out of Fort St. George, but not as a servant of the Company.

INDEX

Made in the USA
Monee, IL
07 July 2026

56646383R00197